Modern ' rations

Modern Migrations

Gujarati Indian Networks in New York and London

Maritsa V. Poros

Stanford University Press
Stanford, California

Stanford University Press
Stanford, California

Printed in the United States of America on acid-free, archival-quality paper

Library of Congress Cataloging-in-Publication Data

Poros, Maritsa V., 1968–
    Modern migrations : Gujarati Indian networks in New York and London / Maritsa V. Poros.
    p. cm.
    Includes bibliographical references and index.
    ISBN 978-0-8047-7222-8 (cloth : alk. paper) — ISBN 978-0-8047-7223-5 (pbk. : alk. paper)
    1. Gujaratis (Indic people)—Social networks—New York (State)—New York. 2. Gujaratis (Indic people)—Social networks—England—London. 3. Immigrants—Social networks—New York (State)—New York. 4. Immigrants—Social networks—England—London. 5. New York (N.Y.)—Emigration and immigration—Social aspects. 6. London (England)—Emigration and immigration—Social aspects. I. Title.
    F128.9.G85P67 2010
    304.8089'914710421—dc22
                    2010027533

Typeset by Thompson Type in 10/14 Minion

*This book is dedicated to the
memory of my greatest teachers,*

Robert K. Merton and Charles Tilly.

Contents

List of Figures, Maps, and Tables

Preface

THIS BOOK IS A STUDY of Gujarati Indian immigrants in New York and London. Gujaratis are part of a long history of migration from a region that has been shaped by early modern and modern economic relations in trade and production, labor, colonialism, educational and professional exchange, and other globalized relations. As shown in this book, those relations demonstrate the historical integration and interaction of individuals, communities, institutions, and states across specific regions of the world where Gujaratis have migrated. Gujarati migrations do not simply represent traditional people moving from a developing country to a developed one, motivated by potential economic gain, as is so often assumed about immigrants from many parts of the developing world. To show how we can see these historical social ties and integration, which cause migration flows and social change, this study argues for a relational approach, which has for the most part been overlooked in migration studies. The relational approach to understanding social life emphasizes dynamic relations over static categories by focusing attention on the kinds of networks and valued goods, such as information, money, resources, and influence, that are exchanged within social ties producing even large-scale processes such as migration. The historical formation of these ties is visible in the social networks that immigrants use to migrate and in the ways in which their economic opportunities are structured by those networks.

Many people might wonder how Gujarati Indians, a seemingly small and insignificant population from the westernmost state of India, can tell us something important about migration processes, in particular, and modernity, in general. Indeed, many of my colleagues shrugged their shoulders when I first decided to study Indian immigrants, and Gujaratis, in particular. Indian immigrants (among whom there were many Gujaratis) did not seem like an important group relative to others, such as Latinos or other Asians, whose numbers had been growing rapidly in the United States throughout the 1990s. In fact, I was once told by a prominent migration researcher and sociologist, someone I admire very much, that "Indians are not a problem." This statement had a double meaning. First, Indians were not a problem in the popular sense in that, as a group, they were not poor, segregated, unemployed, exploited, illegal, criminal, or even culturally different enough to be perceived as one of the more "problematic" immigrant groups in American society. Their presence in the United States neither appealed to any need for social justice nor seemed to spark much anti-immigrant sentiment. Second, they were not a problem in the sociological sense. In other words, their presence in American society, or even the processes by which they migrated to the United States, did not constitute a social problem in that it did not challenge some of the fundamental ways in which we think about the social order. Indians seemed to fit in. Even when they were perceived as culturally different, they still spoke English well, worked hard in professional and entrepreneurial jobs, valued education and American civic practices, and behaved, generally, as good citizens.

These characteristics of Indian immigration were generally true in London as well. By the 1990s, Indians there (among whom there were also many Gujaratis) were known to be stratified more widely along working- and middle-class lines than in the United States. They had also been subject to much racial discrimination, especially during the first half of the twentieth century. Nevertheless, they tended to rank high, often higher than their white British counterparts, on basic measures such as median household income, education, and housing quality. They were also not perceived to be as "problematic" as other South Asian groups, such as Pakistanis and Bangladeshis, or as the large West Indian population in the United Kingdom. In other words, most Indians seemed to assimilate rather quickly, so what could possibly be the problem requiring study?

I shrugged off the indifference of some of my colleagues to the study of Indian immigrants because I thought that they were interesting and important in a number of ways. I had become familiar with Indian scientists and engineers as friends and co-workers of my parents during the 1970s. My parents had migrated from Greece and, with Indians, they were part of the same generation of foreign students and professionals working in the burgeoning scientific fields of computer science, aerospace, and other applied sciences. These fields were at the heart of the post–World War II and Cold War–era race for American hegemony that relied so fundamentally on scientific work. However, these kinds of foreign workers, referred to as high-skill or professional and, nowadays, as high-tech or knowledge workers, were of little concern to most migration researchers in sociology. I thought that they were interesting in their own right because they raised certain questions about how and why international migration occurs. For instance, why did so many of these kinds of Indian workers migrate to the United States but not the United Kingdom? If economic globalization was producing segmented labor markets in which immigrants tended to fill the bottom rungs of the new service industries, where did these professionals fit in? What could we gain by comparing one immigrant group that was well represented in two quite different global cities, New York and London?

In addition to being familiar with these early Indian professionals as colleagues of my parents, we socialized with these immigrant families that, like mine, were spread out in middle-class, suburban neighborhoods where looking and acting foreign was not yet a common sight. Through the common foreignness of our families I became interested in Indian culture, and later, as an adult, in Indian history, philosophy, and religions. Thus, when I first "entered the field," as sociologists and anthropologists like to say about the start of ethnographic research, I was an "outsider." I did not belong to the group that I was studying. But I was also an "insider" with a distinctly personal kind of background knowledge and familiarity with Indian immigrants and culture. Of course, I was never going to be an ethnic insider as are so many migration researchers who study "their own group." Yet, my outsider status and insider perspective turned out to be one of the distinct advantages of this research because it allowed me to enter many different Indian and Gujarati worlds without having constantly to negotiate my identity. And it allowed me to understand more easily where some of the participants came from in cultural terms. In fact, it only helped me when participants learned that I am Greek because they saw me as sharing their roots in one of the world's ancient civilizations. Some participants even knew of the Indo-Greek civilization that existed in northern India during the first few centuries before the Christian era, and they took pride in commenting about it to me. Most importantly, my outsider position encouraged participants to tell me their life stories without fear of repercussion from within their Indian communities. This is not to say that their narratives were somehow more truthful or accurate or that any of us can produce objective narratives about our own lives but only that I quickly gained the trust of participants. All narratives must be understood and interpreted in the particular context of time and space in which they are told, including in relation to the interviewer. The life history interviews I did with these immigrants are no different in that sense.

Indians, perhaps more than other national populations, have significant intragroup differences. They are worthy of study for this reason alone. As a population, they could be sliced up almost endlessly according to region of origin, caste, subcaste, religion, linguistic group, class status, and so on. Thus, even when I decided to focus on Gujarati Hindus and Jains, I discovered not one monolithic group but rather many smaller communities that only sometimes unified and acted collectively under labels such as Gujarati or Gujarati Hindu. This would become a central lesson of my study and lead me to argue for a relational approach in order to examine the historical formation of different social, economic, and political ties that set migration flows in motion and facilitate or constrain the socioeconomic mobility of immigrants in their host societies. The everyday intragroup differences of Gujaratis meant that all those sliced-up static categories, which we so often employ in sociological analysis to understand the social world, made little sense. They were not static at all, and they did not exist as some sort of external, causal characteristic of the relations that actually made up the everyday lives of immigrants and, for that matter, everyone. Class, caste, religion, language, and ethnicity were inherently dynamic phenomena that had meaning only in the context of real human relations, which one could see in these migrants' social networks. Those negotiated relations made the difference in whether to migrate, open a business, move out of an ethnic enclave economy, or pursue further education. These relational phenomena, which became apparent in a qualitative analysis of the migrants' social networks, were an important reminder of the origins of sociology in the work of Georg Simmel, Karl Marx, Max Weber, and so many others. This study represents a small part of this emphasis on the relational approach to social life, which is being renewed today by a new generation of scholars.

Given the multitude of cultures in South Asia, Gujarat may still seem like an unusual place to begin a study of immigrants. Why not Bengalis, I was once asked by a Sikh friend who admired the Bengali reputation for excellence in

art, literature, music, and intellectual life but not the lowly reputation of Gujaratis as shrewd businesspeople and traders. However, Gujarat has an extraor-
dinarily important history of foreign trade that brings to light the question of
modernity. Its long history of migration has been linked to trade for centuries,
indeed millennia. In fact, we now know that Marx and Weber got it wrong
when they claimed that Asian societies and economies, in particular India and
China, could not have become modern capitalist economies as happened later
in the West. The historiography on India, and most intensively about Gujarat,
shows that India was indeed on its way to becoming capitalist and modern,
especially between the 1500s and 1800s when it surpassed Europe in trade, industry, and exports. Furthermore, during this period, Indian traders employed
modern (rational) organizational and financial practices in their firms.

The links to some of that past persist even today in contemporary migrations of Gujaratis to New York and London and other places around the
world. It is not simply the higher education and class status of many Indians
and Gujaratis that make their migration different and less "problematic" than
some immigrant groups. Those static, categorical ways of describing them,
and indeed reducing them to one or two simple characteristics, conceal much
deeper and more specific historical ties between India and the United States
and between India and the United Kingdom. Those historical ties were created
from trade, colonial relations, conflict, religious movements, and, of course,
labor. They do not exist because Indians are simply poorer, traditional people
looking to migrate to richer countries for economic opportunities.

New York and London, furthermore, pose an interesting comparison. On
the one hand, they contain many similarities as global cities that draw immigrants from all over the world, in part as a result of their concentration
of new service industries. Foreign-born Indians rank third among the entire
foreign-born population in the United States and the United Kingdom, and
New York and London are the top cities of settlement for Indians in both
countries. Gujaratis also represent one of the largest regional groups within
the Indian population in each city since the 1960s. On the other hand, London is the center of the U.K. legacy of colonialism, in which India was its
"crown jewel," whereas the United States has never had a colonial relationship
with India. The United Kingdom has also maintained very different immigration policies from the United States, particularly from the 1960s to the late
1990s. During that time, the United Kingdom proclaimed a "zero immigration" policy, with the exception of some asylum. In contrast, the United States

has maintained an "open door" policy of immigration since 1965. Therefore, even though New York and London are both "global cities," we might expect Indian migration flows to and their integration in each city to be very different because of immigration policy and the former colonial relationship between India and the United Kingdom. However, as I will discuss later in this book, the similarities and the differences between the United Kingdom and the United States and between London and New York were not very significant compared to the kinds of network ties that Gujaratis used to migrate to each place and the sorts of relations of exchange that facilitated or constrained their mobility in both cities. Gujarati immigrants with similar kinds of ties looked similar in both cities. They migrated and found employment in much the same ways according to the different composition of their networks. The relational approach illustrates that Gujaratis' network ties rather than their social origins demonstrate variation in the way that Gujaratis are able to migrate to each place and the way in which their economic opportunities are structured. Equally significant, this book historicizes that approach by demonstrating how relational mechanisms link up historically with much larger forces, such as modernity. By looking back in time with a relational lens, we are able to see how, and with what consequences, various historical social ties formed to produce future migration flows to the United States and the United Kingdom.

Acknowledgments

OVER THE LONG COURSE OF THIS PROJECT, I have accumulated many debts of gratitude. First and foremost, I owe my greatest debt to Charles Tilly, who supported, encouraged, criticized, and inspired me from the project's inception to its advanced stages. Sadly, Chuck did not live to see this book come to fruition. Nevertheless, I feel his intellectual presence always. Robert K. Merton was also a constant source of support, encouragement, and enormous inspiration while I knew him during the last years of his life. I am grateful beyond description to have had such great intellectual giants guide my research. Thus, I dedicate this book to both of them.

During the early and later stages of the research and writing, many others also provided needed criticism, guidance, and often friendship; among them are Syed Ali, Anny Bakalian, Mehdi Bozorgmehr, Andrew Kourvetaris, Jack Levinson, Nicole Marwell, Anthony Orum, Margaret Power, Jan Rath, Saskia Sassen, Robert Smith, Arafaat Valiani, Sudhir Venkatesh, and Wen-Ching Wang. In London, I was incredibly fortunate to receive research and intellectual support from Robin Cohen and Peter Ratcliffe at Warwick University and from Steven Vertovec, who included me in the Transnational Communities Seminar at Oxford University, which he convened there. Significant personal aid in London came from Jerry Comati, Violetta Comati, and George Zouros.

I also received significant institutional support to work on the project. The National Science Foundation funded the early stages of the research (SBR 98-11138) with a significant grant that allowed me to live in London for six months and pay for research expenses. Early support also came from the Institute for Social and Economic Research and Policy at Columbia University where I was a fellow. There, Priya Lal transcribed many difficult and long interviews for me, and David Greenberg was a wonderful office mate. I thank them both. Later stages of the research and writing owe support from a PSC-CUNY grant (61712-00 39) at The City College of New York, CUNY. The grant enabled me to fund two wonderful research assistants. Julia Yang carefully updated much of the ever-changing data in Chapter 2, and Virginia Tangel provided important data analysis toward the end of the project. I am deeply appreciative to both of them for helping me push the project to completion.

I feel incredibly fortunate to have found the very professional editorship of Kate Wahl at Stanford University Press. She supported the manuscript from the beginning, read with a close eye, and made insightful suggestions that only helped to improve it. She also directed the manuscript to two excellent reviewers, whom I would like to thank. I am especially grateful to Roger Waldinger, who provided the most thoughtful and productive comments to make the book better than I ever envisioned it.

Of course, this book would never have been possible without the gracious participation of the Indians I interviewed and met in New York and London, whose identities must remain anonymous. They welcomed me into their homes, kept me warm with wonderfully aromatic Indian meals and chai, and allowed me into their lives. I am deeply grateful to each one of them. I only hope that my interpretations of their lives, while not always positive, reflect a just picture of the stories they told me.

Special thanks go to my parents, Daisy Ero Poros and Demetrios Poros, whom I could never repay for all they have given me. They have always been my greatest supporters and a bottomless source of love, aid, and hope. And, finally, my gratitude goes to Vassilis K. Fouskas, who, although he entered the picture late in this project, has become an enormous source of intellectual support and personal happiness for me. Not only did he read the entire manuscript and provide crucial insights that foresaw problems I was blind to, but he also helped push me along in the final stages of writing always with love, laughter, and eternal optimism. I cannot wait to share with him our little bundle of joy, who was mysteriously conceived during this process.

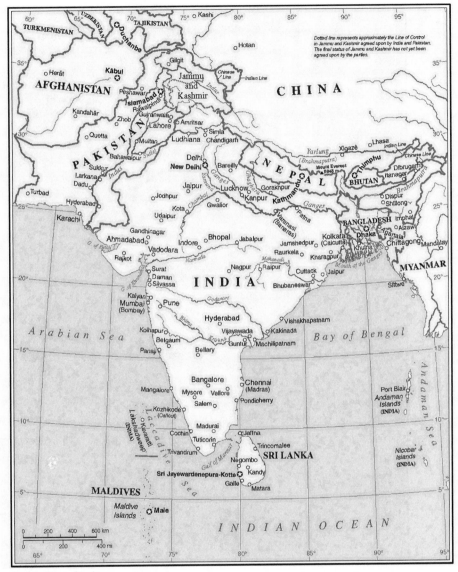

Map 1 Map of India

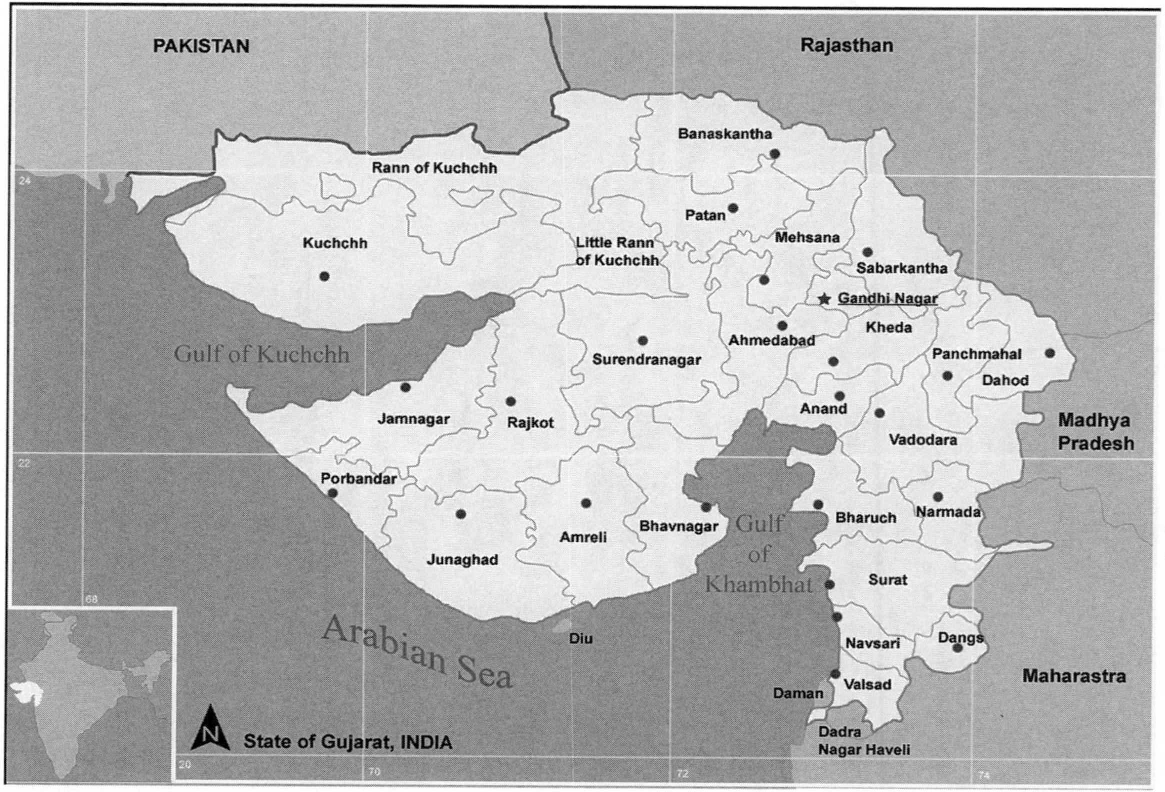

Map 2 Map of Gujarat State, India

Modern Migrations

1 Gujarati Indian Networks in New York and London

1

WHEN I FIRST SET OUT TO COLLECT the life histories of Gujarati immigrants in New York and London, many of them told me that they never expected to migrate to the United States or the United Kingdom. "I never thought that I would come to America," or "We never wanted to go to Britain," they told me. These immigrants' histories, although unique in their own way, had an almost predictable quality to them. Of course, all such stories benefit from hindsight in that they are reflective narratives carefully woven into coherent representations of identity, culture, and life circumstances. Yet, as I listened, it became clear that the stories of their lives, which are intimately intertwined with sociohistorical linkages and relations among India, East Africa, and Britain or between India and the United States, made their migration and occupational histories seem not only likely but even inevitable. The social ties they had to others already living in the United States or the United Kingdom determined where they migrated (for instance, Elmhurst, Queens, in New York, the port city of Mombasa in Kenya, or Wembley in Northwest London) and how they got there, thus confirming many studies of migration that focus on the role that social networks play in the lives of immigrants. Consider the story of Harshad, who was born in Kenya in 1955 as the youngest of six siblings.[1]

In Harshad's generation, most Indians from his ethnoreligious community of Oswal Jains were born in Kenya.[2] Their fathers had migrated there at the turn of the twentieth century after a severe famine in their region of Gujarat resulted in economic hardship and disadvantageous social and economic changes in their class status. Kenya had long been central to Indian

Ocean trade networks that included Gujaratis and was therefore known to this early generation of migrants that included Harshad's parents. Harshad told me that his father "worked for relations or people that we knew, you know, who had set up businesses there." Thus, with the help of others in their community in Kenya, Harshad's family were employed as small traders and shopkeepers in towns that developed along the East African railway, which extended from Mombasa to Lake Victoria in present-day Uganda. They sold all sorts of things—from everyday staples to mattresses that his mother made by hand. Harshad's household had little education or income, but their relatives and coethnic friends often helped with loans and pooled income, which eventually allowed Harshad's parents to invest in dairies and milk bottling plants that served the local district. Because Kenya was a British protectorate when Harshad and most of his siblings were born, they had British passports, whereas their parents had taken Kenyan citizenship in the early part of the century. In East Africa, anticolonial resistance against the British and Asians (primarily Indians) by the native East Africans had been growing throughout the mid-twentieth century. Asians were middleman minorities privileged by the British to suppress the native African population in the economy, education, and, of course, government. The movement for African political independence eventually resulted in a shift in the economic control of Kenya from British and Asian hands to the native Africans. Under these circumstances, Harshad's parents encouraged and financed their children's migration to and pursuit of higher education in London, which was considered superior to education in Nairobi, and financially supported them when they arrived there.

Harshad's middle brother was the first of the siblings to migrate to London with several of his friends from Kenya. From London, he made preparations for the migration of his siblings, who followed him one by one. Their parents bought them a house in London, which Harshad told me served as a "staging post" for all of his siblings and many friends from their Oswal community in Kenya. Despite his initial pursuit of a college degree in London, Harshad was persuaded to join his eldest brother in a prospering garment manufacturing business that operated transnationally in Britain and India through connections to kin and members of their Oswal Jain community in that industry. In fact, Harshad felt obligated to leave his studies at the request of his brother. Later, the firm suffered from a flooding of the market with Indian cottons, and Harshad's brother terminated the business. Harshad was left unemployed but with considerable entrepreneurial experience. He pursued a string of other transnational and local entrepreneurial opportunities that arose from close-knit community and kin relations that sometimes proved obligatory as well. However, when he decided to leave the garment industry, he realized that he had few good opportunities available to him in London's primary labor market because he had not completed his degree in law and economics. He therefore entered a six-month training program in computer programming. Meanwhile, his wife had been working in a large telecommunications firm. She connected Harshad to a job that she heard about from a friend in that firm's human resources department. This distant connection ushered Harshad into a temporary and then permanent technical position consistent with his newly acquired qualifications. Harshad and his wife have no doubt that their three children will complete university and become professionals in London's primary labor market. This belief is pervasive among most other members of their small community, who have made similar transitions from India to Kenya and finally Britain.

Harshad's story illustrates phenomenal generational mobility linked to migration. Kin and community members figured prominently in the ability of Harshad and his siblings to migrate to London, attend university, start businesses, or obtain other types of employment. Money, resources, job opportunities, information, and companionship generously flowed through Harshad's relations with his family and community. And, as in any family or social network, social obligations, negotiation, conflict, resistance, and capitulation were also present. In Harshad's story we see that the premigration histories of immigrants are deeply intertwined with their postmigration lives. His story, however, is not simply a matter of reaping advantages from densely connected networks that span several countries or from solidary networks based on coethnicity and kinship. The types of social ties and the transactions within ties in Harshad's networks provided specific kinds of opportunities that both facilitated and constrained his economic incorporation and mobility. These ties included him in some endeavors, such as partnering with his brother's transnational business, and excluded him from others, such as making decisions about the future of that business or leaving university. As networks change, so do opportunities and the social and economic constraints that accompany those opportunities. Network theories of migration focus almost entirely on interpersonal ties, social ties to kin and community, such as those clearly seen in Harshad's family and highlighted in dozens of studies of immigrants from different countries (for example, Foner 2000; Levitt

2001; Massey, Arango, Durand, and Gonzalez 1987; Menjívar 2000; Portes and Rumbaut 1990; Smith 2006; Tilly 1990). Even when those ties constrain the economic and other opportunities of migrants, they are still crucial for migrants to get from one destination to another and to establish their lives in a new destination. Social ties to family and friends, however, are not the only types of ties that are significant in the migration histories of Gujaratis. Here is a quite different migration story, this one from New York.

Lakshmi comes from a long line of "diamond families" from a small town in Gujarat, now grown into a small city, known for its Jain diamond traders. She was trained early in the business by her uncle, even though women were not often expected to work in the business. They were usually encouraged to marry into other Jain families in the diamond trade and to become mothers and caretakers. The business is mainly centered in Bombay (now known as Mumbai), where Lakshmi was born. Its headquarters, as with most businesses in the diamond trade, are in Antwerp, Belgium. Rough diamonds are bought and sold there and sent to Indian diamond centers, cities such as Bombay in the state of Maharashtra or Ahmedabad and Surat in neighboring Gujarat, for cutting and polishing. Polished stones can be traded again in Antwerp and exported for sale to commercial centers around the world. Lakshmi's uncle sent her and her husband, whom he also trained in the trade, to New York City in 1970 to expand their business to New York's large commercial market. Their firm in Antwerp sponsored them as investors for U.S. immigration, but they still had to start this commercial side of the business from the bottom up. Along with just a handful of other Jain diamond families from Gujarat, they were pioneers among Indians in this new market.

In the early 1970s, Lakshmi and her husband started out in a modest one-bedroom apartment in Queens, in a building filled with many other Indian immigrants. They began navigating the New York market by connecting and partnering with other diamond entrepreneurs and by expanding their business into the production and sale of jewelry—eventually running a multimillion-dollar business. Lakshmi is somewhat unusual in that she plays a central role in an independent operation that she co-owns and in which she works with her husband. However, she also holds a subordinate position to him in most matters of its operation. Lakshmi confided to me that she is careful not to speak back to her husband when they are in the office so as not to cause "major fights" between them. Apart from its overt sexism, this control over her behavior in their office attests to the densely intertwined networks of Jain diamond families who live in diamond centers, such as New York, Antwerp, Hong Kong, Bangkok, and Bombay. Their families have known each other for generations. They share the same region of origin, religion, class status, education, and business interests. Their trade requires huge amounts of trust, in part because it is so risky to trade extremely small and valuable objects around the world on little more than a handshake. And their networks exert strong social controls over their behavior to protect each member's stake in the business.

Lakshmi and her husband are in some ways like many entrepreneurial families whose businesses operate transnationally, often not only between India and the United States or the United Kingdom but also in a number of commercial centers around the world. Clearly, their social networks were instrumental in their migration and in their business opportunities in New York. Social ties to family members, such as Lakshmi's uncle, played a critical role in directing where Lakshmi would migrate, how she would get there, and what she would do once there. Her family and community ties, however, were noticeably different in several respects from the ties that Harshad had. Lakshmi's ties consisted of suppliers and buyers in the diamond trade that were simultaneously family ties—uncles, husbands, and members of their ethnoreligious community in India among whom it would be unthinkable to simply extricate themselves from the diamond industry to pursue other lines of work or interests in the way that Harshad eventually did. Those ties also drove their migration to specific destinations that followed from their business interests, unlike Harshad's migration to London. Lakshmi's dense "trust networks," as Charles Tilly (2005) would call them, are unique in that they are a composite of interpersonal ties to kin and community and organizational ties consisting of those same people within their businesses and industry. These ties are different from those of another kind of migration flow from Gujarat illustrated in this last story from New York.

Kishor and his wife Jamnadevi live in a comfortable home in a wealthy New York suburb. Inside it is adorned with Indian furniture and textiles, which complement its functional American style. Kishor is a pediatrician, and Jamnadevi is a dentist, two common professions of the first large wave of Indian immigration after 1965.[3] I wondered how exactly they got to New York and asked Kishor to describe to me how he became a house physician in a New York hospital:

KISHOR: When I was here in 1974 [the year prior to his immigration on an employment preference visa], I lined up a job in Staten Island with my friend.

MP: *A friend from . . . ?*

KISHOR: Gujarat.

MP: *From school?*

KISHOR: Same college, same college. He said, we have an opening here; why don't you come over? So I said, okay.

In fact, Kishor had been preparing to enter the United States to practice medicine for some time. His brother was the first of two of Kishor's sibling-doctors to migrate to the United States under employment preferences for physicians. When Kishor made a six-month personal visit to his brother in 1974 with a tourist visa, he was encouraged by him to study for the Educational Council for Foreign Medical Graduates (ECFMG) exam, necessary for obtaining a professional visa to the United States. Kishor took a preparatory class, passed the exam, applied for a visa, and returned to India to wait for it. The next year (a mere four months after his application), the visa was granted and, as already mentioned, Kishor had lined up a job through his old medical college friend, a doctor at a Staten Island hospital. That friend also helped him with housing and social support during this major transition in Kishor's life. Kishor had also sponsored Jamnadevi to migrate with him at the same time, as she had applied for a permanent visa under employment preferences for highly educated professionals. However, she finally migrated under family preferences for spouses of employment-preference migrants when that visa approval arrived first. Kishor, his elder brother, and his sister all migrated to the United States, and they are practicing medical doctors there. Their other sister, who is not a doctor or other professional, stayed in India.

The simplicity of Kishor's answer to my initial question about how he migrated to the United States belies a much more complex history that precedes the liberalization of U.S. immigration law in the 1965 Immigration and Nationality Act, which ostensibly opened the doors equally to immigrants from all parts of the world and expanded the number of highly educated people who could immigrate under employment preferences. That history can be traced to the time of India's independence from Britain during Jawaharlal Nehru's term as the first prime minister of a democratic, independent India (1947–1964). Nehru pursued a set of socioeconomic reforms to push India toward Western forms of modernization and to boost the nascent middle class (and the elite) (Varma 1998). Nehru led the development of a set of prestigious institutes of higher education focused on science, technology, and management, which were funded by foreign states, especially the United States, and by American foundations that intended to curb the influence of communism in India. These organizations, such as the Ford Foundation, Harvard, and Massachusetts Institute of Technology (MIT), were instrumental in influencing the structure and curriculum of these Indian institutes during the 1950s and early 1960s and in promoting the study of science, medicine, and engineering among the Indian middle class (Bhagwati 1993; Domrese 1970; Oommen 1987). Nehru intended to bring India closer to the West through a new, highly educated labor force and technological development. Of course, Indian education, including its curricula and organization, was for a long time influenced by the British system. However, after India's independence—as the British were pulling away from India—the United States stepped in to "colonize" India with American-style education and administration at the top Indian Institutes of science and technology, the Regional Engineering Colleges and in medical education (see Magat 1979; Nielsen 1972; Parekh 1985; Sodeman 1971; Weaver 1967). Thus, Nehru's active engagement with the United States fostered Indo-American social ties in which faculty, students, ideas, and resources were exchanged from 1947, long before the 1965 liberalization of U.S. immigration laws, which opened the doors to immigration from Asia, Latin America, and the rest of the world.

The educational ties to specific medical colleges in India, the surplus of Indian-trained physicians, and the shortage of medical personnel in the United States and Britain created open circumstances for the migration of Indian physicians. The United States and Britain actively recruited this high-skill labor force. For instance, the British National Health Service (NHS) in the 1950s and 1960s used ties to specific medical colleges in India, including in Gujarat state (Coleman 1994; Spencer 1997). The NHS also relied on recruited doctors to encourage similarly qualified colleagues in India to help fill the health industry's labor shortage (see Robinson and Carey 2000), a phenomenon similar to the U.S. case. As Kishor tells us, he had lined up his first job in a U.S. hospital through a physician friend from his medical college in India. Large proportions of graduating classes of medical colleges in India left for the United States and Britain (Helweg 2004; Helweg and Helweg 1990; Khandelwal 2002).

More broadly, Kishor's migration history demonstrates how social ties and historical context are inextricable from each other. Without the influence of U.S. development policies on Indian medical schools, social ties between Indian medical students and American institutions may have never formed to encourage this migration of professionals regardless of open or closed immigration policies. Persistent colonial relations in Indian and British institutions perpetuated the same dynamic in Britain. Once begun, Indian physicians themselves continued the recruitment of their colleagues, friends, and family members, who were also certified doctors. Therefore, colleagues as well as kin and friends, who all share the same profession, provided organizational pathways to migration and jobs in their fields. They could not have provided that pathway for others who were not certified to practice medicine in the United States. This is not to say that recruited professionals do not sponsor relatives to migrate on family visas. They often do. However, those kin are more likely to be underemployed in the host country because they do not have to meet the requirements of organizations or institutions to migrate (this is discussed more fully in Chapter 3). Unlike the story of Harshad, for instance, transactions between Kishor and his sibling-doctors and colleague-friends included information specifically about immigration under U.S. employment preferences, professional certification and licensing in medicine, and available jobs equivalent to these qualifications. In addition to that very significant information, their transactions included housing and social support, which are common to all sorts of immigrants. Furthermore, unlike the cases of Lakshmi and Harshad, the certification requirements and mechanisms of organizations such as medical colleges and testing and licensing boards controlled opportunities for migrating and working in one's profession.

The stories of Harshad, Lakshmi, and Kishor reflect the wide diversity of experiences among the Gujarati immigrants whom I interviewed in New York and London. Their experiences of migration and settlement in the United States or the United Kingdom were shaped in large part by the various sorts of social ties that are part of their social networks. Their stories, therefore, reflect many network accounts of migration in which interpersonal ties to family, friends, and community play a central role in shaping whether people migrate, where they go, and what happens to them after they arrive at their new destination. However, in the cases of Lakshmi and Kishor, for instance, their social ties did not only or simply consist of interpersonal ties. Theirs also included ties to institutions, businesses, and state agencies. The historical formation of these different sorts of ties was vastly different for Harshad, Lakshmi, and Kishor, and the relations within their ties furthermore shaped their ability to migrate, where they migrated, and the kinds of lives they have had in East Africa, the United States, or the United Kingdom. These elements of the migration process—different configurations of social ties, the relations within them, and their historical formation—have often been left unexamined or implicit in studies of migration. Although sociologists of migration overwhelmingly agree that social networks are crucial for understanding migration, we still know little about how these networks operate, whether and which kinds of social ties make a difference in the lives of migrants, and how those ties form. The wide variety of migration stories within one seemingly homogeneous group asks us to explain and question anew what is the role of social networks in the migration process and, more fundamentally, how migration happens. What kinds of social networks encourage migration, and in what ways do they do so? Do different kinds of social ties have different effects on migrants' lives and their mobility? How do these ties form historically? What happens within these ties in the lived relations and experiences of migrants? Can social networks explain everything about the migration process, or are they limited in scope?

I explore these questions in this book through an examination of Gujarati Indian networks in New York and London. The migration histories of these Indians opens up the debate between substantialist and relational perspectives of migration, which although it often may be seen as a debate between the economics and sociology of migration, respectively, also highlights weaknesses in network accounts of migration in sociology, which rely on substantialist approaches. That debate is introduced in the following section and elaborated on in Chapter 5.

The Substantialist versus Relational Approach to Migration

On the surface, the migration histories of Harshad, Lakshmi, and Kishor reflect some standard accounts of why and how people migrate and how they become economically incorporated into host societies. All of these immigrants came from a "developing country," either India or East Africa, and migrated to a "developed" one, the United States or Britain. These paths are typically described as East to West or South to North global migration trajectories, which could also characterize the migration of Harshad, Lakshmi, and Kishor. Reflecting these trajectories, individuals or households from poorer countries are portrayed as migrating to richer countries because they are drawn by wage differentials. Certainly, all of the migration stories reflect some anticipation of economic gain in the host society—through education when Harshad and his siblings migrated to London and through work in the cases of Lakshmi and Kishor. Furthermore, this kind of migration from the developing to the developed world is seen as a result of uneven capitalist development around the world, which is evident in India's and East Africa's relative poverty over the past 200 years as they were "underdeveloped" or exploited by British colonial projects there and by American dominance worldwide. The migration literature, notably in economics but also in sociology, also often touts movements from developing to developed countries as common pathways for the migration of the relatively poor and low-skilled to capital-rich countries where there is demand for their labor (Castles and Miller 2003; Massey, Arango, Hugo, Kouaouci, Pellegrino, and Taylor 1998).

Below the surface of these economic and macroaccounts of migration, however, many questions and contradictions form as we consider the life histories of Harshad, Lakshmi, and Kishor. For instance, we might say that Harshad's parents understandably migrated to East Africa during its economic development under the British as they tried to escape the famine that contributed to their own poverty in Gujarat. Ironically, however, colonial India was being "developed" at the same time. Moreover, famines do not occur naturally but rather result from economic exploitation (Sen 1983). Thus, Harshad's parents were pushed out of one colonial context and into another, not from a developing to a developed country. Perhaps Lakshmi and Kishor, too, were "pushed" to migrate in anticipation of their upward mobility through business expansion for Lakshmi and professional demand for Kishor, both of which were linked to capitalist expansion in the United States and United Kingdom. However, Gujaratis have been migrating as part of wide-ranging trade diasporas for centuries, long before capitalist development became concentrated in Europe and the United States (as discussed further in Chapter 2). Some links to that past persist in contemporary trade flows, such as in the diamond and garment industries. Kishor's training as a physician in India and his migration to the United States, where there was more demand for his labor, perhaps better demonstrate uneven capitalist development between core countries (the United States) and peripheral countries (India) in the world economy. However, his medical college ties to U.S. institutions, which encouraged his migration and that of his fellow classmates, indicate a more complex historical integration of these two regions of the world and their economies, ironically during a time when economic globalization was considered to be on the wane compared to the early and latter parts of the twentieth century (see Held, McGrew, Goldblatt, and Perraton 1999; Sassen 2001).

Similarly, among these three cases, perhaps only Harshad's parents and their generation of migrants to East Africa from India can be seen as low skilled and uneducated, poor people migrating to "rich" countries where there is demand for their labor. Harshad's parents even encouraged their children to migrate to London to take advantage of the greater social and economic opportunities of that Western industrialized state. Notably, however, Harshad's parents stayed behind in Kenya as they sent financial remittances to Harshad and his siblings in London. This reverse remittance flow constituted enough money to buy the children a house and send them to university. Typically, if not always, economic remittances are conceived and documented as a one-way flow from migrants in the destination country to nonmigrants in the home country—the newly rich supporting the relatively poor back home. However, cases such as Harshad's indicate that reverse flows also take place, perhaps most prevalently among students or young migrants and investors. This "reverse remittance" phenomenon has not been studied thoroughly and raises the question of whether and how much financial flows follow migrants from sending to receiving countries or circulate in some other manner—not to mention that those remittance flows suggest a counterintuitive logic about people who move from developing to developed countries.

As for Lakshmi and Kishor, they were hardly poor or low skilled. Certainly, many transnational entrepreneurs have lower educational qualifications and, perhaps, could be thought of as low human capital migrants. However, in the case of diamond families, such as Lakshmi's, and other entrepreneurs in transnational industries such as garments, large amounts of financial capital predictably followed them from the parts of the world from which they came, for example, Bombay and Antwerp. Education was hardly a consideration for their success, although they certainly had significant human capital embodied in their business experience in India. Kishor, though not as wealthy as Lakshmi, also defies the stereotype of the poor, uneducated migrant. He comes from a middle-class family, in which his father was a "respected cloth merchant." And he and his sibling-doctors, all of whom attended medical school in India, were obviously highly educated.

Most sociologists and anthropologists have employed network theories to challenge the foregoing explanations of international migration that are typical of economic and "push-pull" explanations of migration (for examples, Borjas 1999; Lee 1966; Piore 1979; Stark 1991; Todaro 1976) and macroaccounts of global migration influenced by world-systems theory (Castles and Miller 2003;

see also Brettell and Hollifield 2000 for an overview of these migration theories). Those accounts often emphasize what have become commonsense sorts of assumptions about immigrants, such as the idea that people migrate solely for economic gain and that people from poor countries are more likely to migrate to rich countries. However, as shown in the histories of Harshad, Lakshmi, and Kishor, economic and macroaccounts of migration leave a number of important questions unanswered, which network accounts of migration have addressed to some degree over the course of almost a century since members of the first Chicago school of sociology began studying the earliest waves of mass migration to Chicago.[4] Among those pressing questions, how do we explain fairly large migration flows of highly educated professionals or of the smaller, but no less significant, flows of transnational entrepreneurs and traders? How do we explain selectivity—the fact that many individuals with ascriptive characteristics similar to those of migrants do not migrate? As an example, a related Oswal Jain sect in Harshad's parents' region of Gujarat did not migrate to East Africa in large numbers (Banks 1994) despite the regional famine. Therefore, the Halari Oswal Jains, Harshad's community, selectively migrated for reasons and in ways that require investigation. Similarly, how do we explain that about half of international migration takes place between developing countries (Martin and Widgren 2002), not to mention within complex diasporas over time (Cohen 1997), such as the Oswal Jain diaspora, which now spans at least three continents over the course of a century, or the Jain diamond traders, whose diaspora across different diamond centers covers much of the world? Network theories of migration have provided answers to some of these questions because they take into account the real connections that migrants have, which create the opportunity to move. As evident in all three stories, network ties were critical to understanding how people move from one destination to another and in defining which potential destinations were possible.

However, network theories of migration have not sufficiently accounted for all sorts of migration flows, thus signaling a broader problem in the debate about migration. The disagreement in the literature between economic or macroaccounts of migration, including world systems theory, and network accounts of migration roughly represents a broader debate between substantialist and relational accounts of social phenomena, such as migration. Generally, substantialist accounts rely on ascriptive characteristics of individual migrants and their households or the countries from which people emigrate for their explanations, that is, the poor, low-skilled male from a developing country migrates seeking economic gain in a capital-rich, developed country. The relational approach rejects these tools of positivism that are now so commonplace in sociological analysis and that treat gender, race, ethnicity, class status, and the like as static, categorical attributes to explain complex behavior. Instead, the relational approach focuses our attention on networks as sets of relations that continually change and that, through the exchange of social goods, such as the passing of money, information, influence, status, and power, shape very specific opportunities for migration and mobility. The relational approach is not new at all. It goes back to the works of Simmel (1955, 1971), Goffman (1967), and Barth (1969), to name a few, and it has been revived recently by a number of scholars who have argued for its return to sociological analysis (for example, Abbott 2001; Brubaker 2004; Emirbayer 1997; and Tilly 1999). For instance, the approach has become prominent in a number of fields, including historical sociology, social movements, and race and ethnicity. However, with the exception of the work of Thomas Faist (2000), in studies of migration, it has remained implicit at most (for example, Bashi 2007; Hernández-León 2008; Mahler 1995; Smith 2006) and therefore has not been developed fully in the context of explaining migration processes.

Most sociologists of migration agree that network theories have long offered more accurate explanations of migration than economic theories and macroaccounts. Nevertheless, their lack of attention to the relational perspective has limited the analysis of migrant networks to migrants' interpersonal ties—the kin and community relations that provide information and critical resources to reduce the risk associated with migrating. That emphasis has sometimes reproduced substantialist arguments in combination with implicitly relational ones because much of migration theory has been developed through the lens of fairly homogeneous flows of relatively poor migrants from Latin America among whom interpersonal ties are crucial for their mobility (for example, Levitt 2001; Massey et al. 1987, 1998; Menjívar 2000; Smith 2006) and who in many ways reflect the assumptions of economic and macroaccounts of migration, which envision the poor huddled masses recalled from the late nineteenth and early twentieth centuries of mass migration to the United States. Thus, for instance, Massey and his colleagues argue that an uneven geography of production brought on by globalization (as put forth in world systems theory) initiates migration flows that are then perpetuated by migrant social networks, that is, interpersonal tie networks. These sorts of combinations of substantialist and relational explanations of migration tend to reflect economic and macroforces that are thought to "push" people to migrate in search of better opportunities and dehistoricize or isolate interpersonal ties from any broader context.

Furthermore, not all network ties are the same. Interpersonal ties were clearly evident in Harshad's migration to London, and, although certainly present in the case of Lakshmi and Kishor, on their own they were not their most important ties. Clearly, for instance, Lakshmi's composite of interpersonal and organizational ties and Kishor's organizational ties made their migrations possible and shaped their opportunities in New York. Interpersonal ties alone would not have sufficed for Lakshmi to be a pioneer in the New York diamond trade among Jain diamond families, and Kishor could not have migrated and preserved his occupational status without organizational ties. These different social ties became apparent in the relations of exchange or transactions within their social networks—for example, when Kishor's doctor-brother shared with him the information about certification as a medical doctor in New York, when Lakshmi's uncle (also her boss) called on her and her husband to expand the family's diamond business in New York, and when Harshad's parents bought their children a house in London as a gift, which also served as a staging post for other close kin and community members.

This book highlights additional kinds of ties that aid the migration process and, along with a consideration of interpersonal ties, more fully explains selectivity and diversity in migration flows within the Gujarati Indian immigrant populations in New York and London. It also examines relations of exchange or transactions within different types of social ties to explain how people migrate and seek socioeconomic mobility at their destinations. It combines our knowledge of migrant networks from migration studies with the study of social networks more generally, as developed in the field of economic sociology, to reach a fuller understanding of how migrant networks and relations of exchange affect the migration process.

In doing so, the book takes a different theoretical and methodological approach from most studies of migration by making migrants' social networks and the individuals and organizations within them its focus of study. Theoretically, it introduces a new typology based on social ties that broadly reflects variation in the composition of migrant networks, which shape migration flows and social and economic mobility in host societies. As we saw in the life histories introduced in the beginning of this book, at least three types of social ties or relations dominate the social networks of the immigrants who, as a whole, make up today's large diaspora of Gujaratis. They are interpersonal, organizational, and composite ties. Briefly, interpersonal ties refer to strong ties (Granovetter 1973) composed of relationships among kin, friends, and community, such as parents, spouses, siblings, cousins, friends, and coethnics. I refer to migrant flows made up of interpersonal ties as *chains* because they most resemble chain migration, as in Harshad's case, which is the most common form of migration from virtually every historical era that has been documented by migration researchers.

Organizational ties, which are typically thought of as weak ties (see Granovetter 1973), exist when individuals are connected or relate to each other through the same organizations and institutions, for instance ties to coworkers, employers, bureaucrats, or community leaders, such as Kishor's ties. Organizations of all kinds, such as schools, government agencies, businesses, voluntary associations, professional organizations, labor unions, places of employment, and religious institutions, mediate relations within these social ties. I refer to these migrant networks and flows as *recruits* because their organizational ties facilitate their recruitment into particular jobs and to particular destinations more than interpersonal ties.

Composite ties are made up of both interpersonal and organizational ties. They are distinct from the two types above because the relations within composite ties are mediated by the organization and the family or community together as a single entity. These relations coexist in such a way that they are inseparable and indistinguishable from each other, for instance in family firms such as Lakshmi's. I refer to these migrant networks as *trusties* because the high-risk nature of their relationships and economic activities require that they continuously place valued goods and activities into the hands of others—often outside any formal means of policing or enforcement. In other words, their transactions require loads of trust.

There is a fourth possibility that contains the smallest proportion of migrants among these flows. That possibility holds that some people may migrate without any ties at all. They are *solitaries*. Typically, we think of these migrants as pioneers—mavericks, adventurers, explorers, even accidental border crossers. More migrants seem to claim to be pioneers than those who really do migrate without ties; therefore, I refer to them as solitaries instead of pioneers to highlight their lack of ties. And our accounts of pioneers are always rare because they are so few in number and their stories are often told in biographies, in legends, or as oral histories.[5] Nevertheless, some solitaries do (and should) exist.

Solitaries, chains, recruits, and trusties are broad, ideal types of migration flows that encompass the wide variety of migrations evident among Gujaratis— refugees from Uganda, recruited physicians, engineers and teachers, students, family reunification migrants, and transnational traders. Some might think that Gujaratis are simply a unique case, unlike other migrants and even, perhaps, unlike other Indian regional groups.[6] However, I contend that they are not and that we see many of the same kinds of network dynamics in Gujaratis as in Indians more generally and many other immigrant groups. (This view is discussed in more theoretical detail in Chapter 5.) For instance, we can explain how migrants as different as refugees, guest workers, and students are linked to organizations and state agencies and as recruits share some of the same characteristics in their flows and mobility. And we can better historicize migration as a process by seeking the origins of different kinds of social ties, not only among individuals, as in interpersonal ties, but also in the development of individuals' relations with organizations, institutions, firms, and the state as represented in organizational and composite ties. These dynamics will become apparent in Chapters 2, 3, and 4, which question how Gujarati social ties are formed historically, what kinds of ties Gujaratis have in their social networks, how those ties contribute to specific migration flows, and what the economic consequences are that accompany those flows. Although we cannot generalize knowledge about the Gujarati case to all immigrant groups, Gujaratis are a critical case with which we can compare other immigrant groups (via the rich fieldwork studies on migration that already exist) to develop a more empirically sound model of the role of migrant networks in migration flows and mobility. Thus, the theoretical significance of the case of Gujarati migrations is elaborated in Chapter 5. In that chapter, the book advances a relational perspective to understanding migration, which challenges standard network accounts of migration and provides a way of thinking about international migration more generally, not only in the case of Gujaratis. Methodologically, the book also uses a novel approach to investigate migrant networks and their role in shaping migration flows and mobility in New York and London. Detailed in the following pages, it uses a qualitative network method for sampling migrant networks and for collecting data about the relations of immigrants within their networks.

A Qualitative Network Method for Studying Migration

This book is based primarily on eighty interviews (fifty-six life histories and twenty-four interviews with organizations) and participant observation in

New York and London during 1998 and 1999. At that time, I also read much of the ethnic media serving the Gujarati and Indian populations in both cities on a daily basis while engaged in fieldwork. Over the last ten years, I have been in regular contact with some of the original participants in the study and have engaged in informal conversations with numerous new contacts on regular visits to New York and two visits to London, while I lived away from each city. I have often attended Indian festivals and cultural events, mostly in New York, and kept up with some of the ethnic media that serve the Gujarati and Indian populations in both sites. Those media have grown exponentially, especially via the Internet, since I first began this research.

Sampling Networks in New York and London

The life histories of Gujarati immigrants presented in this book are based on a novel methodology that, unlike other studies of migrant networks, samples networks for comparison. Examining the role of networks requires comparing more than one network, as does examining relations within social ties in networks and across them. However, conventional snowball samples, used in virtually every qualitative study of migration, often result in the sampling of one large network that is relatively homogeneous because everyone is connected to one degree or another. For instance, collecting a nonrandom snowball sample begins by targeting individuals who fit the specific population criteria to be sampled (for example, first-generation Gujarati Hindus or Jains living in New York or London) and then asking each new participant in the sample to refer the researcher to someone else who also fits the criteria. Key informants are also used to build qualitative samples; however, snowball sampling generally results in a long, fairly homogeneous chain of persons who are linked to each other to a greater or lesser degree. For instance, although Vilna Bashi (2007) began her study of West Indian immigrants in New York and London with two "unrelated persons" to sample two separate networks, this nonrandom snowball sample resulted in essentially one large network in which some participants in New York and London were linked to each other. I sought to avoid this long chain effect to compare distinct networks that might or might not be connected to each other, but I also needed to be able to examine relations of exchange within network ties to understand their role in the migration process and their effect on mobility. Therefore, I began with a random sample of individuals and then used "short-string" snowball sampling to gain access to the networks of those randomly selected participants.

To do this, I began by selecting four of the most common Gujarati surnames from which to draw a random sample of participants for conducting life history interviews in New York and London.[7] Those surnames represent three of the four *varna* castes (Brahmins, Kshatriyas, Vaisyas) and specific subcastes or *jati* (*jatni* in Gujarati), thus drawing from a range of caste groups. In reality, varnas as functioning caste divisions are virtually meaningless, especially in the case of Gujaratis, who in recent times have at least twelve caste divisions of the first order and numerous second, third, and fourth orders of division within those, resulting in hundreds of castes and subcastes (Shah and Desai 1988).[8] Two of the surnames are common not only among Gujarati Hindus but also among Jains, Parsis, and Muslims. Jains and Parsis, when encountered, were kept in the sample because of their history of relatively close relations and equivalent position vis-à-vis middle- and high-status Hindus in Gujarat, India, and the diaspora. Muslims, on the other hand, hold a generally subordinate position in Indian society, much like ethnic minorities in Western countries (Brass 1994). Therefore, they were removed from the sample to limit the analysis to a purportedly homogenous but clearly complex socioreligious group from India.[9] Limiting this study to one regional and religious group from India allowed me to keep constant some of the effects of culture so that the effects of networks could be distinguished more readily. Focusing on Gujaratis also permitted a more in-depth analysis of intragroup differences, which have often been overlooked in studies of Indians and other nationality groups.

To collect a random sample using the four common Gujarati surnames, I used census data from 1990 for the New York Consolidated Metropolitan Statistical Area (CMSA) and from 1991 for Greater London to identify the top residential areas for Indians in those cities. The top residential counties in the New York CMSA in declining order were Queens and Manhattan in New York City, suburban Nassau-Suffolk (NY), suburban Middlesex-Somerset-Hunterdon (NJ), Bergen-Passaic (NJ), and Newark (NJ). In Greater London, the top boroughs of residential concentration were Ealing, Brent, Harrow, Hounslow, Newham (Inner London), Redbridge, and Barnet (Ratcliffe 1996; Rees and Philips 1996). These counties and boroughs of residential concentration remained much the same in New York and London in the 2000 and 2001 censuses.

With names and counties in hand, I turned to public telephone directories that corresponded to these top residential areas of Indian immigrant settlement to draw a random sample from each county or borough and to send initial contact letters to potential participants in the study. I then followed up by telephone to recruit participants to meet with me for a life history inter-view. This was not an easy path to participant recruitment, and the positive response rate was fairly low (18 percent in New York and 12 percent in Lon-don); however, it was higher than in some other studies of Indian immigrants. Padma Rangaswamy's (2000) nonrandom sample survey of more than 500 In-dians in Chicago, for instance, produced a response rate of only 11 percent.[10]

A random sample of six potential networks in New York and ten poten-tial networks in London was obtained from the recruitment method. This sample of sixteen individuals or married couples lived in Queens, Manhattan, Westchester, and Nassau counties in New York and in the boroughs of Barnet, Brent, Harrow, Hounslow, Newham, and Redbridge in London. After inter-viewing each of these randomly selected participants, I asked them to refer me to as many as four people whom they knew as colleagues, friends, or acquain-tances, whether at their workplaces, schools, community associations, neigh-borhoods, or places of worship (excluding their households). Those contacts comprised the short-string snowball sample. Often, I was not able to interview all of the contacts participants referred to me. Some participants also chose to refer me to fewer than four people in their networks. Therefore, I sought addi-tional members of the network from the second- or third-order contacts. (See Figure 1.1.) Six short-string snowball samples were successfully obtained from the initial random sample. The random and short-string snowball samples re-sulted in a total of fifty-six life history interviews in both sites (thirty-three in London and twenty-three in New York) of which forty-three, or 77 percent, were part of networks that I interviewed (four networks in London and two in New York). The samples within each city were evenly divided between males and females. The London sample contained a wider age range than the New York sample. London's participants migrated to the United Kingdom mostly in the 1960s and 1970s, reflecting the fact that many were either born in East Africa or had first migrated to East Africa from India in the 1950s. The par-ticipants in the New York sample, on the other hand, migrated throughout the 1970s and 1980s to New York from India. New York's Gujaratis were, on the whole, more educated than London's, including eight participants who had finished a postgraduate degree. Only one person in the London sample held a postgraduate degree. London's sample was almost evenly divided be-tween those who had matriculated or completed A-levels and those who held a college degree. Interestingly, New York's sample is skewed toward the more highly educated (college degree and higher) even less than it might be because

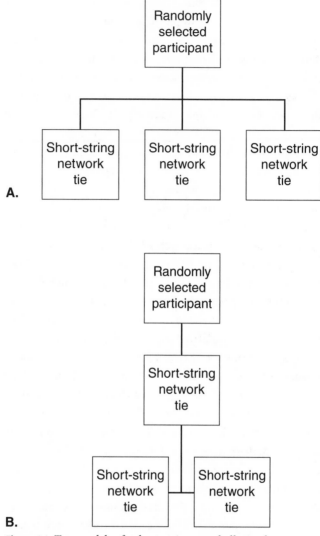

Figure 1.1. Two models of a short-string snowball sample.

many of the transnational entrepreneurs in the diamond and garment industries found there did not attend or complete college. Most unusually, one participant, who attended school in India, did not matriculate.[11]

Sampling networks by using short-string snowball samples drawn from randomly selected participants allows researchers to compare distinct networks. It also illustrates the structure of social networks and how social networks represent different configurations of social ties. Qualitative network studies, furthermore, can demonstrate relations of exchange, such as the exchange of information, resources, money, power, influence, persuasion, and status that pass through network ties. This approach can be more effective than survey methods, which are often used in social network analysis, because survey methods, although they capture the structure of networks very well and produce generalizable results, often do not capture relations of exchange as well. The approach is also better than conventional ethnography because it can better describe the structure of networks of relations and provide a comparison of networks, which "long-string" snowball samples cannot accomplish. The qualitative network method is, of course, limited by lack of generalizability and small sample size. The method is also extremely difficult and time consuming and cannot produce samples from a known universe of social network ties. However, its initial random selection ensures diversity in the sample that conventional snowball sampling does not, and it permits researchers to treat network theories of the migration process and associated dynamics, such as mobility, as empirical questions about relational processes. Therefore, it generates new theoretical insights about network processes that quantitative studies often lack.[12]

The Life History Method

Life histories are quite fascinating as stories and as tools for learning about the migration process. They also have several advantages that make this study distinctive. For instance, the life histories of Gujarati Indians span four continents: Asia, Africa, Europe, and North America. Without traveling to India or East Africa, I was still able to capture some of the dynamics of the migration process that occurred in those places by collecting life histories that reached back in time to the beginning of participants' lives and along the way told the story of related others, often from earlier generations.[13] That retrospective view provided another methodological advantage because it allowed me to see how change occurred in the lives of the participants, whether related to family, education, work, health, political turmoil, social unrest, religious dynamics, or the like. Finally, life histories illustrate relations with others, which permit the gathering of relational data not only from each individual interviewed but, most importantly, from other individuals in the networks of participants. Relational data, therefore, were sometimes primary data, in that I collected the life histories of people connected to each other in the same network (via the short-string snowball sample); or they were secondary, in that stories about relations of exchange within the networks of individuals were narrated to me, such as the story of how Harshad and his brother went into business together. This method allowed me to learn about dozens of connected others in the lives of the immigrants who comprised the primary sample, albeit from the perspective of the narrator.

Voluntary Association and Organization Interviews

The Indian and Gujarati immigrant populations in New York and London and the United States and the United Kingdom more generally are highly involved in voluntary associations of all kinds. In fact, the proliferation of such associations over the years became impossible to keep up with. In the late 1990s, it seemed possible for me to catalog the many associations that operated in New York and London, dividing them into categories based on the variety of purposes they served. For instance, occupational, philanthropic, cultural (pan-Indian and region-/language-/caste-specific), political (transnational and American-focused), religious, special needs or services, and umbrella organizations constituted the most common purposes for voluntary organization. I compiled a list of hundreds of these organizations from ethnic media, directories of large organizations that were affiliated to smaller ones (these directories were provided to me by organization leaders), the life history interview participants, association interviews, and informal conversations. However, after a few years, the task clearly exceeded my abilities, as the population and its associational life have grown dramatically over the last ten years. Today, hundreds if not thousands of Indian associations, including many smaller chapters of national-level and regional associations, exist in New York and London.

Nonetheless, I interviewed leaders and members from nine associations in New York and fifteen associations in London to better understand their role among immigrants. Some of these were newspaper editors, philanthropists, and prominent businesspeople (mostly men) who held formal positions in their organizations and were sometimes rivals; others were local community leaders and members. I attempted to sample a wide variety of associations and their members and leaders to form a broader picture of their role within Indian communities and to understand the religious, regional, and linguistic variation in the population, which is not captured by census data. The interviews also provided important information about the different occupational, political, and sociocultural interests within the Indian and Gujarati immigrant populations in New York and London.[14]

Participant Observation

The life history and organization interviews brought me into the homes, neighborhoods, schools, temples, workplaces, and other private and public spaces where Gujaratis and other Indians lived, worked, and congregated. This provided multiple opportunities to engage in observation and participant observation. I also sought out such spaces, primarily neighborhoods known for their Indian concentrations, such as ethnic enclaves in Jackson Heights, Queens, in New York City and Edison, New Jersey, or Wembley and Southall in Northwest and West London, respectively. In particular, I sought out Indian retail traders whom I met informally while living in London and New York. In my own neighborhood in London, for instance, the local post office outlet, hardware store, chemist (pharmacy), newsagent shops (there were two), and small grocery were all owned and operated by Gujarati families from East Africa. This was unremarkable even in a quiet, lower-middle-class neighborhood that was inhabited by whites and African Caribbeans or West Indians. I also regularly visited one newsagent in a tourist area of Central London, who taught me rudimentary Gujarati and about the ins and outs of owning a small shop. Thanks to the many Gujarati newsagents in New York and London, I read ethnic media regularly—newspapers and magazines such as *The Asian Age* (India and United Kingdom), *Asian Times* (United Kingdom), *Eastern Eye* (United Kingdom), *Garavi Gujarat* (United Kingdom), *Gujarat Samachar* (including *Asian Voice* and *Asian Business*) (United Kingdom), *India Abroad* (North America), *India in New York* (United States), *India Link International* (United Kingdom), *India Today* (North America), *International Indian* (United Kingdom), *SiliconIndia* (United States), and many Indian websites to gain a broader sense of community concerns, popular discourse, and media representations of the Indian and Gujarati populations in both cities (see also Peak and Fisher 1998).[15] And I attended festivals, cultural events, neighborhood meetings, religious celebrations, and informal gatherings. Participating in and observing these activities gave me the opportunity to contextualize the Gujarati population in New York and London within the wider Indian population and American and British society from a perspective that was close to the ground.

New York and London: Gujaratis in Two Global Cities

In choosing to focus my research on one regional, linguistic, and religious group from India, I sought to control the effects of culture as much as possible. However, studying Gujaratis in only one place might have led to erroneous conclusions about the role of networks without accounting for place-specific effects. Comparing Gujarati immigrants across more than one location addressed this problem and kept open the question of the role of networks in the migration process. New York and London are obvious (but not the only) comparative sites for studying Gujaratis. They share a number of important similarities, such as their role as "global cities" (Sassen 2001). Their immigrant, Indian, and Gujarati populations are also similar in size. However, they do have important historical differences related to the national immigration policies of the United States and the United Kingdom and each state's relation to India (and East Africa) (these factors are discussed more extensively in Chapters 2 and 6).

London and New York are immigrant cities. One can feel, see, and smell every corner of the world just by walking London's High Streets or New York's Broadway. Immigrants comprise high proportions of their populations. Of London's approximately 7.2 million residents in 2001, 27 percent were foreign born. In New York, 28 percent of its 18.3 million residents were foreign born in 2005.[16] Indian immigrants contribute significantly to each city's diversity. The foreign-born populations from India and Kenya make up about 3.5 percent of London's population and 12 percent of all immigrants in London. In New York, Indians from India make up 1.5 percent of New York's population and 5.2 percent of the foreign born in New York. New York and London are also the top destinations in the United States and the United Kingdom for Indian immigrants. Even though foreign-born Indians in both cities are among the top immigrant populations (the top in the case of London), they clearly comprise only one of many immigrant groups within two incredibly diverse, polyglot urban contexts.[17]

New York and London have continued to play dominant roles in their respective national economies and in the global economy (Sassen 2001, 1999). They are capitals of culture, tourism, information, trade, finance (despite its uncertain future), and immigration. They continue to be major centers of manufacturing, retail and wholesale distribution (even as these decline), and air and sea travel. With the largest metropolitan populations in their respective countries, they also remain important markets for consumer products both nationally and globally (Fainstein and Harloe 1992). In large part, they resemble each other in the global economy. As global cities, New York and London have undergone significant restructuring of their economies since the 1970s. Once large manufacturing centers, both cities have experienced steep declines in manufacturing and a rise in producer services (for example, accounting, financial, legal, and professional services that necessarily accompany production) as their economies (especially finance) internationalized and headed toward the current crisis.[18] Immigrant labor played a central role in these dynamics as many low-skilled immigrants were needed to provide personal and other services for workers in the high-skilled producer services, which widened the economic and social inequalities of each city (Mollenkopf and Castells 1991; Sassen 2001).

Most Indians, however, bypassed many of these dynamics as they migrated and became employed in New York and London. High public-sector employment in London and professional employment in New York in the 1970s, followed by an upturn in retail and wholesale trade in both cities in the 1980s, protected and facilitated many Indian and Gujarati economic niches. Although many of the small retail and wholesale shops of these Indians are now in decline as chain and superstore retailers have come to dominate many commercial areas of New York and London, this development will probably matter less and less as the second-generation children of these immigrants become college educated and pursue professional careers in fields highly regarded by their parents, for example, medicine, pharmacy, engineering, computer science, and accounting. Indians are highly represented in growing industries such as health and education and in the public sector, sheltering them from some of the effects of today's economic crisis. The early decline in manufacturing, however, did affect many of London's immigrants from India and Indian women from East Africa.

The United States and the United Kingdom have important differences that may affect how Indian immigrants are incorporated into American and British society. First, India's history as a British colony implies obvious historical ties between today's independent India and the United Kingdom, which makes contemporary migration from India to Britain seem more likely than from India to the United States. The quite different policies of the United States and the United Kingdom toward immigration since the 1960s seem to set different conditions for the migration of Indians (and others from around the world) as well. The Immigration and Nationality Act of 1965 purportedly flung open the doors of the United States to potential immigrants from all over the world as if it were a free market for migration. In the meantime, the United Kingdom had been closing its doors since the Commonwealth Immigrants Act of 1962 began restricting the number of new Commonwealth immigrants to the United Kingdom. These are somewhat contradictory forces—historical colonial relations on the one hand possibly pushing Indian immigrants to Britain as its immigration policies push them away and, on the other hand, U.S. immigration policy inviting Indians to immigrate seemingly without any prior connection between the United States and India. These contradictions leave open the question of how and how much prior colonial relations and immigration policy matter. As evident in the case of Kishor, organizational ties between India and the United States had already been forming for almost twenty years when the 1965 act took effect. Those kinds of ties made the early wave of Indian mass migration possible. As also discussed in more detail in Chapter 2, the United Kingdom's immigration policies could hardly keep out Indian immigrants with strong interpersonal ties linking them to family and friends already living there. Thus, colonial ties persisted in a new manner.

Plan of the Book

The chapters that follow center around several specific questions. Chapter 2 asks how social ties form historically and who migrates, thus providing important background material for the discussion of particular life histories of Gujaratis presented in Chapters 3 and 4. It asks how the migration of Gujaratis has been selective under different historical conditions. In doing so, it considers the history of Gujarati migration flows since about the 1600s, when India and Gujarat were at the center of lucrative trade routes connecting Europe, Asia, and the Americas in a global economy. It discusses the important trade networks in Gujarat and western India that helped to establish early capitalism in the region and what happened to those networks as they came under British rule and after India gained independence from that rule. The chapter looks at the social ties created from trade, colonialism, labor, education, and development, connecting the history of Indian and Gujarati migration from India to East Africa, Britain, and the United States to these relations up to the present day.

Chapters 3 and 4 are two of a piece. They present the life histories of individual Gujaratis and their networks to address the question of how migration happens, what migration flows look like, what is the role of social ties in forming the selectivity of these particular flows, what are the economic consequences of these flows, and how does destination matter in the lives of these immigrants. Chapter 3 traces the migration of Gujaratis to East Africa, London, and New York to the first jobs held by these migrants at their destinations. It shows how migrant networks link local labor markets transnationally, setting up the conditions for migration and selecting particular migrants to move and work in a distinct set of occupations and industries. Chapter 4 continues the life stories of Gujarati migrants in New York and London, describing further the kinds of occupations they have and how they have settled into their host societies. Gujarati immigrants have consolidated their presence in certain jobs and industries forming what are called economic or occupational niches. These ethnic niches refer to the overrepresentation of a particular ethnic group or population in certain occupations, industries, or economic sectors—in this case, health services; the diamond, garment, and textile trades; hospitality; and small retail. Thus, many of us have become familiar with Indians as newsstand agents on London's High Streets and New York City's Broadway; or as diamond dealers in Antwerp, New York City, and Hong Kong; or as doctors and other health care professionals in American and British hospitals.

In Chapter 3 we can see how local labor markets become linked transnationally through the migration histories of the Gujarati immigrants whom I interviewed. Labor markets have generally appeared and flourished under industrial capitalism, and most explanations of how labor markets operate suggest an efficient market mechanism for how workers are matched with jobs. Workers are thought to be matched according to their human capital, which consists of skill level, experience, and education. However, many sociological studies have found that labor markets are embedded in networks of social relations that often do the business of matching (Granovetter 1974; Tilly and Tilly 1998). Among Gujaratis, specific networks of interpersonal and organizational ties channel immigrants into particular occupations and destinations and link local labor markets in the process. These labor markets are further conditioned by historical, political, and economic relations among the geographical regions encompassing those markets. Immigrants not only create or become subject to the nonrational economics of labor markets, but that process also alters the role of human capital in matching them with jobs. For instance, the question of underemployment is often explained by focusing on the specific individual characteristics of immigrants that may make them subject to racial discrimination—their brown skin or cultural foreignness in American and British society. However, the underemployment of only some of these Indians instead highlights the limitations of their interpersonal ties in contrast to the organizational ties of their coethnics who have equivalent education and skill levels but who are not underemployed. Our understanding of human capital, therefore, requires revision by taking into account how the differences in interpersonal and organizational ties can affect occupational outcomes for immigrants rather than the seemingly straightforward effects of human capital or racial discrimination.

Once local labor markets become linked and whole networks have been transplanted to another place or exist transnationally across sites, some migrants can consolidate their position in particular economic niches. The visibility of economic niches often fuels a contentious popular discourse about whether immigrants are taking native jobs, especially among those natives who no longer find it easy to reap the benefits of a capitalist economy that is in search of cheaper labor and production costs. Chapter 4 shows that the picture is far more complex than this apparent zero-sum game. As in the research of other sociologists, such as Roger Waldinger and Ivan Light, we see that Indians occupy significant economic niches or concentrations in a number of industries or occupations. In some cases, this phenomenon does mean that Indians have taken native jobs. But they have also filled labor shortages in response to recruitment by the American and British governments. And they have stimulated economic growth by creating jobs and revitalizing urban neighborhoods. Migrating to New York and London and hoarding opportunities in economic niches occur when Gujaratis mobilize their social networks for these activities. While other authors have documented the importance of interpersonal networks for similar kinds of niches within other immigrant groups, this study shows that organizational ties can result in niches that make the difference between a dead-end job and economic mobility in an ethnic economy. It also shows us how and why some individuals within a network can escape the limitations and constraints of their network ties while others cannot. In other words, because economic activity is embedded in social networks it can produce inequalities within the networks of Gujaratis as well as among them, other Indian and immigrant groups, and natives.

Chapter 5 develops the theoretical implications of the case of Gujarati migrations to New York and London and shows how migration research can benefit from adopting a relational approach to understanding migration and migrant networks. It considers the social networks literature in economic sociology together with network studies of migration to form a more complete picture of the structure of networks and the kinds of transactions that take place within networks to show how migration flows occur and the role of migrant networks in mobility. Although network theories of migration have offered the most empirical evidence to explain migration flows, they have conceptualized networks in a fairly homogeneous way. The role and meaning of networks as they affect migration have been taken for granted. The chapter explains how we might conceptualize networks differently so that we understand how coethnicity operates within a network, for instance. The relational view also expands our idea of networks in migration research to include formal network ties such as those found in organizations, institutions, and the state. In doing so, it overcomes the false separation between the idea of network ties as interpersonal ties and larger structures of power, such as states and institutions.

Chapter 6 concludes the book by discussing the implications of the relational approach to migration and how we think about immigration debates in the United States and the United Kingdom and policies that regulate immigration. Immigration debates in many countries focus on the problem of how many immigrants to accept, from which parts of the world to accept them, and what to do about them after they arrive. These concerns of nation-states are no exception for the United States and the United Kingdom. The policy histories of both countries have differed somewhat over the last fifty years, with the United States generally liberalizing but also retrenching periodically and the United Kingdom generally restricting immigration since decolonization in the 1960s. Both countries, however, have encouraged migration either explicitly through labor recruitment programs, fairly liberal reunification and asylum policies, and, especially in the U.S. case, by looking the other way at unauthorized migrants.

The schizophrenia of migration policies begs that we understand the contradictions of the power and authority of states and the social mechanisms that encourage migration. These mechanisms lie not in the problem of supply and demand as much as in the social networks that allow specific people to migrate to specific destinations. These ties are formed from communities of people who are linked by colonial relations, trade, labor, educational and professional exchange, war, religion, and a host of other globalized relations between countries. Indian immigrants in the United Kingdom and the United States provide a particularly interesting lens on the future of immigration because their population includes virtually every type of migrant from refugees; temporary high-skilled workers; students; recruited professionals, such as doctors, scientists, and engineers; entrepreneurs in garments, diamonds, and various other trades; and finally family reunification migrants. The huge range of migrants in this population provides us with an unexpected view on directing future policy efforts. A relational perspective demonstrates that these "types" of migrants represent the historical formation of different sorts of social network ties that cause migration flows and patterns of economic and social integration in the societies where migrants live. To rediscover how those ties have formed historically and the early modernity of Indians, this story about Gujarati immigrants in New York and London travels back several centuries to the 1600s to Surat, one of Gujarat's and India's most important cities.

2 From Arab Dhows to Jet Planes

*The immigrant is often perceived by
the host as "a man without a history."*
—Alfred Schütz (1944, 502)

THROUGHOUT ALL OF HUMAN HISTORY, people have been migrating all over the world
to one degree or another (Cavalli-Sforza and Cavalli-Sforza 1995; Hoerder
2002). International migration, however, is thought to reflect a unique historical period in which the movement of people has been driven by the need
for labor associated with the rise of industrial capitalism and in which the
modern nation-state has increasingly regulated people's movement (Castles
and Miller 2003). This understanding of international migration rests on two
assumptions—first, that international migration has grown up with the rise
of industrial capitalism and the modern nation-state; and, second, that modern capitalism rose in the West, thus creating a demand for labor migrants
there. Gujarat's history of trade, commerce, and capitalism challenges these
assumptions. Its history of extensive overseas trade networks linked to highly
developed commercial and productive economic activities from at least the
1500s suggests that trade migration linked to capitalist activities was prevalent until Britain colonized Gujarat and India. As India fell under British rule,
the British used Indian labor in many of its overseas colonies for a variety
of purposes that served its imperial project. Postindependence India created
new conditions for international migration that were based on a new relationship to the former empire and to other nation-states in the international
system. Gujarat's long history of migration linked to trade, colonialism, and
capitalism raises the question of the historical origins of particular migration
flows and how the social ties of Gujarati migrants have formed under different conditions. I am not suggesting that we can somehow trace contemporary

migration flows directly to early trade networks, for instance, but rather that we might benefit from a long view of Gujarat's history instead of assuming that the origins of all of Gujarat's migration flows begin and end with modern Western capitalism's demand for labor, whether during the colonial period or more recently. Gujarat's history also asks us to think about who migrates and to explain the selectivity of social ties that encourages the migration of some but not of others. This chapter explores the historical origins of Gujarati's social ties and how those ties shape selection through an investigation of migration flows associated with Gujarat's important early history of trade, its history under British colonialism, and the period after independence in 1947. The postindependence period forms the content for most of the chapter, focusing on the relationship between immigration policy and social ties and using much of the ethnic media or "grey literature" that I collected while doing fieldwork in London and New York over the past ten years. This historical account is not meant to be an exhaustive discussion of Gujarat's history of emigration during the three periods; rather it is purposive in that it seeks to uncover how social ties have formed and shaped the selection of contemporary Gujarati migration flows.

Trade, Early Capitalism, and Modernity in Gujarat

The interwoven relationship between trade, industry and craft production in Gujarat contributed to its early urbanization and relative prosperity so that by the time "the British arrived on the coast of Gujarat, houses in Surat already had windows of Venetian glass imported through the Ottoman Empire" (Goody 1996, 113). Surat, an industrial and commercial city, was a central trading port for large numbers of Arab, Persian Portuguese, Dutch, and English traders during the Mughal Empire (1526–1707). From December 20, 1662, to February 5, 1663, for instance, Father Manoel Godinho, a Jesuit, who had been in India's Portuguese colony of Goa, visited the Gujarati port city, arguably the most important city in western India at the time and for centuries a center of trade. Godinho estimated that Surat's population was more than 100,000, with people from all over the world residing in the city or frequenting it for business. He even claimed that it "surpasses our Evora in grandeur" (Lach and Van Kley 1993, 741).[1] Godinho was very impressed by Surat's trade:

> Goods arrive at Surat by land and sea. The English and Dutch bring merchandise from Europe, the ships of the Red Sea carry the products of Africa and

the native (Indian) merchants import the merchandise of Asia Minor. The Indian merchants of Surat are rich and they have "fifty ships of their own going out to all the countries." Goods from inland production centers are carried into Surat by caravans, bullocks, and camels "which enter its gates every hour." The country around Surat produces wheat, pulses, and rice, as well as the date palm, from which a wine is produced by the Parsis. (quoted in Lach and Van Kley 1993, 742)

Surat was also a commercial and industrial center for silks, textiles, diamonds, gemstones, and pepper. In 1674, Dr. Fryer, a merchant with the French East India Company, was ordered to take a ship to Surat. He described its trade in and production of such luxury goods:

Trading ships arrive at Surat from the Persian Gulf in February and from the Red Sea in August. Like the European ships they buy indigo and textiles; in the main they bring precious metals and pearls as well as lesser-valued dates, drugs, and horses. Most of the world's gold supply ends up in India because of the need for its textiles. Even the proceeds from the spice trade are used to pay for Indian textiles. Surat also profits from the jewel trade. Its artisans cut stones with many fewer tools than the gem-cutters of Europe. All stones except diamonds are cut on a wheel made of lac and a stone obtained only at Cochin. Diamonds are cut "with a Mill turned by Men" but they are mostly sent to Europe for cutting and setting. (quoted in Lach and Van Kley 1993, 752)

Indeed, Fernand Braudel likened Surat to some of the great mercantile cities of Europe and Asia, such as Venice and Beijing (Braudel 1981a). Not only did Surat attract Europeans who wanted its many precious goods, but its traders also traveled extensively. During the Mughal period, and even up until the early nineteenth century, Indian traders and merchants were operating over land between northern India through to Iran and even as far north as Russia and Poland. By sea, they traded far more extensively throughout Asia, the Mediterranean, the Indian Ocean region, and Africa (Braudel 1981a; Dale 1994; Frank 1998; Goody 1996; Ludden 1999; McPherson 1993).[2] India maintained a central position in the three gigantic world economies of Islam, India, and China in part because of its merchants in Gujarat (Braudel 1981a). Surat's trade with Europe and Asia was the greatest of any city in the Mughal Empire and its economic influence may have equaled other world cities. Braudel referred to Surat as the "gateway to the Mogul Empire . . . the rendezvous for all

India" (1981a, 583).[3] It was the preferred center of shipowners and investors in high-risk maritime trade,[4] a place of religious and ethnic cosmopolitanism, and early capitalism.[5]

From about 1500 to 1800, India experienced massive population growth; urbanization; intense production in manufacturing, especially of textiles; and export of both manufactured goods and raw commodities. In fact, India was ahead of Europe throughout these centuries in all areas of material life—trade, industry, and exports. Europe sought greater access to the dominant markets of Asia, whose sought-after goods, especially textiles, it paid for using silver and gold bullion from the Americas (Frank 1998). Recall that Dr. Fryer, the French East Indies merchant, wrote: "Most of the world's gold supply ends up in India because of the need for its textiles." Even until the 1700s, however, the European traders of the Great Indies Companies owed great sums of money to the Banyans (the name that the English used to describe merchants in Gujarat and western India); they often borrowed more than they could pay in return (Braudel 1981a). Nonetheless, Europe's eventual ascendance was made possible through the payment for such goods in gold and silver brought from the Americas. Andre Gunder Frank (1998) argues that these economic flows between the Americas, Europe, and Asia represented one world or global system in which Asia played a dominant role until about the 1800s because Europe could not compete with Asia until then (see also Chaudhuri 1990).

There is much debate about why India (and China for that matter) declined economically and how Europe rose in world dominance. Both Karl Marx and Max Weber were concerned with this question and tended to see India and China as traditional or premodern economies that could not advance technologically when compared to modern capitalist economies of Western Europe. They argued that the Asian economies were organized around "traditional" values and practices. Marx's and Weber's views influenced later scholarship, which claimed that India was not able to compete technologically with Britain during the early Industrial Revolution because it was simply backward and premodern—this despite the fact that India was technologically ahead of Britain until the early 1800s (Braudel 1981b; Frank 1998).

Recent research on this question shows that India was well on its way to capitalist modernity had it not been for a number of factors: internal political conflict in the late Mughal Empire coupled with the predatory colonial project of Britain, especially as Britain became more competitive with Indian textile manufacturing. For instance, some historians have argued that Britain was able to outcompete other rising European powers in India, for example the Dutch and Portuguese. Britain also "outcompeted" India by imposing unfair trade restrictions on Indian exports to protect British markets (Braudel 1981b). It also banned exports of new technology to India (Richards 1993). Others have shown that the Mughal Empire declined on its own because of internal conflict, especially after the death of Aurangzeb in 1707, which created the opportunity for rule first by the Marathas and then the British (Richards 1993). Regardless of the position one takes in this debate, it is clear that India fell into a state of dependence under British colonialism, and its early capitalist practices diminished under the new regime. Britain underdeveloped India to a great degree (Frank 1998). It also used the Indian population as a surplus labor force for expansionist purposes in its other colonies. For instance, there was debt bondage and labor migration from India to Trinidad, Fiji, Guyana, East Africa, and other parts of the Empire from the 1800s into the early 1900s.

The debate about the modern origins of capitalism also focuses on the financial instruments of capital and the organization of merchants' firms. Although India may not have reached fully modern capitalist practices (in the Marxist sense) by the time it was colonized by the British beginning in the mid-1700s, it had developed rational financial practices. The organization of Indian merchants in Eurasian commerce, such as those of traders in Surat, was as important as the extensiveness and products of their trade. In fact, contrary to the belief that Indian firms were not organized for capitalist practices, the organization of Indian businesses as family firms and their financial practices largely resembled the Italian Renaissance firms of Genoa and Venice (Dale 1994; Goody 1996), which have often been touted as examples of early modern capitalist firms. Codified structures in Indian family firms, such as the Hindu Undivided Family, or managing agencies (subsidiaries of parent companies overseen by family members similar to the Italian *commenda*) were organizational forms of early capitalism that allowed extensive trade. Early capitalist financial practices, such as the selling of futures and double-entry bookkeeping, were also common among Indian merchants, as they were in Renaissance Italy. In essence, the control of capitalist endeavors by interpersonal networks among Indian merchants allowed for long-distance trade, especially in textiles and finance (Dale 1994; Goody 1996). In fact, these interpersonal networks seemed to resemble composite networks of family members who were simultaneously business associates. The interpersonal dimension of these ties was central to capitalist endeavors in both Europe and Asia as they are today—despite the claim that capitalism in the West is purely rational and does not involve any "irrational" personal elements. For instance, Ritu Birla's (2009) study of the far-reaching Marwari merchant group, also from western India, offers an important view of how, during the colonial period, economy and culture were intertwined in the organization and practice of merchant firms. She argues against the notion that Indian firms were too personalistic to be truly capitalist. Her study shows that colonial governance enforced, indeed, created a distinction between economy (firms and markets) and culture (family), which has been used ever since to relegate Indian economy and society to premodern history. Birla's work, along with other studies of Indian firms and their practices, shows that Indian cities such as Surat were clearly central to an earlier global or world capitalist system not only in their reach but also in their practices. Surat and its merchant capitalism were becoming modern long before the British began to rule India.[6]

Trade and commerce in Gujarat were also undeniably significant because they contributed to long-distance diasporas. India's central position in trade relations created the early diasporas, which extended over land through much of the Middle East and north toward the Caucasus Mountains and, by sea, throughout the Indian Ocean region and Southeast Asia. Gemstones, garments, and textiles were some of the most important products in these trade systems, as they are among many contemporary Gujarati traders in New York and London. Many of these traders were merchant middlemen in India who came from different castes, religions, and regional groups and whose status was fundamentally associated with trade. These early trading groups formed the same kinds of composite ties we see in contemporary family firms of transnational traders from Gujarat, such as in Lakshmi's diamond family.

Merchant Groups, Religion, and Emigration

Traders have often suffered from low status around the world (Curtin 1984). The occupation of merchant was held by a small minority in most societies where land-based production was widespread and necessary. Traders were not considered productive in the way that farmers or laborers were nor in any noble sense such as the educated and priestly classes of society. A prominent Dutch merchant who resided in Gujarat during the 1630s remarked of the Parsi traders of Gujarat: "They are greedy and sharp traders like the Chinese and Banians" (cited in Lach and Van Kley 1993, 665–666).[7] The term *Bania* included all merchants the British encountered in western India, regardless of religion or caste, and is still used today. A revealing contemporary example of the lowly reputation of merchants occurred when I was recruiting participants for life history interviews in London. I misdialed the telephone number of a potential participant (I instead dialed the adjacent phonebook entry with the same surname) and found myself in a conversation with a retired Punjabi Hindu professor, who wasted no time in telling me about his loathing for Gujaratis—"especially the Banias."

Despite the lowly reputation of merchants, Gujarat was unique in that merchant ideologies were prevalent in many communities throughout the region, not only among merchant castes. Certainly merchants, but also farmers, artisans, and even sometimes the priestly, educated castes engaged in trade in the region. Merchants simultaneously drew respect and resentment for their wealth and dominant status. Their dominant status was not hegemonic, however. The Vaniyas (Banias) were an intermediary group, a middleman minority, not a ruling class. "On the one hand, they accepted the hegemony of the class which controlled the state, and on the other hand they had their own distinct moralities which were accorded a certain amount of legitimacy by those subordinate to them" (Hardiman 1996, 4). Hardiman also emphasizes the caste and class antagonisms that resulted from the status of merchants, which was sometimes even higher than that of Brahmins. He argues that these antagonisms and the associated stigma against moneylenders probably reflected the real debt of some Brahmins to Vaisya merchants because orthodox Brahmins were generally not permitted to practice usury, unlike those of the Vaisya caste.

Mercantile ideologies were often incorporated into religious doctrine as many temples were dependent on the philanthropy of merchants to feed their endowments and activities (Hardiman 1996). Owing to the great economic success of merchants in Gujarat and the blending of interests between merchants and religious authorities, merchants enjoyed higher status than the two caste groups above them, Kshatriyas and (some) Brahmins. Landowning castes, who were simultaneously involved in trade in Gujarat, also exploited landless laborers, which greatly enhanced their dominance in the region (Breman 1985, 1993; Rutten 1995). Among Gujarat's most prominent merchant groups are many minority religious communities, who are overrepresented there and have also played an important role in its history of trade and commerce. In particular, sectarian Hindus, Jains, Parsis, and Muslim merchant groups, such as the Shi'ite Bohoras and Khojas (also known as Ismailis) and the Sunni Memons (see Engineer 1980, 1989), are known for their widespread trade diasporas. Today, the Ismailis, too, can be found in East Africa, Britain, Canada, and the United States, and many Memons migrated to and remained in South Africa (Dwyer 1994). These dominant castes of traders and landowning peasants were precisely the groups who had the resources and social ties (through trade and status) to migrate overseas for trade and other related economic endeavors. The rise in status (if not always reputation) of these merchant groups is closely linked to the history of emigration from Gujarat to many overseas destinations.

Caste emulation further demonstrates the importance of merchants' status and is linked to the migration of landless peasants. Peasant farmer and artisanal communities often tried to emulate merchant castes and groups in an attempt to raise their status and wealth. For example, the Hindu Kanbis, a low-status peasant caste, collectively accumulated much wealth after migration to East Africa in the early 1900s to engage in commerce. On their remigration back to India, they successfully legitimated their claims to higher Patidar caste status (Chandra 1997; see also Pocock 1972). Many of these new Patidars became devout followers of the sectarian Hindu Swaminarayan movement in India and the diaspora (discussed in Chapter 4). The success of the Swaminarayan movement in Gujarat was an expression of social change there as people were trying to upgrade their caste status. In a recent twist, the success of the movement in the United States and Britain has been a consequence of class dominance brought about by entrepreneurial success and the increasing professionalization of their membership (Bharot 1999). Thus, in Gujarat, peasant communities often emulated higher merchant castes by engaging in commerce overseas and by adopting upper-caste practices. The emulation of merchant castes coupled with economic success as migrants have especially contributed to upward caste mobility and higher class status among those groups who migrated to East Africa and then to Britain.

Of course, not all of Gujarati's historical ties to trade are evident going back several centuries. Some historical ties have formed far more recently and from quite different conditions than trade and commerce. Thus, merchant castes and groups were not the only migrants to be found in Gujarati diasporas even though they predominated throughout the seventeenth and eighteenth centuries while India played such a dominant role in the world economy. By the time Britain had fully colonized India in the mid-1800s, migration often became a solution for those less fortunate than merchants. The Hindu Kanbis are one such example of landless peasants who migrated under conditions of poverty, as are the Halari Visa Oswals, the Jain community that Harshad belongs to. The fathers of Harshad and Dinesh (a friend of Harshad's whose story I tell in the next chapter) for instance, were just young boys when they climbed into small, wooden Arab boats, called dhows, for the dangerous thirty-day journey across the Indian Ocean from Gujarat to East Africa. Dinesh told me that his father did not even have a pair of shoes to wear when he embarked on that perilous journey as a boy of thirteen. In Gujarat, the Halari Oswals were Jain peasant farmers around the city of Jamnagar, where the related higher-status Jamnagari Oswals were traders. The Halari Oswals began migrating to East Africa to escape the famine of 1899 around the area of Jamnagar, which harmed their community much more than the higher-status Jamnagaris. They had heard that life was better across the Indian Ocean in East Africa, where trade had been carrying on for centuries. There, they established themselves in commerce, raising their status above the Jamnagaris back in Gujarat (see Banks 1994). They also achieved enormous generational mobility in East Africa, as we saw with Harshad's family, and after a secondary migration to London, where their raised status has put them in direct class competition with their Swaminarayan neighbors.

Eventually, many different communities of Indians from Gujarat settled in today's Kenya, Tanzania, and Uganda, mostly during the first half of the twentieth century (Gregory 1993). Some, as with the Halari Oswals, were petty traders with no prior experience in commerce. Yet they set up small shops along the East African Railway. Others contributed a large industrial presence in East Africa. For instance, the Madhvani family in Uganda, whose enterprise was founded in 1905, produces sugar, tea, glass, cooking oil, soap, metals, and even financial insurance and television broadcasting.[8] Educated migrants hired by the British to become civil servants would take the same trip by steamship across the Indian Ocean in the middle of the twentieth century. A few decades later, most of these East African Indians, from railway workers and petty traders to civil servants and professionals, would voluntarily and involuntarily migrate to the United Kingdom after Kenya, Tanzania, and Uganda gained independence from the British in the early 1960s. Now, most Indian migrants— even the poorest ones—board airplanes for at least part of their journey to a new land, today the United States, the United Kingdom, Australia, Canada, the Middle East, and increasingly the European Union.

Composite ties embodied in family firm organizations such as the HUF were prevalent in the early migration history of traders and merchant castes.

This prominent class of merchant-usurers had established the foundations for a significant middle class in Gujarat by the time of India's independence from Britain in 1947. They had exploited landless peasant castes and had capitalized on the development of industry, trade, and craft production in earlier centuries, creating widespread diasporas linked to trade. Some landless peasant castes had emulated these merchant groups and raised their status via migration using interpersonal ties within their caste communities. Nonetheless, the development of a middle class was not some linear economic progression over hundreds of years of dominance by foreign empires. However, the money-lending merchants had always aligned themselves with successive Mughal, Maratha, and British ruling classes to preserve their economic power (Hardiman 1996); and, as a result, Gujarat had become one of the most economically developed Indian states around the time of independence, with an influential middle class. This middle class stood ready to reap the advantages of a newly independent India and its relationship to the United States and Britain. The remainder of this chapter discusses the selectivity of those flows within this new political context.

Selectivity and Social Ties in the Migration of Gujaratis and Indians after 1947

Not just anyone migrates from India to the United States and United Kingdom, or more directly to particular neighborhoods in New York and London. The question of who migrates is about a process known as selectivity. In other words, immigrants in countries all over the world are rarely representative of the populations from which they come. They are positioned in their societies to be more likely to migrate because of their social ties to institutions, states, and individuals in other countries. For instance, a highly educated English-speaking middle class could be found all over India from the time of independence, but they did not all leave India. The question of who migrates depends on how social ties are formed and how they affect selectivity. Here, I examine why we see certain "kinds" of Indians in New York and in London today. The exchange of ideas, education, money, and resources between India and the United States and among India, East Africa, and Britain contributed to the formation of interpersonal, organizational, and composite social ties in specific arenas of society. These factors affect the location of potential immigrants in particular configurations of ties that shape migration opportunities. Once ties are set in motion, that is, once transactions within ties begin to promote the process of migration, potential migrants must face external aids and barriers, such as immigration policies.

In the next section, I examine select relationships between Indian and American and Indian and British educational institutions, philanthropic sources of investment in India, and the exchange of ideas and resources. Rather than focus on the "thin relations" of foreign direct investment, foreign policy, and other macrorelations, I instead focus on "thick relations" (Malik 1997), primarily in education, where we can better see how social ties are formed and how they relate to immigration policies in the United States and the United Kingdom. This emphasis shows that particular relations promoted the formation of distinct types of social ties that only later were affected by policy. The different immigration policies of the United States and Britain did not cause their different migration flows, as might be expected. Rather, the two countries invested money, resources, and political influence differently in India, which resulted in the formation of organizational ties between the United States and India in the early flow of recruits in the 1960s and 1970s and of primarily interpersonal ties of chains to Britain during approximately the same period. These flows, in addition to the policies of the two countries, then conditioned the selectivity of later migrants. The flows of trusties, transnational traders, and entrepreneurs were formed from the composite social ties of their early trade activities.

The Migration of Ideas, Money, and Resources from the United States to India

Although the United States and India do not share a long colonial history (such as that of India and the United Kingdom) linking their governments, institutions, corporations, and people, American governmental and private organizations became heavily involved in India's development after independence in 1947. This was partially a result of Jawaharlal Nehru's openness to Western forms of modernity as a model for India's future. Nehru's vision of Indian modernity was based largely on Western science and rationality (Khilnani 1999); therefore, his reform policies pushed India toward Western forms of modernization. Those reforms lifted the nascent middle class (and the elite), which probably did not exceed more than 10 percent of the population (Varma 1998) and which, in Gujarat, was dominated by traders and the middle-level landowning peasantry. That middle class excluded the agricultural poor, unskilled, and semiskilled workers and included those in government service, qualified professionals such as doctors, engineers, and lawyers, business entrepreneurs and the more well-to-do traders, teachers in schools in the bigger cities and in the institutes of higher education, journalists, the partially or fully educated among the middle-level peasantry, the white-collar salariat in the private society, legislators, and a substantial section of university students. (Varma 1998, 26–27)

This middle class stood ready to reap the benefits of Nehru's modernization programs, U.S. influence, and transnational ties created from these developments. Nehru's reform program rested partly on the creation of a set of prestigious and superior educational institutes that were funded by foreign states, especially the United States (but also the United Kingdom and the Soviet Union). The Ford Foundation, Harvard, and MIT, for instance, were instrumental in influencing the structure and curriculum of these Indian institutes during the 1950s and early 1960s (Bhagwati 1993; Domrese 1970; Oommen 1987). The focus of these new institutes of higher education centered on science, technology, and management. As a result of this focus, the middle class especially valued degrees in the fields of medicine and engineering (Varma 1998). Nehru intended to bring India closer to the West with a new, highly educated labor force and with the technological development of the country. He accomplished this with the help of active engagement by the United States, which fostered these Indo-American social ties in which faculty, students, ideas, and resources were exchanged long before the 1965 liberalization of U.S. immigration laws. This influence heightened the exchange of ideas, money, and resources between India and the United States and, in turn, created organizational ties through which many Indians migrated to the United States after 1965.

The Influence of American Educational Institutions

Organizational ties are especially prominent in the migration of students and have often led to more permanent settlement. The United States receives by far the most Indian students at its universities, and it is the most expensive destination for higher education. Approximately 84,000 foreign-born Indian students (14 percent of all foreign students in the United States) were enrolled in American universities during 2006–2007 (Institute of International Education 2007). In comparison to the United States, Britain had 23,835 and Australia 39,166 students that same year (UK Higher Education Statistics Agency 2008 and Australian Education International 2006); Canada had only 2,515 Indian-born students in 2006–2007. Indian foreign students in the

United States make up the largest proportion of foreign students from a single country, followed by China (11 percent), South Korea (10 percent), and Japan (7 percent) (Batalova 2007). U.S. governmental organizations located in India, American universities, and American philanthropic foundations reach hundreds of thousands of students in India and Indian educational institutions directly each year to recruit them to American universities. Indian diaspora press, Indian websites, and American private institutions also disseminate information on educational opportunities in the United States. The primary governmental organizations involved in India–U.S. educational exchange are the U.S. Agency for International Development (US AID) and the U.S. Educational Foundation in India (USEFI), founded in 1950. In addition to administering the Fulbright program in India,[9] for a fee USEFI offers a variety of educational advising services through Education USA, advising centers to Indian students who wish to pursue higher education in the United States (Federal Register 2007). In recent years, they have held educational fairs in many Indian cities, including the U.S. Electronic Education Fairs since 2006, which use the Internet, television, and on-the-ground activities to disseminate information about attending university in the United States (Federal Register 2007; U.S. Embassy, New Delhi 2007). Fairs are also common practice by the British Council, the Canadian Education Centre, and the Australian Education Centre. Among USEFI's services are help with applications to universities, student visas, travel arrangements, entrance exams, and academic credentials.

Recently, websites have been developed to aid students seeking higher education in the United States. The U.S. Department of Commerce funded the development of the website www.namastestudyusa.com, which provides links to a range of useful sites about various colleges and universities, visa information from the U.S. Embassy in New Delhi and Indian consulates, the TOEFL (Test of English as a Foreign Language) and other standard examinations, financial aid, and the USEFI. Dozens of private, online, fee-based overseas educational consultants who target Asians have recently added to the advising services aimed at attracting Indian students to American and other universities.

Advertisements and articles in Indian and ethnic press also provide information on admissions into American universities. For instance, an article in *The International Indian* (Ronad 1998) gives a detailed discussion of what to expect on the Graduate Record Examination (GRE) and how university admissions evaluate test scores. Reflecting the widespread migration of Indian engineers to the United States, the article lists contact information for the top fifteen U.S. engineering schools. HT Horizons (2008), based in Delhi, India, recently contained advertisements for American universities and articles about Stanford Business School's new campus and the Test of English for International Communication (TOEIC), which is authorized by the Educational Testing Service and is geared toward establishing English proficiency for work in multinational companies (Sarkar 2008). These kinds of print articles and advertisement are becoming more and more obsolete. In the ten years since I began this research, the placement of advertising and discussions about becoming a student in foreign universities has changed dramatically from print media to Internet-based websites, blogs, chat rooms, and most importantly YouTube.

Local, face-to-face contact has its place, however. American universities, such as the New York Institute of Technology, also recruit directly by sending their representatives to India (Pais 1998). Even some Indian parents of current U.S. students arrive in India armed with lists of families to contact on behalf of particular universities. These schools have high proportions of Indian students and have invested heavily in Indian management education. For example, the son of one participant attends the University of Pennsylvania. When I interviewed her, she told me of her plans during her next trip to India:

> R: In fact, just now we're going to go back [to India] and we're going to be canvassing for UPenn [University of Pennsylvania] . . . I've got a whole list of parents who are there, in different states in India, whom I have to contact and talk to them. And give donations.
>
> MP: *And how is this organized?*
>
> R: Uh, well, I'm trying to find contacts in India. I'm calling up my different friends in India, sending them this list of parents, which the college has given me.
>
> MP: *Was this an initiative that began with the college?*
>
> R: Yes. We take part in the UPenn phone-a-thons . . . Because I'm very fond of the school, I think it has a lot to offer and, as you said, if I can get a few scholarships and all that for India, I'd love it. If I could establish that, or do something like that. In fact, I want it in my will that if anything happens to all four of us, I would like a part of my estate to go to UPenn, and all that money put aside in a fund.
>
> MP: *In a scholarship fund for Indian students?*
>
> R: Yeah, for me it's a dream to do that.

Prestigious American universities also enlist their Indian alumni to sponsor annual gala events to encourage the Indian applicant pool. At the institutional and curricular level, American influence is also pervasive:

> The highly prestigious Institutes of Management, as they have developed in India, are also American in inspiration. The spectre of MIT haunted the Indian industrialists and educationists for a long time, and has inspired the Indian Institutes of Technology . . . The Regional Engineering Colleges are, again, not British but American in inspiration. The idea that there should be Institutes of Advanced Research wholly or partially independent of the universities is, again, an American import . . . In the Indian Institutes of Management, for example, the managerial, business and other practices are taught which have no connection with the traditional Indian methods of running a business. They teach American business practices and American theories about how industry and business should be managed. It is, therefore, hardly surprising that the students of the Indian Institutes of Management look upon America as their spiritual home . . . A large number of them end up in America or in the Indian subsidiaries of American multi-national companies. Many traditional Indian business houses remain sceptical of the products of the Indian Institutes of Management and refuse to absorb them. (Parekh 1985, 268–269)

Some of the migratory trends reflect a continuation of relationships forged between particular Indian and American universities, which encouraged migration over the last half century. From 1968 to 1976 approximately half of those graduating from the Indian Institutes of Technology, and between 10 and 15 percent of the graduates of the Indian Institutes of Management emigrated (Helweg and Helweg 1990, 60–61).[10] Harvard and MIT had a close hand in influencing the development of these prestigious Institutes.[11] The integration, even interdependence, of U.S. firms and Indian educational institutions met with misfortune recently, however, as the U.S. banking sector has begun to collapse. Lehman Brothers and Merrill Lynch, for instance, had been offering graduating students from India's prestigious IIMs and IITs preplacement offers (PPOs) for associate and analyst positions in recent years (SiliconIndia 2008). The 2008 financial crisis, which has spread throughout the banking sector in the United States and Europe, has eliminated those offers. Medical schools were similarly tied to the United States. One doctor claimed that forty-five graduates from his class of 120 at Bombay Medical School left for the United States (Helweg and Helweg 1990). Other universities, such as Bombay and Baroda (in Gujarat), also had close connections with American universities, which heavily influenced the immigration of their students to the United States. These included Kishor's medical college friend and his brother, both of whom also graduated from the Government Medical College in Ahmedabad.

Recently, many prestigious American universities, such as Carnegie Mellon, Cornell, Harvard, Princeton, Purdue, University of California, State University of New York, University of Washington, and Yale, have set up educational joint ventures in India with Indian educational institutions (Terhune 2007). This continuing "Americanization of Indian education" has ranged from educational and faculty exchange at Rice University, to research collaborations at Cornell, to partnerships for joint degree offerings in India through Carnegie and Champlain College, to name a few examples. Even California State University, Long Beach, has agreed to train faculty and form the curriculum for a four-year degree program at Lucknow University in northern India (Sengupta 2007).

The information technology sector in India has been the focus of investment from not only foreign firms but also the Indian government. As India is now the world's largest exporter of software, Indian firms and educational institutions have benefited from investment by multinational firms, such as Microsoft, Oracle, and Hewlett Packard. These companies have been instrumental in the development of software technology parks on the outskirts of high-tech cities like Bangalore. Together with the administrators of the top U.S. business schools, they have also influenced and funded a new set of prestigious Indian institutes. These Indian Institutes of Information Technology (IIITs) are producing the most recent crop of labor for export to the United States and several other burgeoning information technology sectors in the developed world.[12] Thus, the close interrelationship between educational institutions and industry has provided significant organizational ties for the migration of students and others influenced by American educational institutions.

American Philanthropic Activity in India

American philanthropic foundations have been instrumental in the development of India's economy and educational institutions since independence. As part of the activities of the Ford Foundation, it spent $919.2 million on aid for less-developed countries. Within its mission was to develop "American university resources for overseas technical assistance" (Magat 1979, 189). It poured $38 million into overseas university development between 1955 and

1977. It also established the Institute of International Education (1951–1977) at a cost of $7.1 million as part of its objective to improve American university cooperation with foreign counterparts. "The Ford Foundation quickly became the giant in the international educational field. It launched a vast Overseas Development Program and an International Training and Research Program" in support of educational, training, and research institutions that would advance the native economic, social, and educational programs of each recipient country (Weaver 1967, 420). India was a major recipient of these kinds of funds (Nielsen 1972). Ford's investment in India also had negative political consequences. In the 1950s, during the notorious McCarthy era, the foundation was investigated by a committee of the House of Representatives led by Eugene Cox, for "subversion of Communist penetration" (Nielsen 1972, 82). The Cox Committee accused the Ford Foundation of investing in a procommunist India. Ironically, the Indian Communist Party was simultaneously demonstrating against the foundation's community development program in India (MacDonald 1989). Ford was not the only foundation investing in Indian economic and social development. The Rockefeller Foundation, headed by Dean Rusk in the 1950s, launched a program to aid developing countries, especially India (Nielsen 1972). Part of its aid to India was a grant for the Indian Association for the Advancement of Medical Education (Sodeman 1971). The Danforth Foundation in 1959 also installed its first foreign program in India by "offering graduate fellowships in the United States to young teachers in thirty private colleges in India" (Nielsen 1972, 103).

From these few examples, we can see that India has received enormous amounts of educational investment from the United States. Although much of this investment was financial, it also greatly influenced the structure of Indian higher education and curricula. Medicine, science, and engineering, in particular, were the primary recipients of this money and influence. Most recently, American multinational computer and information technology corporations are investing heavily in India's economy and educational system.

These American-influenced institutes, colleges, and firms have been the loci of organizational ties that cause migration flows of recruits. For Gujarati recruits, only the middle and upper castes and classes were in a position to be influenced by exchanges between American and Indian institutions. In fact, many of the professionals I interviewed came from merchant backgrounds and the middle classes of Indian society. Their fathers encouraged them to enter the professions. For instance, Kishor was the son of a cloth merchant who encouraged all of his children to become doctors. A friend in his social network, Kamlesh, similarly became a mechanical engineer. Among these middle and upper castes and classes, only Gujaratis studying appropriate fields, such as engineering, medicine, management, and information technology, would furthermore be affected by this exchange. Therefore, individuals in these positions within organizations, notably universities, were most likely to develop the social ties necessary to take advantage of new immigration policies in the United States that favored highly educated professionals and attempted to fill labor shortages with them. A brief account of those policies and their effects on social ties is given in the following section.

Asian Indian Migration to the United States

Among the first Indians to arrive in the United States were Punjabi Sikhs, who crossed the border into California from British Columbia, Canada.[13] Sikhs were heavily recruited into the British Army during colonial rule because they had a reputation for bravery and a militaristic ideology embodied in the ideal of the soldier-saint (Cohen 1997). Some of these soldiers were being returned to the Punjab via Canada after Queen Victoria's jubilee in 1897. As British subjects, they had the right to reside in any part of the empire. Thus, several thousands of these returnees stayed in British Columbia, eventually making their way into California as they were attracted by employment opportunities in agriculture and on the Western Pacific Railroad. From 1905 through 1913, an estimated 7,500 to 10,000 Sikhs resided in the United States, mostly in California (Cohen 1997, 110). These Sikh migrants did not have an easy time settling into a new life in the United States. By 1917, U.S. immigration policy became explicitly anti-Asian, barring all Asians from further immigration and denying present ones from naturalization rights.[14] In 1923, the Thind case of the Supreme Court (*U.S. v. Bhagat Singh Thind*), which hinged on the argument that Indians are "Caucasian," decided that "Hindus" were not "white" and therefore not free persons eligible for naturalization and immigration (LaBrack 1988). The immigration of Indians would not resume again until after World War II. At that time, the former legislation, which excluded Chinese and other Asians, was repealed, and annual quotas of about 100 persons from each Asian country were instituted. Thus, up until the 1960s immigration policy was quite effective at controlling the quantity of Asian immigration, especially because there were also few ties among Indians to encourage migration. In 1965, a significant shift in immigration policy and flows occurred,

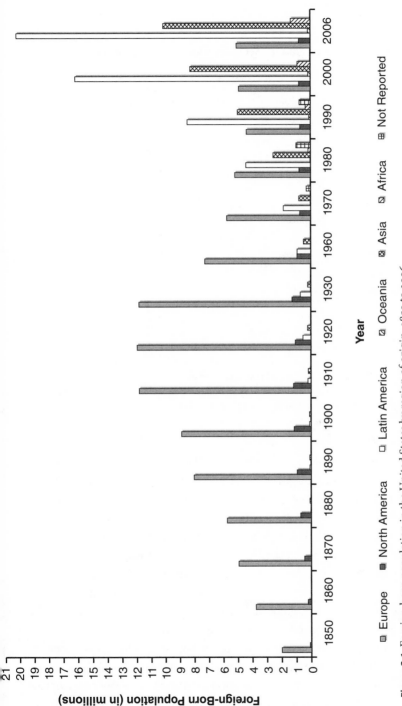

Figure 2.1 Foreign-born population in the United States by region of origin, 1850 to 2006.

SOURCES: Data for 2006 are from the 2006 American Community Survey. Data for 2000 are from the 2000 Census. Data for earlier decades are from Campbell Gibson and Emily Lennon. 1999, U.S. Census Bureau, Working Paper No. 29, Historical Census Statistics on the Foreign-Born Population of the United States: 1850 to 1990 Washington, DC: U.S. Government Printing Office, 1999; available at www.census.gov/population/www/documentation/twps0029/tab04.html)

Table 2.1 Total and Indian foreign-born populations in the United States, 1850 to 2006.

Year	Foreign-born	Rank	Indian-born share of foreign-born	Number
1850	2,244,602			N/A
1860	4,138,697			N/A
1870	5,567,229		0.01%	586
1880	6,679,943		0.02%	1,707
1890	9,249,547		0.02%	2,143
1900	10,341,276		0.02%	2,031
1910	13,515,886		0.03%	4,664
1920	13,920,692		0.03%	4,901
1930	14,204,149		0.04%	5,580
1960	9,738,091	42	0.1%	12,296
1970	9,619,302	30	0.5%	51,000
1980	14,079,906	16	1.5%	206,087
1990	19,797,316	12	2.3%	450,406
2000	31,107,889	3	3.3%	1,022,552
2006	37,547,315	4	4.0%	1,519,157

SOURCES: U.S. Bureau of the Census. Data for 2006 from the American Community Survey, 2006. Data for earlier decades from Campbell Gibson and Kay Jung. 2006. U.S. Census Bureau Working Paper No. 81, *Historical Census Statistics on the Foreign-Born Population of the United States: 1850 to 2000.* Washington, DC: U.S. Government Printing Office.

widely opening the door to immigration. The Hart-Celler Immigration Act abolished the national origins quotas for a system of preferences favoring family reunification and some immigrants with special skills (mostly professional and technical workers). Although the act intended to draw more immigrants from Europe so as not to disturb the racial homogeneity achieved by that time among "European" and "Caucasian" immigrants, it unintentionally promoted mass flows from Latin America, the Caribbean, and Asia. Indians were no exception.[15] Although in 1970 the U.S. population born in India was only 0.5 percent of all the foreign born, by 2006 they ranked fourth and comprised 4 percent of the foreign-born population. See Figure 2.1 and Table 2.1.

The dramatic rise in the number of foreign-born Indians since 1965 reflected in Table 2.1 represented only in part the liberalization of U.S. immigration policy. The policy enabled pioneer migrants to take advantage of new quotas favoring professional workers and their sponsorship of family members, such as Kishor and his wife and brother. The policy also encouraged the migration of entrepreneurs who, with sufficient capital, could qualify as "investors." Indians, such as Lakshmi and her husband, seeking to expand their businesses into the American market for diamonds, garments, and other goods, pioneered these flows of trusties. Although the 1960s pioneer stage of Indian migration and the decades before it were heavily restricted by immigration policies, in a few short decades this situation changed considerably. It did not change, however, simply because immigration policies were more open than they had been for several decades. The formation of distinct types of social ties had already been forming for two decades between India and the United States just after India's independence from Britain. Those organizational ties, with the help of a more open immigration policy, caused the pioneer flows of the 1960s and 1970s.

The Pioneer Flows of Recruited Professionals and Students

The first Indians to arrive after 1965 were mostly professionals who had no ties to the Sikh migrants in the earlier part of the century. Engineers, natural scientists, and medical professionals predominated in these early flows (Fisher 1980; Helweg and Helweg 1990). In 1974, of 46,000 employed Indians, more than half were professionals in the sciences; 16,000 were engineers, 4,000 were scientists, and 7,000 were physicians and surgeons (Fisher 1980, 20). The story of Indian medical doctors is particularly instructive of how relations between and within sending and receiving countries affect selectivity.

In 1970, India was estimated to have an excess of 81,900 physicians relative to its population (Mejia, Pizurki, and Royston 1980, 109). Indeed, the number of medical schools had been growing rapidly—thirty-two in 1949, eighty-six in 1966, and ninety-four by 1970 (117). The development of Indian medical education was a priority of the postindependence Nehru government. Higher education, in general, catered to the urban, middle-class, upper-caste, English-speaking elite. However, the problem for doctors was not only that there were too many of them but also that Indian doctors did not want to relocate to rural areas in India to practice medicine. Hospitals in cities held fewer chances for employment. Therefore, when recruitment mechanisms for overseas work were put into place by Indian medical colleges and American foundations, many doctors became open to the idea of pursuing their profession abroad.

In the meantime, the health care industry was expanding rapidly in the United States. Although in the 1940s less than 10 percent of the American population was insured for hospital, surgical, and regular medical expenses, by the 1970s a full 70 to 85 percent were covered (Mejia et al. 1980, 73). Similarly, Britain launched its National Health Service after WWII and, as in the United States, experienced a shortage of doctors. These factors emanating from all three countries—India, the United States, and Britain—created open circumstances for the migration of Indian physicians. By 1972, India had approximately 15,000 medical doctors abroad and 42 percent in the United States alone, reflecting a great rise in the Asian origins of foreign medical graduates (FMGs) there (Mejia et al. 1980, 146, 187). Britain had been the other major receiving country for Indian doctors, but it soon became a way station for entry into the United States. Over two-thirds of U.S. FMGs from the United Kingdom were born in an Asian country, and almost half were from India alone. Thus, not only were Indian FMGs migrating directly from India, but they also arrived via Britain. In 1976, the U.S. Health Professions Education Act also amended prior immigration legislation to restrict the entry of professionals to only those who could show they had an offer of employment. By that time, however, organizational ties between doctors in India and the United States had already been well established, and many physicians easily met the new policy restrictions.

The 1976 act also abolished the preference for medical professionals declaring an end to the labor shortage and preventing the overallocation of these visas to India and the Philippines (Lobo and Salvo 1998). Some 3,000 to 4,000 physicians practicing in Britain rushed to meet the 1977 deadline of the act. Ironically, many of those British doctors were not, in fact, English, but rather Indian and Pakistani:

> Many of them, once they have established residence and registered in the United States, are expected to return to the United Kingdom to complete their commitment to the National Health Service, and then emigrate to the United States within 364 days after their initial departure from the UK. A number of those involved are physicians who came to the UK from India and Pakistan. (Mejia et al. 1980, 194)

Despite the early policy restrictions, Indian physicians continued to enter the United States to practice medicine. This was possible using long-established organizational ties and some interpersonal ties. Although it has become increasingly difficult for foreign doctors to practice in the United States, today over 47,500 Indians are doing so (American Medical Association 2007, 6). They make up a full 5 percent of all doctors in the United States, a formidable occupational niche that has been recognized by the American Medical Association

(AMA). It is now customary for the president of the AMA to give the keynote address at the annual American Association of Physicians of Indian Origin (AAPI) convention. Indians are also active in the AMA's activities: During 1999–2000, four of seven elected members of the International Medical Graduates (IMG) Governing Council were Indian. Indians make up 20 percent of the IMGs in the United States, more than double the number of Filipinos, the next highest group (American Medical Association 2007).

Indians have also continued to be prominent in immigrant flows of science and technology workers from the early pioneer days. In 1988 through 1990, India led in the number of engineers and natural scientists, surpassing other foreign-born groups from the Philippines, China, Taiwan, and Iran. Indians were second to Filipinos in medical fields and second to Taiwanese among math and computer scientists (Kanjanapan 1992). More recently, Indians lead the number of foreigners who have been given nonimmigrant H1-B visas to work in the U.S. information technology sector. The H-1B visa was capped at 65,000 in 1990 but raised significantly during the high-tech boom years from about 1999 through 2004. For instance, in 2000 it was raised to 195,000 visas through fiscal year 2003. As of fiscal year 2004, it reverted back to 65,000 despite active attempts by technology leaders, such as Bill Gates, to persuade the U.S. Congress to raise the cap (Chisti and Bergeron 2008). During the peak years, about half of all of these visas were given to Indians, even though only 7 percent could be allocated in any one year to persons from a particular country of origin (Robinson 2000). In 2006, approximately 25 percent of H-1B visas went to Indian immigrants (McGee 2007). Remarkably, in the same year, seven of the top ten companies that received the most H-1B visas were actually headquartered in India, for example, Infosys, Wipro, and Tata Consultancy Services. The top U.S. technology companies that received the most H-1Bs were Microsoft, IBM, and Oracle. The temporary character of the visa is ignored in many cases, as firms seek to recruit workers by promising them aid for immigration. Bodyshoppers, or labor brokers, have become staple middlemen in the global labor market as they recruit workers in India's high-tech cities, such as Bangalore and Hyderabad in the southern part of the country, to work in the information technology (IT) sectors of the United States, Australia, and other Western countries (see Biao 2006; Lubman 2000).

Students (recruits) were also among the early pioneers who established the basis for later chains of kin. The number of foreign-born U.S. students of Indian descent has been steadily increasing since 1980 and reached 14 percent

Table 2.2   Foreign-born Indian students in the United States, 1980–1981 through 2006–2007.

Year	Number of students from India	Percentage of total foreign students in the United States
2006–2007	83,833	14.4%
2005–2006	76,503	13.5%
2000–2001	54,664	9.9%
1995–1996	31,743	7.0%
1990–1991	28,860	7.1%
1985–1986	16,070	4.7%
1980–1981	9,250	3.0%

SOURCES: Institute of International Education 2007; National Center for Education Statistics 2006.

of all foreign-born students in 2006–2007 (see Table 2.2). Although foreign students are not technically immigrants (they typically enter the country on nonimmigrant F-visas), the majority have plans to stay in the United States for postgraduate study or employment and can eventually become immigrants by changing their visa status. This trend is even more prevalent among students in the natural sciences, computer sciences, and engineering (U.S. Department of Education 1997).

The pioneer professionals and students migrated to the United States with organizational ties. These early flows were composed of educated professionals and students in particular fields, most of whom came from urban, middle-class, higher-caste backgrounds in India. Rather than having family ties as do most chains, recruits were linked to organizations that encouraged their migration. These organizations consisted of Indian and American educational and cultural institutions, firms, government agencies, employment agencies, and the like. Many of these early immigrants were also Gujarati as a result of ties with particular universities in Gujarat, such as medical colleges and the IIM in Ahmedabad. Although chains now make up the bulk of Indian immigration and, indeed, of all immigration to the United States, the organizational ties linking Indian immigrants to the United States have been underexamined in migration research or denied altogether (for example, Portes and Rumbaut 1996). In particular, social network theories of immigration have typically pointed to interpersonal networks, not organizations, as the mechanism that encourages and reproduces most migration flows (see Massey et al. 1987, 1998; Portes and Rumbaut 1996). This emphasis on interpersonal networks is accurate for chains but not for recruits or trusties. Those

theories do reflect, however, the observation that flows of recruits and trusties often become chains. This transformation demonstrates the importance
of interpersonal ties even for those flows that are not initially driven by them.

Recruited Indian professionals, therefore, established the basis for later
chain migration of their close kin to the United States. Chains still comprise
the majority of immigration to the United States, a flow that is encouraged
in current policy. Organizational ties, thus, set the stage for recruits, while
interpersonal ties continue the chain. Because organizational ties historically
came first in the process of Indian migration to the United States, they also
greatly affected the selectivity of future migration among those professionals
and their families. In contrast, Indian migration to Britain was more diverse
and contained many separate and independent flows of chains and fewer recruits and trusties as discussed below.

Forging Links between India and the United Kingdom in an Era of Unwanted Immigration

Although active engagement by the United States in India's educational institutions and economy had been occurring since independence, Britain was
instead retreating from India. The marks of empire were surely still present in
the structure of India's government, military, educational system, and politics. However, Britain had to surrender its earlier colonial role. Britain still
retained some political influence over India through foreign aid but quickly
withdrew that aid when there was a lack of political agreement. This was especially apparent in the 1980s during the Thatcher administration, when India's
stance on international issues before the United Nations and attractiveness as a
trade or economic investment partner were perceived negatively (Malik 1997).
Nonetheless, some links still endured, though usually at the topmost levels
of society. The binding links between India and Britain were symbolized in a
shared language, Indian graduates of elite English universities, Anglo-Indian
literature, business, and tourism (Malik 1997). Immigrants and low-skilled
labor from India and the colonial diaspora (much of it made from indentured
servitude during the early twentieth century) constituted the darker, binding
links. Britain could not simply ignore its former subjects, who, in the post–
World War II period, were becoming a permanent part of the center of the
former empire. Two centuries of colonial relations created durable social ties
between Britain and the former colonies. One restrictive immigration policy
after another failed to break those ties.

The Early Years, Pre-1947

"With one exception, there has never been an official immigration policy to recruit or encourage immigrants, only to keep them out, starting with the Aliens Act of 1905" (Coleman 1994, 38). Here lies the major difference between U.S. and U.K. immigration policy, especially in the last half-century. Perhaps the only exception to Britain's persistent obstacles to immigration has occurred in the last ten years, during which time immigration has risen dramatically as Tony Blair sought to encourage certain kinds of economic migrants and to reform and limit asylum claims. Nevertheless, as the United States opened its doors after 1965 (despite a subsequent tightening of restrictions in recent decades), the United Kingdom sought to close its doors. Ironically, both countries suffered from similar unintended consequences of their policies. The United States received immigrants from more unwanted origins—Latin America, the Caribbean, and Asia—while Britain conceded to accepting both more immigrants and more from the equally undesirable New Commonwealth countries.[16] Indian migration was at the heart of Britain's contentious policies.

Indian migration to Britain has been occurring for several centuries. In the earliest years of the eighteenth and nineteenth centuries, Indians from very diverse backgrounds arrived in Britain: nannies, princes, students, seamen, and soldiers (see Tinker 1977; Visram 1986). Many of India's most prominent leaders of society, such as Mahatma Gandhi, Mohammed Ali Jinnah, and Jawaharlal Nehru, went to England to be educated, especially in law. Others, such as Dadabhai Naoroji, a Parsi, traveled to London in 1855 for business and settled there permanently. He was a partner in Cama and Co., the first Indian business house in England, and became very active in social activities for Parsis and Indians in London and Britain (Holmes 1988). In the early 1860s, he established both the London Zoroastrian Association and the London Indian Society. Among many other elite Indians, he was instrumental in the fight for India's independence from the geographic center of the empire, London.

The early Indian migration to Britain was far more diverse and numerous than the early Punjabi Sikh migration to California. The former colonial and now postcolonial relationship between India and Britain created a continuous but ever-changing relationship for Indians migrating to Britain and its other colonies, notably East Africa, Trinidad, Fiji, and Guyana. Students, military personnel, businesspeople, princes, nannies, indentured laborers, and servants were part of these early circulatory flows to Britain and the colonies. Permanent settlement occurred mostly among indentured and free laborers, who migrated between Britain's far-flung colonies but not to Britain until the latter half of the twentieth century. In contrast, Indian immigration to the United States did not rely on, nor stem from, any colonial relationship between the United States and India. However, ironically, the early migration of Sikhs to the United States was, in fact, a result of British imperialism that had found its way there.

Social Ties and Settlement, Post-1947

Before 1948, those persons living in the empire were British subjects. India's independence in 1947 was one of the primary motivations for defining British citizenship over subjecthood in Britain's 1948 Nationality Act. Indians from India and other parts of the New Commonwealth comprised a small proportion of the foreign population residing in the United Kingdom prior to 1955. British subjects were afforded rights or residence anywhere in the empire, but without citizenship. The 1948 Act established a new status of "Citizen of the United Kingdom and Colonies," while continuing the privileges of free entry, even to former colonies that had gained independence (for example, India and Pakistan). This free entry facilitated migration during the next few decades, showing a steady rise in the proportion of foreign born in the U.K. population (see Figure 2.2).

During the 1950s and early 1960s, a time of general labor shortages in the manufacturing, service, transport, and health industries, the United Kingdom actively pursued labor migration—first from Europe via the European Volunteers Workers, 1946–1951, and afterwards from the West Indies and South Asia (Holmes 1988). This was the only time during which immigration was explicitly encouraged. Labor recruitment during this time was arranged privately by specific companies such as the NHS, London Transport, the British Hotels and Restaurants Association, and British Railways. Even though only about 10 percent of migrants were recruited this way (Coleman 1994), many of these recruits then sponsored or informally recruited their kin, friends, and co-ethnics in a further chain flow of migration. Gujaratis and Punjabis were the main sources of low-skilled labor. Gujaratis and other Indians were also especially present in the mill and textile factories in the West Midlands (Holmes 1988). The word that there were many job opportunities for Asians and African-Caribbeans spread quickly, and firms relied on this word-of-mouth method of obtaining new labor. Certainly organizational ties were initially formed through direct contact with recruiting firms; but, unlike professional organizational ties,

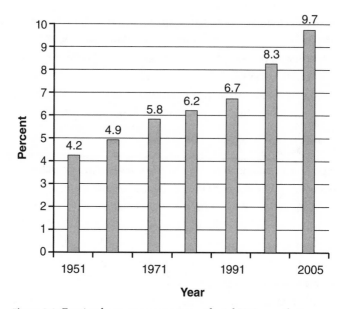

Figure 2.2 Foreign born as a percentage of total U.K. population, 1951 to 2005.
SOURCES: Office for National Statistics, United Kingdom; Migration Policy Institute.

these organizational ties for low-skilled labor in manufacturing firms quickly became supply networks composed of interpersonal ties.

Organizational ties for recruited professionals endured longer. The United States and Britain actively recruited this high-skilled labor force that it had helped to create. In the 1950s and 1960s, recruitment was arranged privately by the British NHS (Coleman 1994), which used ties to specific medical colleges in India, including Gujarat state (Spencer 1997). In addition to direct links between the NHS and specific medical colleges in India, the NHS could also rely on recruited doctors to encourage similarly qualified colleagues to help fill the health industry's labor shortage (Robinson and Carey 2000). Again, Gujaratis were prominent in this stream of recruits (see Spencer 1997). Similar to the case of American physicians, professional organizational networks reproduced themselves through ties formed in organizations, whereas supply networks of low-skilled labor reproduced themselves through interpersonal ties.

Although there has long been a significant flow of students from India to Britain (see Holmes 1988; Malik 1997; Visram 1986), organizational ties promoting such flows were developed through several newly formed institutions.

Most prominently, the British Council, established in 1948, is one of the "three pillars of British foreign policy" along with the British Foreign Office and British Broadcasting Corporation (BBC) (Malik 1997, 242). The council promotes educational, cultural, and technical cooperation between Britain and 109 countries and is a division of the British High Commission. The council in India offers British examinations on-site, scholarships, English classes (especially business English), and fairs about British higher education. The council also manages a variety of scholarships for Indian students wishing to study in Britain. The Chevening scholarships program, for instance, is jointly funded with British universities, Indian trusts, and U.K. industries (*Gujarat Samachar* 1999, 49).

Other such collaborative efforts include the Department of Trade and Industry's Indo–British partnership. In fact, Gujarat is the focus for a new vocational training initiative among the Confederation of Indian Industry (CII), the state government, British Training International, and U.K. colleges and consultants. The project aims to assist Indian industry by introducing the British approach to competence-based National Vocational Qualifications (NVQs).

Indian Migration from East Africa

The influx of new commonwealth immigrants from disparate cultural, ethnic, linguistic, and religious backgrounds promoted a contentious discourse on the integration of immigrants into British society. Immigrants were blamed for putting undue pressure on available employment and housing. In response to a heated public debate, the Commonwealth Immigrants Act of 1962 sought to curb the number of new Commonwealth immigrants but did not dispose of their privileges of free entry. Labor migration did continue after 1962, and new Commonwealth immigrants were required to obtain employment vouchers. However, it was not until the 1968 act that these immigrants were subject to immigration control, even though they held British passports. This act was especially crucial for the tens of thousands of Indians living as British subjects and citizens in the decolonizing states of Kenya, Uganda, and Tanzania. These three colonies gained independence in the early 1960s—Tanzania in 1961 (with Zanzibar in 1963), Uganda in 1962, and Kenya in 1963. The subsequent Africanization policies of these newly formed states sought to limit and exclude Asians from the economic dominance they had held as middlemen minorities during colonial rule (see Gregory 1993). As political and economic tensions swelled in East Africa and the debate over racial and ethnic minorities simmered in Britain, the 1968 act could not have been more damaging to these African Asians.[17] These citizens of the United Kingdom and colonies held "D" passports, which restricted their "free entry" to Britain.

One participant, Kanti, insisted that I take the passport of his wife (Uma) and his Ugandan identity card for use in this research. He seemed almost relieved to hand them over—as if finally he and his family would be recognized for the second-class citizenship they experienced during their painful expulsion from Uganda and subsequent immigration to Britain. Most interesting about the passport is that, rather than being issued a new passport after immigrating to Britain, the profession and country of residence on the second page were simply crossed out and filled in with new information. With a stroke of black ink Uma had gone from being a teacher to a machinist and from a resident of Uganda, where all of her belongings and properties had been confiscated, to one of England, where she and Kanti and their two children had to start life over again. Her second-class citizenship status became even more pronounced with this bureaucratic touch (see Figure 2.3).

The 1968 act further reduced annual quotas of new Commonwealth immigrants and required these British subjects and citizens to apply for entry vouchers. The 1971 act also stiffened the requirements for obtaining work permits and the annual quotas for entry. In the face of severe political and economic difficulties faced by Asians in East Africa, these acts were at the very least irresponsible and, at worst, flagrantly discriminatory. Even the European Commission on Human Rights considered the legislation "racist" (Mattausch 1998). As tensions worsened with the impending expulsion of Asians from Uganda by Idi Amin, Britain was forced to confront its responsibility to its former subjects. Thus, from 1965 through 1974, Britain saw a large influx of immigrants (mostly Indians) from the East African countries of the New Commonwealth (see Table 2.3). During those same years, 113,000 of the 509,000 New Commonwealth and Pakistan (NCWP) immigrants entered Britain from East Africa, and 148,000 Indians from India also migrated. Together, they constituted more than half of the NCWP entrants and the majority from any part of the former British Empire. The policies had finally been thwarted, but the Ugandan refugee flow in 1972 would be the last year that such high numbers of Indians would enter Britain. According to the 2001 U.K. Census, 11.6 percent of the foreign-born population was Indian and born in either India or Africa (Rendall and Salt 2005). India has consistently ranked among the top three sending countries to the United Kingdom since the early 1990s.

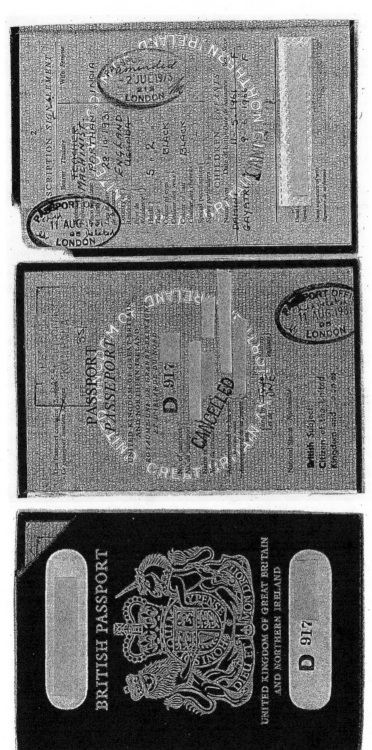

Figure 2.3 "D" passport, Citizen of the United Kingdom and Colonies.

Table 2.3 New Commonwealth immigration, 1961 to 2001 (in thousands).

Country of birth	1961	1971	1981	1991	2001
NCWP	360	699	924	1,013	1,198
Caribbean	172	237	295	265	255
India	157	322	392	409	468
Bangladesh	—	—	49	105	154
Pakistan	31	140	188	234	321

SOURCES: U.K. Census country of birth tables; Rendall and Salt (2005).
Bangladesh came into existence in 1971. It was previously part of Pakistan.

Nearly all of the migration of Indians from East Africa was a chain migration, such as with Harshad and his siblings. The refugees from Uganda, such as Kanti and Uma, in some ways also resembled a chain flow, even though the British government was instrumental in accepting and resettling them in the United Kingdom. Unlike most African cases of war-affected refugee flows (for example, Somalis, Sierra Leonians, Sudanese, Liberians, and so on), Ugandan Indians emigrated as entire families or households under conditions of relatively less violence. Many stayed in the refugee camps for just one week until some family member or friend provided them with temporary housing. Remarkably, the camps virtually emptied in three months. The refugee status of Ugandan Indians was short lived because so many of their kin and coethnics from all three of the former East African protectorates had already settled in Britain and were able and willing to help them. Nonetheless, the most durable effect on the refugees' economic adjustment to life in Britain was the confiscation of their livelihood and assets in East Africa.

Gujaratis were most prominent in the flows from East Africa to Britain. They also came from fairly diverse origins in Gujarat. Lower-caste groups of landless peasants had migrated to work as laborers on the railways or on other colonial development projects. Certain caste or community groups, such as Patidars and Oswals, had become small shopkeepers and engaged in trade. Anavils had been recruited to teach in East African schools that the British were developing (see Gregory 1993). Thus, after the political exodus from East Africa to Britain, Gujaratis became one of the largest regional groups of Indians represented in Britain.

Forging New Links between India and Britain

During the 1980s, Britain's immigration policy was one of containment, rationalized by a discourse about the need for improving race relations. The general immigration policy represented an understanding that further immigration was not needed or desirable. The work-permit system could handle specific labor needs. Nevertheless, family reunification and legitimate refugees remained exceptions to the general restrictiveness of the policy. This "understanding" was a very racialized one because Britain was still looking to the free entry of European Union (EU) citizens to fill its labor needs. This racial and political bias resulted in complaints by employers of not being able to locate sufficient high-tech labor from Europe. Ironically, they wondered: Where are all the engineers (Salt 1992)? During the last ten years, however, Britain has experienced a dramatic rise in the number of immigrants and a change in its policies toward immigrants. Prime Minister Tony Blair led four major immigration acts in 1999, 2002, 2004, and 2006 to encourage "economic migrants" (both high and low skilled) in particular economic sectors and to reform asylum laws to hasten procedures for asylum and deportations (Somerville 2007).

These major legislative changes in immigration policy signal Britain's coming to terms with its economic competitiveness and its historical legacy of colonialism, which has created durable social ties resulting in immigration. The European talent shortage, for example, is forcing Britain to look into its excolonial backyard in a very different way now that employers have finally realized that high-tech workers in India's computer industry have been providing labor to that sector in the United States for at least two decades. For instance, up to 32 percent of Silicon Valley's IT workers are from India and Taiwan (Saxenian 1999). Germany began to recruit Indian labor in this sector beginning in 2000, although it now hopes to recruit European high-tech workers through the EU's recently proposed Blue Card scheme (Collett 2008). Finally, Britain is also catching on to the desirability of Indian high-tech labor.

In 2000, Britain appointed its first e-minister, Patricia Hewitt, to promote stronger relations in the IT sectors of the two countries. Hewitt described the necessary change in the old colonial attitude toward Indian labor—an attitude that American employers would reserve for only Mexican labor—in this way: "We need to get ourselves out of mentally thinking of India as a third world country or a poor country. What struck me is the strength of their [India's] engineers and technical training, and their world-class IT institutes" (quoted in Daniel and Merchant 2001). By 2001, Britain had invested $3 billion in several sectors in India, including IT (*SiliconIndia* 2001). New policies to help the effort have included doubling the number of visa permits for Indian students over the next three years. IT categories were also added to the list of labor shortages so that firms can obtain work permits in less than two weeks to fill these slots.

Wipro, one of India's largest IT companies and third largest software exporter, opened its first European Development Centre in Reading, England, in 2001, along the M4 corridor just west of London. (Reading has been set to become the new center for Britain's young IT sector.) Wipro's European headquarters in the United Kingdom has allowed it to service its U.S. clients more easily and to create a launching pad for its European operations (UK Trade and Investment 2006). Thirty percent of Wipro's revenue comes from Europe, with about half of that from the United Kingdom alone (Daniel and Merchant 2001; UK Trade and Investment 2006).

Conclusion

The immigration policies of the United States and Britain have been significantly different, at least during the last half century. This is not the reason, however, for the divergent migration histories of Indians in both countries. Distinct relationships between India and the United States, and between India and Britain, affected the types of social ties that formed to create migration flows of predominantly recruits and chains. During the postindependence period, the United States invested heavily in Indian higher education, thus promoting the formation of social ties for highly educated Gujaratis and other Indians in medicine, engineering, and management. Those migrants had origins in the predominant merchant castes and groups of the region and were poised to benefit from those transnational relations between a newly independent India and the United States. Recently, similar organizational ties have been forming in the IT sector. However, significantly fewer Gujaratis are connected to this sector. These organizational ties within networks of professionals and students, who benefited from an open immigration policy in the United States, then created a flow of recruits to the United States. Those recruits, in turn, sponsored their interpersonal others resulting in a chain flow of migrants.

In Britain, similar organizational ties were promoted through long-standing colonial relations and labor recruitment, particularly in the medical professions and low-skilled manufacturing work. Gujaratis were prominent in these flows directly from India. They were also prominent in streams arriving from East Africa, where several generations of Indians had settled since the turn of the twentieth century, many of them coming from both merchant groups and landless peasant castes. Those immigrants worked in diverse occupational backgrounds that supported the British imperial project in East Africa—shopkeepers, manual laborers, teachers, clerks, and the like. However, these immigrants and their children later migrated to Britain, primarily through interpersonal networks.

In this chapter, we can see how social ties have formed from specific relations of trade, colonialism, foreign development programs, and philanthropy to form distinct flows of Gujaratis and other Indians to the United States, East Africa, and Britain. Those relations also represented specific ties that migrants had to states, organizations, firms, and interpersonal others. Thus, we can see how organizational, composite, and interpersonal ties shape the selectivity of migration flows from India and East Africa to Britain and the United States. These different configurations of ties that led to the migration of recruits, trusties, and chains to the United States and Britain also aided the formation of particular economic niches. Middleman shopkeepers in East Africa used their interpersonal networks not only to migrate to London but also to reestablish themselves in retail and wholesale trades there. Formidable niches developed around medical professionals recruited to practice in the United States and Britain. Transnational traders (trusties), who are numerically much less significant than recruits and chains, also established niches as they sought to develop new markets for their goods in the garment and diamond trades. Relations of exchange were crucial to the formation of these niches. The next chapter describes how migrant networks link local labor markets, creating these economic and occupational niches, and how the relations of exchange within their networks have affected their mobility in their new destinations: East Africa, London, and New York.

3 Linking Local Labor Markets

IN 2001, GERMAN NATIONALS took to the streets shouting "Kinder statt Inder" (children not Indians) to protest the German government's effort at recruiting foreign high-tech labor. However, between August and December 2000, only 946 Indians (7 percent of all applicants) of an anticipated 20,000 Indians and Eastern Europeans had responded positively to the German government's offer of employment in high-tech jobs for the next five years.[1] By 2004, when the program ended because the German government thought it was unsuccessful, 3,926 Indians (26.4 percent) had received green cards, the largest number of any group (Kolb 2005). Why didn't Indians race toward this great opportunity? The scheme was criticized for being too bureaucratic, with salaries too low compared with those in the United States, visa terms too short, and restrictions on bringing family too difficult (Harding 2000). Large multinational corporations may have been unlikely to use the program because they already recruit workers internally (Kolb 2005). Although these are all credible reasons, they mask the underlying mechanism that explains how recruited professionals end up migrating to and working in other countries. On the one hand, there is a global labor market for certain types of labor such as computer scientists and software engineers. Often states think that they know where that labor should come from—IT specialists from India, nurses from the Philippines, or teachers from Europe. On the other hand, flows of these professionals and other kinds of workers, such as entrepreneurs or unskilled laborers, reveal very specific patterns that make the international circulation of labor a very local process that links labor markets. Contrary to most explanations, which suggest an efficient market mechanism for how workers

are matched with jobs, labor markets are embedded in networks of social relations (and vice versa) that often do the business of matching. Specific networks of interpersonal and organizational ties channel immigrants into
particular occupations at particular destinations and link local labor markets
in the process. High-tech workers, such as the Indians sought by the German
government, rely on organizational ties to migrate and secure employment,
which is why, perhaps, non-Indian workers are recruited to and transferred
within the largest multinational firms, according to Kolb (2005). The narrow
and translocal character of this occupational channeling further illuminates
how social networks facilitate and constrain the movement and economic incorporation of immigrants.

This chapter demonstrates how local labor markets become linked transnationally through specific network mechanisms that are roughly distinguished
by different configurations of social ties. In doing so, it clarifies the role and
meaning of networks as they affect different types of migration and the occupational outcomes of immigrants. The prominence of these network mechanisms
also challenges the role of human capital in producing distinct migration flows
and occupational outcomes. The chapter presents the life histories of Gujaratis
and their networks to illustrate what specific migration flows look like and
what the role of social ties is in those flows. It follows these immigrants' stories up to their first jobs at their destinations in East Africa, London, and New
York, showing what kinds of social ties facilitated or constrained the mobility
of these immigrants. One significant consequence of that process was that different configurations of social ties channeled immigrants into particular occupations and destinations, linking local labor markets in the process. As a result
of this occupational channeling, some Gujaratis became employed in jobs that
were occupational niches while others were left out of those niches. The linking
of labor markets is not a rational economic mechanism, as usually portrayed
in modern Western societies, but rather one located in "irrational" network
mechanisms. Labor markets are embedded in social networks that match employers and workers, a process that is often ignored or invisible to native workers who may fear that foreigners are taking away their jobs in a rational labor
market, as native Germans feared in 2001.

Linking Local Labor Markets

Labor markets have generally appeared and flourished under industrial capitalism (Tilly and Tilly 1998). In labor markets, recruitment and supply networks

provide information that links workers with jobs. Employment networks, therefore, reduce hiring costs but also limit the "market efficiency" of matching workers with jobs. Because these networks provide restricted types of information, resources, and outlets for such matching, specific categories of workers are often reproduced to fit particular jobs. Notwithstanding some control over differences in human capital, these categories might be based on gender, race, ethnicity, community of origin, or religion. Labor markets thus become highly segmented and highly localized. These categories or static characteristics seem to provide credibility to substantialist arguments that highlight them as causes or predictors of migration. Therefore, this chapter examines the composition of social networks and whether particular characteristics of immigrants do indeed provide reliable ways of explaining how people migrate and become employed in specific jobs.

Furthermore, the localization and segmentation of labor markets does not always require geographical proximity of workers to jobs, as is often the measure of a local labor market. Sassen (1995, 90) instructively proposes a return to the original concept of a local labor market, which centers on employers and then extends the concept by examining the "workplace–household nexus" in immigrant labor. Her conceptualization holds well for the way that local labor markets become linked. As employment networks connect workers with jobs in one local labor market, two or more local labor markets can become linked through transnational recruitment and supply networks that aim to fulfill labor demand. Local labor markets are further conditioned by historical, political, and economic relations between the geographical regions encompassing those markets. Where labor markets are linked transnationally, some international migration is bound to occur. An examination of recruitment and supply networks that connect potential migrants with jobs shows how local labor markets become linked and how they are embedded within migrant networks. This examination also reveals how recruitment and supply networks operate through different configurations of social ties in the migrant networks of recruits, trusties, and chains.

The life history profiles of Gujarati immigrants (individuals or married couples) and their social networks presented in the following pages illustrate the differences in the networks and occupational outcomes of recruits, trusties, and chains. The narratives of solitaries are not presented because the sample did not include any Gujarati immigrants without some type of social ties; however, theoretically solitaries should exist. The narrative profiles show, first, the historical, political, and economic linkages connecting local labor markets in origin and destination countries pertaining to each network; second, the structure of those social networks, which facilitates migration within that larger context; and third, the ways in which those individual immigrants and their networks are channeled into particular jobs or occupations as a result of the linkages and structure. Despite differences in the socioeconomic context of New York and London, the structure of Gujarati migrant networks was similar for each type of migration stream across sites. In other words, networks of recruits in New York, for example, resemble their counterparts in London but not other trusties or chains in New York.

Recruits: Professionals in New York and East Africa

Health Professionals in New York

In the previous chapter, I recounted that the first significant Indian migrant stream to the United States since the turn of the twentieth century occurred in the 1960s. This pioneer flow was composed largely of professional workers. Several historical circumstances facilitated the migration of health professionals in particular: the 1965 liberalization of U.S. immigration laws, which abolished national origins quotas; the national labor shortage of doctors in the United States, which resulted in the recruitment of foreign professional labor from India and other countries; and an examination process for foreign medical graduates that could take place in India or the United States to obtain a labor visa or green card before actually migrating (see Bowers and Rosenheim 1971). The development of medical education in postindependence India (after 1947) also created an enormous surplus of doctors (Mejia et al. 1980). For many potential immigrants, however, these conditions were probably not sufficient encouragement to migrate. Organizational ties to educational institutions, professional organizations, and employers were crucial for recruited professionals to retain their professional status after migration to the host society. The following narratives of Kishor and Jamnadevi, who were introduced in Chapter 1 and whose story I continue here, show how U.S. immigration policy and organizational ties facilitated their migration and linked professional labor in India with corresponding demand in the United States.

Kishor, the son of a respected cloth merchant, was a practicing medical doctor in Gujarat. Kishor's father wanted Kishor and his siblings to become doctors rather than continue in their father's business. In the 1970s, shortly after graduating from medical school in Gujarat, Kishor visited his brother,

Mahesh, a practicing medical doctor in the United States. Life in the United States made a positive impression on Kishor. Thus, during a subsequent six-month visit, he lived with and worked for his brother while taking classes in preparation for the ECFMG exam. The exam would qualify him to practice as a physician in the United States. During his studies, Kishor made contact with a friend from their medical college in Gujarat, who was working as a physician at a New York hospital. Kishor's friend informed him of an opening at that hospital and arranged for him to work there. On passing the exam, Kishor applied for a green card and returned to India for four months pending its approval. In 1975, he reentered the United States to begin a job as a house physician. Kishor entered the country just one year before the enactment of the Health Professions Educational Assistance Act, which declared an end to the national shortage of physicians and surgeons. The act eliminated the automatic labor certification granted to foreign medical graduates and prevented the overallocation of these visas to certain countries, such as the Philippines and India (Lobo and Salvo 1998). Kishor's doctor-friend, doctor-brother, and a receptive immigration policy, therefore, helped Kishor migrate directly to New York to practice medicine, all of which was made possible by organizational ties formed since 1947. Today, Kishor is among the 47,581 practicing medical doctors of Indian origin in the United States, or 5 percent of all medical doctors there (American Medical Association 2007). Like him, the majority of these doctors are first-generation immigrants; most of their second-generation children have barely come of age.[2]

Organizational ties alone would probably have sufficed to encourage Kishor's migration and employment, such as the recent pioneer migration of Indian IT workers to Germany. Fortunately, both interpersonal and organizational ties assisted Kishor in meeting the requirements for entry as a professional doctor and provided him with more personal needs such as housing and companionship, a combination of ties that signal a mature migrant stream of professionals with well-developed supply networks. In the case of Jamnadevi, Kishor's wife, both kinds of ties also helped her to complete her education and to establish her own dental practice in New York—her first job in the United States.

Jamnadevi and Kishor had an arranged marriage while Jamnadevi was still finishing dental school in India. To join Kishor in the United States, she applied for a green card under the immigration statute's allotment for professionals. Kishor also applied to sponsor her immigration. Both approvals arrived simultaneously, and Jamnadevi was officially admitted under the family-preferences provision. That year, Jamnadevi entered dental school in New York to complete her training. By 1979, she finished dental school, passed her board examinations, and began her own practice. The owner of Kishor's practice helped her to set up her own office. He offered Jamnadevi the opportunity to establish her practice near their office, consisting of three pediatricians. The two medical practices strategically banked on the idea that by having neighboring pediatric and dental offices, they could share clients needing both of these health services. Jamnadevi's ties to medical professionals, such as her husband's professional partners, and organizations, such as the Indian Dental Association of New York, provided important information and resources for her employment. Her status as a qualifying dentist and her professional degree from a prominent university in New York also aided the creation of those organizational ties.

Jamnadevi's and Kishor's migration experience is, in many ways, mirrored in the experience of Indian doctors in the United Kingdom. In their interviews with Indian doctors in a British teaching hospital, Robinson and Carey (2000) emphasize the role that social networks played in their migration. Although they highlight the role of interpersonal ties, their interviews show that those interpersonal ties were only to other doctors who could strategically help them to navigate the NHS and British society. For instance, "Dr A described how a friend in Bradford had paid his air fare and PLAB fees and had given him accommodation and food during his first few months in the UK. Dr A had then done the same for two other Indian doctors" (Robinson and Carey 2000, 101). (The PLAB is the Professional and Linguistic Assessment Board test for international medical graduates.) "Dr C told us how he had corresponded over a three years period with friends from medical school who were in the UK" (101). Dr C was also helped by a doctor friend when he arrived in Britain. The authors also emphasize that "social networks become migration networks" through these relational ties that are first formed from institutional relationships and the legacy of colonial relations between India and the United Kingdom (100). Although Robinson and Carey do not name these colonial institutional relationships organizational ties, they clearly resemble the organizational ties of recruits such as Jamnadevi and Kishor.

Jamnadevi and Kishor arrived on the heels of the pioneer stream of health professionals to the United States in the 1960s. Thus, they were able to take advantage of linked labor markets between India and the United States. They arrived at a time when supply networks of Indian immigrant health professionals were already in place to recruit them and ease their transition, as also happened with Indian doctors who had been recruited to the NHS in Britain. An open immigration policy and demand for medical labor contributed to the functioning of those networks, which consisted mostly of organizational ties from their educational institutions and workplaces. Similarly, the recent migration of Indian IT workers to Germany represents an early stage of migration of recruited professionals where supply networks are still few and underdeveloped. However, in time, this flow could mature into a stream of professionals, who will be recruited by Indian colleague-friends and not only by German institutions.

Umashankar and Kirtiben are part of Jamnadevi and Kishor's network of friends, but their migration history did not carry the virtual guarantees of recruitment as in the health professions. Umashankar was educated in Ahmedabad, Gujarat, with two bachelor's degrees, in commerce and in law, and a master's degree in commerce. After graduating with the master's in 1962, he worked for the Bank of Baroda, a large bank in Gujarat, as a clerk. He was later promoted to officer (equivalent to an assistant manager) and then manager of the bank. A friend from his commerce college told him and his wife (who also attended the same college) that the United States was favoring the immigration of Indians with master's degrees under the preference three category for professionals. In 1970, after applying for a U.S. green card in India, Umashankar was approved to immigrate. However, as the first son of six siblings, he chose to stay in India to care for his family. That year, he had also married Kirtiben after they had been introduced by Kirtiben's cousin, who worked at the same bank as Umashankar. Finally, in 1985, he migrated to the United States with the help of his wife's sister, who had gone to New York on a tourist visa. She had received a green card through a general amnesty and subsequently sponsored two of her brothers to immigrate to New York. Thus, when Umashankar and Kirtiben left for New York, they first stayed with Kirtiben's brother in New York for six months. When Kirtiben found a job as a telex operator in a bank before Umashankar, he was reassured that he would also find employment. Subsequently, he resigned his post in India to take an entry-level position as a clerk at the New York branch of the Bank of Baroda. Organizational ties in India and interpersonal ties in the United States encouraged Umashankar's and Kirtiben's migration and settlement in New York. However, it was not Umashankar's interpersonal or organizational ties that helped him get his first job but more likely his prior organizational *affiliation* with the Bank of Baroda. His organizational ties to key personnel at the bank were too few and distant to channel him into a new job commensurate with his Indian qualifications. Umashankar therefore had to rely on strong interpersonal ties in a kin-based network and organizational affiliation to migrate and obtain employment in the United States.

Anavils in East Africa

Administrators, clerks, and educators are the typical occupations of the Anavils, a lower-status subcaste within the high-status Brahmin caste. Four members of the Anavil network of friends whom I interviewed in London were teachers. As part of an educated middle class, many Anavils were unsurprisingly employed in educational, administrative, and professional positions in the East African protectorates of the British Empire. Teachers were in demand in East Africa during the first half of the twentieth century as a result of the British development of a formal educational system for European settlers, the African population, and a growing Asian population. Gregory (1993) reports that Asians far outnumbered Europeans and Africans as teachers in the East African protectorates of Uganda, Tanzania, and Kenya. He states that "although the proportion of Asians to Europeans in the overall population was approximately three to one, the teacher ratio was five to one" (228). Gregory found that Goans, Gujaratis, Punjabis, and Mahratis were among the most numerous Indian regional communities represented by the teachers, especially those who were educated and expatriates. The Anavils, therefore, probably constituted a high proportion of those Gujarati teachers because most of them were expatriates with a college degree. India's proximity to Africa and its British-influenced educational system also made it favorable to teacher recruitment. Representatives from the Ugandan, Kenyan, and Tanzanian High Commissions regularly recruited teachers during visits to India. They circulated advertisements, held interviews, and visited colleges and universities to recruit students. Colonial links and formal recruitment mechanisms, therefore, shaped the way in which the Anavil network I interviewed in London first migrated to East Africa. Here is the story of Kanti and Uma.

Kanti and Uma had an arranged marriage in India. Kanti received his BSc in 1950 from Bombay University and found work as a teacher. Uma taught primary school in Gujarat after she matriculated. Kanti informed me that at that time there were many advertisements circulating in local Indian newspapers for available work in East Africa. Gregory (1993) also confirms this account. Kanti and Uma answered an advertisement for teachers that was placed by the Indian committee members of a Ugandan private school serving mostly Asian children. (Students were racially segregated into European, Asian, and African schools throughout the British colonial period.) Kanti had a BSc with second-class honors; therefore he was hired to be the headmaster of a small staff of twelve teachers. Uma was hired to teach the primary grades. Kanti recounted that the salary in Uganda was better, although "not that much, but still I wanted to change the country so I went there . . . just to live in a different place, explore the new things." In addition to their desire to have new experiences, the opportunity was attractive to them because teaching contracts in East Africa paid higher salaries than those in India and provided free first-class travel and six months' leave every four years. In 1953, they left together for a small town outside Kampala to begin their new jobs.

Similar to Kanti and Uma, Pravin also answered an advertisement to teach in East Africa, though in Tanzania. Pravin was born in Gujarat in 1925 but spent his early childhood in Bombay, where his father was an engineer. When his father lost his job, they moved back to their village near the coast, and Pravin matriculated in another village several miles away. He then left to study science at a college in the city of Surat, where he lived in a hostel, and which is the home region of many Anavil Brahmins. He had difficulty with his studies. His father also ran out of money before he could finish his degree, but Pravin was able to obtain a job teaching in a private school. Later, he worked as a customs officer, a common job for Anavils in India.

In 1952, Pravin and his wife left for Tanzania. While still in India, Pravin had met an official from Dar es Saalam who was recruiting teachers for Tanzanian schools. Pravin was hired along with three others. In Tanzania, Pravin was appointed by the government to teach in a primary school for Asian children. The opportunity was attractive because the salary was better than in India and every four years they gave teachers six months' leave to return to India.

Bharat was more directly recruited to teach in Uganda in 1953. Born and raised in Bombay, he completed a postgraduate degree in Gujarati and English and was a lecturer in a college in Bombay. An overseas officer from the Ugandan High Commission, in conjunction with the Indian High Commission, came to his college in 1953 to recruit teachers through advertisement and recommendations from various college administrators. In addition to advertisement in local newspapers and announcements, visits to colleges were common recruitment strategies. Bharat's principal recommended him for the position in Kampala, and he was persuaded to migrate there by his distant aunt and uncle, who were already working as teachers there. During their six-month leave, when they lived across the street from Bharat in Bombay, Bharat's aunt and uncle gave him firsthand information on what their lives were like in Uganda to convince him to migrate there. Bharat, urban and educated, thought that "Uganda must be a jungle, and who would want to go—leave Bombay and go to a jungle," but eventually he was persuaded by his relatives and his principal at the college where he taught. Added incentives, of course, were that teaching positions in Uganda were fairly well paid with free, first-class passage and six months' leave every four years, exactly as with the situation of Pravin, Uma, and Kanti. In fact, Bharat became the headmaster of a public school in Kampala that was educating the children of civil servants, ministers, and other high-ranking colonial officials.

The Anavils, on the whole, are recruits. Their prior experience as teachers in India allowed them to take advantage of organizational ties within local labor markets produced by colonial relations linking India and East Africa. Bharat's organizational ties were probably the strongest of the four. Those ties, coupled with Bharat's higher educational achievement, resulted in his attainment of the most prestigious teaching position within the Anavil network. (The durability of his organizational ties would also reappear almost twenty years later to influence his migration to and employment in London, as discussed in the following chapter.) Nevertheless, demand for teachers and formal recruitment mechanisms carried out by governing officials influenced the formation of transnational recruitment and supply networks between India and East Africa and aided their migration and employment opportunities.

Significantly, interpersonal ties also play an important role in the migration and occupational histories of recruits. However, without organizational ties, interpersonal ties alone would not have preserved the occupational status of these immigrants. Furthermore, despite the different historical contexts of the cases of the Anavil teachers in East Africa and medical professionals in New York, organizational ties to professional and educational colleagues and to government and institutional representatives led to a similar process. With the exception of Umashankar, these recruits were channeled into occupations that were consistent with their Indian education and their training before leaving India.

Trusties: Transnational Entrepreneurs Create
New Markets for Labor and Consumption
Oswals in East Africa and London

In the previous chapters, I introduced the Halari Oswal Jain community, in which the majority of young men sailed in small Arab dhows to East Africa, specifically to Kenya, around the turn of the twentieth century. At that time, most Halari Oswals were struggling economically as small farmers in their fifty-two villages surrounding the western Gujarat city of Jamnagar. A severe famine in the region, which lasted from 1899 to 1901, resulted in the Halari's decline in status relative to the urban trading group of Jamnagari Oswals (Banks 1994). The resulting class division, in addition to the hardships created by the famine, contributed to the migration of many Halari Oswals to East Africa but not that of Jamnagari Oswals. At the time, many regions of Gujarat were already experiencing substantial out-migration to East Africa, as the word spread that good opportunities for trade and commerce existed there. By 1972, half of the almost 15,000 Oswals in East Africa had settled in Nairobi; the others had settled elsewhere in Kenya (Banks 1994; Gregory 1993). In Kenya, Oswals were primarily small shopkeepers dealing in textiles and household goods because their Jain practices conflicted with the handling of meat, fish, and liquor.[3]

The migration of Oswals to East Africa began as a turn-of-the-century free migration that eventually became a chain migration and settlement. Pioneer male migrants returned to India to recruit family and community members to work for them and to marry and bring their wives to East Africa. Indian and British organizations played a very limited role in that chain migration flow and in the Oswals' economic development as small shopkeepers and traders. Kin and community networks in India were initially sustained throughout their settlement in East Africa and provided labor for their shopkeeping niche. These networks would serve them later, when many members of the community migrated to London and reestablished themselves in small shops and trade, thus resembling trusties rather than chains. Some of these chains, who migrated within East Africa and/or to London, became trusties as they expanded their markets for production and consumption. The following profile of Mahendra, an elder in the Oswal community in London, shows how he became a transnational entrepreneur in East Africa and in London, linking local labor markets for commercial trade in India, East Africa, and Britain.

Mahendra was born in Kenya, the eldest of twelve siblings. He received a seat to study dentistry in Edinburgh, but he was too poor to pursue an education abroad. Instead, Mahendra had been keeping accounts for a businessman (who would soon become his uncle-in-law) in exchange for living with his family. That uncle asked Mahendra to become a partner in his confectionery business. Later, they began a food manufacturing company that made curries and other Indian foods for export and local sale. Thus, Mahendra soon acquired the necessary experience and ties to suppliers and buyers to operate a transnational business in the food industry. Until at least the mid-1900s, Indians were trading throughout East Africa, in particular Uganda, where agriculture and industry were well developed. Therefore, Mahendra migrated to Uganda to start an independent business with the help of his brother, who was living there. Colonial links to Britain, particularly London, also opened opportunities for trade. Among other pioneers of the ethnic foods industry in the 1960s, Mahendra and his brother bought a shop in London to sell curries made in their factories in Uganda. They also imported indigenous Indian and African vegetables and flowers grown in East Africa. While Mahendra stayed in Uganda, his brother and a partner ran the London end of the business. In addition to difficulties with food spoilage and developing a new consumer market in London, the shop failed because of mismanagement and conflict between Mahendra's brother and his partner. In 1972, when Idi Amin expelled the Asians from Uganda, Mahendra and his family immigrated to London as refugees. Even though Amin's government seized all of their property, technology, and capital, Mahendra and his four brothers were able to start new businesses together in London. They not only had preexisting ties to suppliers and buyers in India and Europe, but they also had experience in the London retail market. They imported silk saris from India, Japan, and Paris. They had twelve sari shops at one point, but Mahendra eventually sold them because of family conflict.

In Kenya, Uganda, and Britain, Mahendra owned several transnational businesses. Each migration and transnational business was facilitated by his interpersonal ties to his younger brothers, who had to oblige him with labor. His brothers and other Oswals also served as organizational ties of suppliers and buyers in the various industries represented by their businesses. Such dense networks of composite organizational and interpersonal ties were crucial to run their risky and lucrative transnational businesses. As the eldest, and the holder of the family's wealth, Mahendra had the power to intensely monitor the behavior of his network of brothers and business partners and to dominate decision making for their businesses. This dense transnational business network also directed Mahendra and his brother's migration to Uganda and London.

In Chapter 1, Harshad's story highlighted how interpersonal ties promote migration flows as Harshad and his siblings, following their middle brother, migrated to London "one by one," as Harshad put it. Part of Harshad's life story, however, also demonstrates the role of composite ties in his migration history and that of his brother.

Harshad, the youngest of six siblings, was born in Kenya in 1955. Like many other Oswals, his father, at the young age of fourteen, migrated to Kenya around the turn of the twentieth century to earn a living and help the family back in India. After working in the shops of other relatives and friends from their community, Harshad's father had enough money to buy his own business, build a house, and send money for his younger brother, wife, and eldest son to join him. First, he had a general store selling locally produced goods to local residents. Harshad's mother also made household goods to sell in the family shop. Later, the family bought dairies and a bottling plant, supplying milk to the local district's hospital, school, and government.

Their small town had only a primary school; therefore, all of Harshad's siblings attended secondary school in Nairobi, fifty miles away, and some went to university in London. In 1962, at the age of sixteen, Harshad's middle brother went to London in the company of four friends from their town to take their A-level exams and attend university. They had British passports from birth, and their families considered education in Britain better than that in Nairobi. Harshad's brother was at first a paying guest in a private home while he pursued his studies. However, as each sibling migrated to London for education, their parents, still in Kenya, bought them a house and paid regularly for their expenses. Harshad was the last to arrive in 1968 at the age of twelve.

By the time Harshad arrived in London, his eldest brother, Mahesh, had moved out of the family home, bought his own house with a shop underneath, and begun selling fancy goods. He had initially come to London with a friend from Kenya in 1963 on a "fact-finding" tour for investment possibilities. They were interested in a petrol station. More importantly, Mahesh knew before migrating that he wanted to own a small business and that he could realize this ambition by using his experience and capital from Kenya. Harshad had been studying law and economics at a university in London when his brother Mahesh summoned him to work in his prospering business. By that time, their parents had migrated back to India, and Mahesh had switched to a clothing manufacturing business. Harshad and Mahesh had a factory in London. They were also importing raw fabric from India through connections with other members of the Oswal community. In a short while, they were able to obtain jobs for their maternal cousins and uncles in the same factory in India from which they were importing. They were even able to buy those relatives a factory in India from which Harshad and Mahesh imported more fabrics. Eventually, in the late 1970s, the British market became flooded with Indian cottons. To diversify their goods, they started buying fabrics locally in Europe, but Mahesh finally sold the business. In the meantime, they had found new buyers for their relatives in India, who still have a successful business of about 400 employees in Bombay and Jaipur.

In this story, Harshad's brother resembles Bashi's (2007) concept of a hub or, in network terms, a central actor in this interpersonal network. Centrality measures the degree to which an actor is connected to other actors in a network. Central actors often control crucial resources that are exchanged within network ties, such as money, information, and influence. Bashi's central argument, based on the case of West Indian immigrants in New York and London, is that these hubs control the process of migration rather than demonstrating a chain effect in which each subsequent migrant can promote the migration of the next person. Mahesh's central position in his network of kin, however, does not necessarily represent the typical organization of networks of trusties or chains.[4]

Even though Harshad and his siblings migrated as chains, composite ties aided Harshad's brother to establish a transnational business from London and to employ Harshad in his first job. As the eldest son in the family, Mahesh had persuaded Harshad to leave university and work for him in this garment business. When the business faltered, however, Mahesh decided to sell it. Harshad was not influential in that decision and was left unemployed because of his brother's decision. Trusties in transnational trades such as the garment industry involve dense network ties in which family members are simultaneously buyers, suppliers, and business supervisors in the family firm. These ties spanned India, East Africa, and Britain in Mahesh's family firm, which was organized vertically connecting production—the factories where their cousins and extended kin supervised and worked in the production of garments—to consumption—the markets in Britain and Europe where Mahesh and Harshad sold their products. Although the organization of these businesses as family firms provides economic advantages to kin, it also allows key actors in these firms to control and monitor the behavior of those they recruit to work for them. The mobility of these trusties, furthermore, is controlled by actors such as Harshad's brother—those who dominate their economic niche.

Jain Diamond Traders in New York

New York is one of the major diamond markets in the world, along with Antwerp, Hong Kong, Bangkok, and Tel Aviv. Ninety percent of uncut diamonds and 50 percent of all polished stones sold in the world are traded in Antwerp alone (duBois 1997; Westwood 2000). India's $4.5 billion industry is the stone-cutting center for 80 percent of the diamonds sold around the world (Karp 1999). Uncut diamonds are traded in Antwerp and sent to Bombay and other cities, where they are carried by *anagadias* (the Gujarati word for a person who carries valuables and therefore is trustworthy) to stone-cutting and polishing centers such as Surat and Ahmedabad in Gujarat. Then they are exported for sale to major diamond markets such as New York. The United States is viewed as a very large market for selling diamonds, accounting for over two-thirds of cut and polished diamonds exported from India according to the Indian Diamond and Colorstone Association. India's advantage in the market for stone cutting and polishing is, in part, the availability of cheap, skilled labor that "can put 56 facets on a stone the size of a grain of salt" (McDonald 1996, 4). Other advantages include the tight-knit networks of the diamond industry in Gujarat.[5] The following profiles of Jain diamond dealers in this close-knit community show how migration is encouraged through transnational trade, channeling entrepreneurs directly into emerging industries and markets dominated by their community.

Lakshmi and Narendra, whose story I began in Chapter 1, were pioneers of the American market for Indian diamonds. In India, they had a love marriage combining similar class backgrounds but different religions. Narendra is Hindu, whereas Lakshmi comes from a Jain diamond family. Narendra left his natal family's business as a result of interpersonal conflict and was adopted and trained in the diamond trade by Lakshmi's uncle. Lakshmi had been working in her family's business in Bombay since she was eighteen. In the early 1970s, her uncle sent them to New York to expand the family business. They migrated under U.S. visa allocations for investors with sponsorship from the family firm's headquarters in Antwerp. They were also among the first Jain families to establish diamond businesses in New York. They forged new ties with other

Jain pioneers in the American diamond market and with American buyers. Members of their community of diamond traders provided them with a directory of all of the jewelers in the United States, which included names, locations, and ratings. Based on those merchant's ratings, Lakshmi and Narendra spent their first two years in the United States by traveling throughout the country to meet potential customers. Their composite ties to other traders in New York and Antwerp and exporters in India helped the firm to grow and allowed them to build more factories in India to expand into jewelry manufacturing and sale. They had a series of partnerships, always with Jain diamond families, until they could make their business independent.

Networks of Jains in the diamond industry include ties to family and friends in the trade, all of whom are also members of the Indian Diamond and Colorstone Association. Lakshmi and Narendra met Sadvati and Arun this way. In 1985, Sadvati migrated from Bombay to New York with her husband, Arun, whose parents had pioneered their family business in Bombay and New York. Their marriage was arranged; therefore they come from the same community of Jain diamond traders in India, who have established businesses in the major diamond centers of Bombay, Antwerp, and New York. Arun inherited the business and their exclusive Manhattan apartment from his parents, who first established their firm in New York in the early 1970s. They sell diamonds and sometimes jewelry from stones cut and polished in their factories in India, and they have organizational networks of producers, buyers, and sellers that span most of the major diamond centers (cities) around the world.

Sadvati's cousin, Chandrika, also migrated to New York in the 1980s to join her husband, Madhu. Chandrika and Madhu own a profitable manufacturing and retail business in New York, specializing in high-end casual menswear. Both of their families come from the same region in Gujarat, where, like other Jains, they began work in the diamond industry, eventually taking that work to Bombay, Hong Kong, Antwerp, and New York. Although Chandrika's family had migrated first to Hong Kong, where she was born in the early 1960s, and later settled in Antwerp, where she grew up, Madhu's family stayed in Bombay, where his father began his own clothing manufacturing business. Madhu's father first began operating the business transnationally with a partner who ran the New York branch. Madhu, a self-proclaimed mischief maker and school rebel, was sent by his father to New York to study clothing design, planning all the while to return to Bombay and work in his father's business.

Perhaps fortuitously, a $300,000 debt incurred by his father's partner led to Madhu's stay in New York to take over and rescue the New York operation. Therefore, he immediately became president of the U.S. branch of the company. Madhu's company is still in partnership with his father's company in Bombay. They own several factories in India and Africa and have contracts with factories in Bangladesh and Pakistan. The New York branch also makes its own private label clothing, which it sells in North America and Europe. The rest of their clothing is manufactured and sold to medium- and high-end fashion labels.

Madhu's marriage to Chandrika was arranged through members of their small community, who knew both families in Bombay and Antwerp. In this way, Chandrika migrated to New York on a family visa sponsored by Madhu. She did not attend college, and her family expected her to marry shortly after completing secondary school. Thus, when she arrived in the United States, her first job was in a diamond company that was owned by a partner of her parent's diamond company in Antwerp. Chandrika and Madhu's network of dense, composite ties between kin and community and ties to firms in the diamond and clothing manufacturing and retail industries resulted in their employment in transnational family businesses consistent with their family's occupational status.

Kin, community, business, and trust are carefully interwoven in these social networks of trusties, preserving and enhancing their high occupational status in the New York diamond trade. Those ties preserve and enhance their occupational status in lucrative, yet risky, transnational trades. They also control the recruitment of labor and the kinds of labor members of those networks perform. Their financial success is evidence not only of the large market demand for their goods but also of their ability to dominate the trade through dense networks of composite ties.

Chains: "Business in Their Blood" or the Limits of Interpersonal Ties?

Gujaratis often say they have "business in their blood" when they explain why they own or are employed in various retail and wholesale trades. That belief persists as a collective myth owing to the centuries of successful merchant and trading castes from Gujarat (Tripathi 1984). On the contrary, this research shows that some Gujarati immigrants are entrepreneurial not because they have business in their blood but rather because of interpersonal ties that channel their entry into business niches controlled by others in their network. Conversely, other Gujarati chains have interpersonal ties that aid their entry into the dominant labor market, albeit in lower occupational positions than those they held prior to migrating.

Organizational ties typically play a very limited role in channeling chains to particular destinations and into occupations. Without such ties, these immigrants have instead used their interpersonal ties to move to Britain and the United States. Although U.S. immigration policy since 1965 has substantially increased the number of high-skill visas, the majority of immigrants still enter the country on family visas. In Britain since the 1960s, most Indian immigrants came from East Africa with British passports in hand and family to help them settle. Once they arrive in the host country, chains also use interpersonal ties to seek employment. However, interpersonal ties limit their employment opportunities because kin and community can rarely provide new and better information and resources, a well-known limitation of "strong ties" (Granovetter 1973, 1974). Because reliance on interpersonal ties produces few new possibilities, chains must resort to public advertisement and employment agencies. Whether chains rely on interpersonal ties or on formal means to become employed, their occupational status is typically downgraded to entry-level positions at the time of their arrival in the host society. Their lack of organizational ties significantly affects their ability to achieve parity with their home-country status. Nevertheless, some chains can compensate for lowered status if they are part of interpersonal networks that dominate occupational niches. This is a significant factor in channeling some chains into niches while excluding others. The following narratives of chains in the Patidar, Oswal, and Swadhyaya communities show how interpersonal ties limited their employment opportunities to small business or entry-level positions in the dominant labor market.

London's Patidars

The Patidar community has origins in the Charotar region of central Gujarat. The Patidars are a peasant landowning caste who have been economically and socially influential throughout Gujarat since the early twentieth century (Gregory 1993; Patel and Rutten 1999).[6] Their immigration to East Africa began around the mid-nineteenth century when many Patidar men migrated to work for British infrastructural projects and administration, such as the railways and civil service. Many also engaged in commerce as small shopkeepers.

In Uganda in 1950, Patels (the most common surname of the Patidar caste) numbered 41 percent of Hindus who held trading licenses (Gregory 1993). Although some second- and third-generation East African Patidars rose into the professional occupations, the community retained a significant shopkeeping niche until the 1960s. Around that time, the Africanization policies of Tanzania and Kenya and the expulsion of Asians from Uganda prompted or forced most Patidars to migrate to London or back to India. In London, their tight-knit community based on interpersonal ties helped them to reestablish themselves in local retail trade. Consider the case of Raj and Parvati, who run a small shop in East London.

Raj was born in Kampala, Uganda, to a father born in Gujarat and a mother born in Kampala. His father had a bachelor's degree in commerce and was a certified accountant on a coffee plantation in Kampala. However, the 1972 Asian expulsion suddenly transported Raj's family to a refugee resettlement camp in Britain. Like all Ugandan refugees, they were allowed to bring £150 per person into Britain; and unlike the wealthy businesspeople of Uganda, they had no overseas bank accounts to buffer their loss. Raj's family stayed in the camp for a week until a cousin offered them housing. Although Raj and his family were refugees from Uganda, in many ways they resemble chains. The refugee status of many Ugandan Indians was short lived because so many of their kin and coethnics throughout East Africa had already settled in Britain and were able and willing to help them. Nonetheless, the most durable effect on the refugees' economic adjustment to life in Britain was the confiscation of their livelihood and assets in Uganda.

Raj's parents found their first jobs in factories doing assembly work. Raj's father was unable to transfer his educational qualifications to London's dominant labor market. Therefore, he attained the same occupational status as Raj's mother, who had only matriculated. Raj's father also kept the account books of local Indian shopkeepers to gain extra income informally. After more than a decade of working on assembly lines, Raj's parents bought a shop in the confectionery/tobacco/newsstand (CTN) industry, which is dominated by Patidars across London (Lyon and West 1995). Relatives living in the United States and bank loans helped them to buy the shop. Prior experience keeping the accounts for other CTN shopkeepers made the transition into a small business easy. Raj's father died shortly after Raj finished his A-level high school qualifications and while his sister was still unmarried. Raj then inherited the shop, which he presently runs with the help of his mother and his wife, Parvati. Parvati has a bachelor's degree in social studies. She completed her degree in the same year that she was introduced to Raj, while he was in Gujarat for his father's funeral. They were married in four days, after which time Parvati migrated to London, where she began work in the family shop. Raj's overwhelming obligations as the new head of the family included providing his sister with all the obligatory expenses of a Patidar wedding.

For Raj and Parvati, interpersonal ties channeled their opportunities for small business. Although inheriting the family shop was economically advantageous, their economic opportunities to expand their shop, for instance, were severely limited by family obligations and a short supply of capital. Similar conditions of limited capital and a lack of organizational ties instead led Minesh into manual work.

Minesh was born in Kampala, Uganda, in 1955 but was sent by his parents to India to study, eventually attaining a BSc in electrical engineering in Gujarat. Anticipating political difficulties in Uganda, his parents joined him in India in 1971, one year prior to the Asian expulsion. From India, his parents entered the visa queue for refugees holding British passports to migrate to London. After completing his schooling, Minesh joined his parents in London in 1976. Minesh's father had a small shop for retail trade in Kampala and in India, where Minesh sometimes helped him on his days off or during school vacations. Minesh, however, had acquired his family's middle-class and high subcaste status and an engineering degree. Therefore, he sent out some fifty applications for engineering positions in London rather than go to work in an "Asian shop." One employer responded by offering him a job as a porter in a canteen, which he swiftly rejected. Still despondent from the lack of recognition of his qualifications and inability to meet the three-year residency requirement for a council educational grant, Minesh took his first job doing assembly work for a prominent auto company. Padma, Minesh's wife, was born in Kenya and migrated to Britain with her parents at the age of four in 1962. She completed her secondary schooling in London and went to work as a clerk in a prominent British bank. Native educational qualifications and a broader incorporation into British society led her to seek employment through institutional channels rather than interpersonal ties.

As a chain migrant and having escaped much of the anguished conditions of Ugandan refugees, Minesh used his interpersonal ties to migrate. He lacked organizational ties in his professional field because most of his community and family were involved in retail trade in London. Thus, limited wealth to gain higher educational qualifications, the absence of organizational ties to firms in his field, and restrictive interpersonal ties in the Indian ethnic economy led Minesh into low-status manual work. In contrast, family circumstances, limited wealth, and interpersonal ties, which allowed Raj to inherit his father's shop, channeled his and his wife's opportunities for work in that direction. Here, we see that interpersonal ties, while providing for some opportunities, as in the case of Raj and Parvati, can also be very limiting. They restrict new kinds of information from passing within ties, which are necessary for entry into a field where no network niches exist.

The Oswals in London

Dinesh's father came from a poor family in Karachi (now in Pakistan). He migrated alone to Bombay as a child in the early 1900s and found work in the building trade. He migrated again to Kenya in the early 1930s around the age of thirteen. Aided by other members of their community already in Mombasa, Dinesh's father worked in various shops and eventually returned to India to marry and bring his wife back to Kenya. He then began a one-man operation as a traveling salesman, where he would rewholesale products to warehouses in the various villages and towns around Nairobi. At different times, he bought both local and foreign products from such places as Switzerland and China, where he and others like him from the Oswal community had developed business connections. Dinesh, the second son of seven siblings, was born in Kenya in 1954. His younger brother was the first to migrate to London for further studies, and Dinesh followed him in 1973 after completing his A-levels in Kenya. Dinesh originally wanted to attend university in London, but he was not eligible for a council educational grant without at least three years' residence in Britain; therefore, he began looking for a job. Within a week of arriving in London, he obtained a job as an insurance evaluator through a public employment agency. As he put it to me, "That time it was very easy because I had good A-levels, so it was quite easy for me. Maybe at that time my English wasn't . . . spoken English. I had a very heavy accent, but my written English was very good, so, and I was good at Maths, so . . . it was very easy for me to get a job."

Jayant and Parul, a married couple, also from the Oswal community, reported similar strategies and outcomes. They were each born in Kenya in the 1950s to families of modest means. Their fathers owned small clothing shops in a small town along the railway. They finished their O-levels in Kenya and migrated to London with their families, where they completed their A-levels. The three-year residency requirement for educational grants also kept them from pursuing a university degree, but Parul qualified as a nurse's aide and through an employment agency found her first job. Jayant began as an entry-level telephone exchange planner with British Telecommunications, a job that he also found through a public agency. Both had family already living in Britain when they arrived with their respective parents, and they both have strong interpersonal ties to members of their Oswal community and its formal association. However, like other young migrants who finished their education in Britain, they pursued institutional routes to locating employment rather than community ties. They did so during a time when jobs commensurate with their modest qualifications were readily available in London, especially in the public sector. Had these advantages not existed for them, it would be fair to speculate that their interpersonal ties to their community would have produced information and aid about employment opportunities limited to the small businesses and shops, which many Oswals owned or where they were employed.

Public-sector employment remained strong in London throughout the 1970s and employed many Indians, particularly those from East Africa, who had college degrees. In the years before the 1976 Race Relations Act, which banned racial discrimination in employment, public-sector employment often resulted in underemployment. One participant in this study, Kamlesh, came to London from Kenya in 1967. In those early years, he experienced blatant racial discrimination at a public employment agency. Kamlesh had earned a bachelor's degree in commerce at the University of Bombay in 1955 and had worked as an accountant in Kenya and in Tanzania for a large English motor corporation. The job placement officer in Britain had been suggesting low-level clerical positions from the list she had in front of her, where certain jobs were marked with red and others black. Kamlesh pointed out accounting positions from the list that he might qualify for, but the officer admitted that those jobs were reserved for white candidates. Through that agency, Kamlesh became underemployed as a clerk with the Post Office and Telegraph, which later became British Telecommunications. Despite instances of racial discrimination, London provided significant public sector opportunities for East African Indians, such as Dinesh, Jayant, and Parul, before its recession from 1979 through 1982.

Dadaji's Pilgrims in New York

Unlike the Oswals, Patidars, Jain diamond traders, and Anavils, the Swadhyayees are bound together by their common beliefs and practices rather than community of origin. They are a fairly heterogeneous group in terms of their caste association and class composition in the United States. That diversity is in keeping with the religious philosophy of Swadhyaya (self-study), which binds them together as a network of friends, who participate in this socioreligious movement led by a teacher whom they fondly and respectfully refer to as Dadaji. The eight Swadhyaya members whom I interviewed were born and raised in Gujarat in relatively urban middle-class families. Their Indian educational qualifications range from associate's degrees to postgraduate master's and medical degrees. Equally important, they each had at least one close family member living in the United States before they migrated. Five of the eight Swadhyayees I interviewed arrived in the United States on family visas—as chain migrants with family already residing there. However, without organizational ties, finding employment that would honor these qualifications proved difficult. Ashok and Hansaveni provide a typical example of the limits of interpersonal ties.

Ashok and Hansaveni are from educated, middle-class families in the Anavil community. Ashok has a bachelor's degree in commerce but found economic prospects in Gujarat unsatisfactory. In the late 1970s, he immigrated to the United States on a family visa sponsored by his sister. Ashok's sister was sponsored by her husband, who entered the United States from Britain by taking advantage of immigration preferences for health professionals, a common pathway described in the previous chapter (see also Mejia et al. 1980). Ashok was introduced to Hansaveni by her brother, and they had an arranged marriage in Gujarat. In their first years in New York, the couple relied on Ashok's sister and brother-in-law to house them and to help them adjust to life in the United States. Ashok's sister also provided Ashok with his first job; she asked her supervisor to hire Ashok at the nursing home where she was employed. Even though Hansaveni has a bachelor of science degree from Gujarat, she took her first job as a clerk at a large New York bank. Ashok arranged for her employment after he began working there. Ashok and Hansaveni became employed in a string of similar entry-level positions. After more than a decade, they obtained jobs that were consistent with their educational background and experience.

Interpersonal ties helped Ashok and Hansaveni to become employed, even though using those ties resulted in a significant drop in their initial occupational status. Age and familial obligations further limited their economic activities, such as pursuing American educational qualifications to obtain professional status. Thus, interpersonal ties facilitated and constrained Ashok's and Hansaveni's employment in the dominant labor market just as it did Raj's and Parvati's employment in small business.

In a similar case, Nathubhai, a friend of Ashok and Hansaveni, finished an associate's degree in electrical engineering in Gujarat and migrated to the United States in 1978 on a family visa. His visa was sponsored by his wife just after they were married. She had been living in Chicago with her family since 1972. Before migrating, Nathubhai had worked as a farmer (the traditional occupation of his family and of the Patidar caste to which he belongs) and as an engineer with supervisory status in various Indian firms. Lacking a bachelor's degree, however, significantly disadvantaged him in the United States. Thus, he took his first job as a pump repair technician in a chemical plant. Simultaneously, he pursued a degree in computer science after learning that his course credits from India could not be transferred into an engineering degree program. Like many chain migrants, Nathubhai had close interpersonal ties to help him migrate but much more distant organizational and interpersonal ties to aid his employment opportunities.

The city of New York faced bankruptcy by 1975, which resulted in job losses and many retirements that opened up public-sector employment to immigrants in the 1980s when the city began to recover. Thus, many Indians, such as Ashok and Hansaveni, first found jobs in the private sector and later in their occupational histories entered the public sector, during the city's recovery period. Indians such as Nathubhai had been building a small niche in engineering and accounting positions that would serve as supply networks for the recruitment of newer arrivals in the 1980s during the economic recovery (Waldinger 1990). Nevertheless, during those years, the majority of Indian immigrants, such as Jamnadevi and Kishor, had professional skills and worked as doctors, engineers, computer scientists, and accountants (Kanjanapan 1992; Minocha 1987). Thus, public sector employment was less crucial as a gateway for Indian employment. In fact, about 13 percent of New York's Asian Indians worked in the public sector—at the local, state, or federal levels of government—in 1990, according to the U.S. Census Bureau.

These stories of chains in New York and London illustrate the limits of interpersonal ties in preserving the occupational status of Gujaratis, many of whom had college-level qualifications and experience in India. Many chains are not channeled into occupations unless their interpersonal ties lead them into niche employment. As with Raj and Parvati, for instance, chains with interpersonal ties in niche employment were channeled directly into those occupations in ethnic economies. Other chains, such as Ashok and Hansaveni, used similar ties to obtain employment, though in nonniche occupations and at levels below their human capital qualifications. Those immigrants who used formal means to locate work, such as advertisements and employment agencies, also became employed in nonniche occupations. Thus, overall, chains have more varied but less stable occupational outcomes than recruits or trusties. Marriage and marriage opportunities also create distinct opportunities as interpersonal ties and deserve special attention, as in the three cases discussed in the following section.

Marriage Patterns and New Occupational Opportunities

Marriage is an economic act, in addition, of course, to its various reproductive, social, and personal functions and meanings. Although economic concerns may not be the primary reasons for marrying or intermarrying a particular person in a particular family, gains or losses in economic status and opportunities often find their way into the calculus of marriage decisions. Most of the marriages among the Gujaratis I interviewed were arranged by a relative or friend well known to both families. Or, as many participants put it to me, "We were introduced." In the case of the arranged marriage of one young couple in London, the husband was introduced to and "interviewed" about twenty women during a brief stay in India, while his wife had an astounding forty-some introductions before choosing him. In these cases, caste endogamy is almost always preserved. Even though caste endogamy is still the norm for many Gujaratis, and indeed Indians, intermarriage does occur and at different orders of division. It also occurs mainly among the urban, professional classes in India (Shah 1998), a pattern that seems to hold for both New York's and London's Indian immigrants. Most interestingly among the Gujaratis I interviewed, marriage (whether caste endogamous or not) can lead to enhanced social and economic status through new economic networks and opportunities, and the marriage can produce breaks in other marital norms, such as patrilocality, which anticipate or create improved economic opportunity. Thus, marriage can be a form of brokerage even though it is a strong tie. These marital patterns are not necessarily typical of Gujaratis or Indians. However, the following profiles show how nonnormative patterns of marriage can foresee positive occupational opportunities, which then change the occupational trajectories for some individuals.

Narendra, whom we met earlier, comes from a very prominent Hindu family of merchants, most of whom had settled or had been born in East Africa since the turn of the twentieth century. They amassed great wealth in a family business of industrial, commercial, and agricultural enterprises. As a result of a falling out with his owner-relatives, Narendra returned to Bombay, where he met his future wife, Lakshmi. They lived in the same neighborhood and spotted each other on the street. Lakshmi comes from an upper-class family of Jain diamond traders and certainly would have had her marriage arranged to a man from another family of the same origin and similar class status had it not been for her meeting Narendra. Narendra and Lakshmi broke several marital norms—across religion, caste, patrilocality, and occupation or trade. First, a marriage between a Jain and Hindu is an interreligious marriage, even though it would certainly not cause the kind of family anguish that a Muslim–Hindu or, perhaps less so, a Sikh–Hindu marriage might. Second, unlike Hindus, Jains are not bound by any prescribed caste system; thus, class divisions play a heightened role among them. Narendra and Lakshmi could flex some of the rules in this matter and push caste concerns to the side because they came from similar class backgrounds. Third, Narendra was further adopted into the diamond business of Lakshmi's family rather than staying with the business of his own family. Lakshmi's uncle taught and trained Narendra in everything there is to know about their business. He gave Narendra the human, financial, and social capital necessary to eventually break into a new market in the United States during the early 1970s, when very few Indians were involved in the diamond trade there. Narendra's adoption into the trade meant that not only had he become a fully fledged member of the family but also that he could be surveyed more closely and that Lakshmi's economic future would be secure. Thus, Lakshmi's and Narendra's intermarriage resulted in the breaking of several norms, which opened a new and promising occupational door for Narendra in keeping with his premarital social status. As often happens in arranged marriages, these possibilities certainly did not go unnoticed by Narendra, Lakshmi, and her family during discussions about their desire to be married. Thus, the potential conflicts of an exogamous "love marriage" were overcome by breaking traditions of patrilocality and being accepted into the family business by Lakshmi's uncle. This effectively changed Narendra's occupational trajectory and likelihood to migrate to the United States as opposed to East Africa or later to London where his natal family now resides.

As noted previously, Patel is a common surname among the Patidar caste in Gujarat and can belong to one of at least two caste divisions of the first order. Even within these divisions are further subcastes, which define marriage circles or *gols* and patterns of caste endogamy. These marriage circles are hypergamous—that is, women or girls are permitted to "marry up," while men or boys are not. The love marriage between Nathubhai and his wife broke two traditions. Nathubhai "married up" into his wife's caste from a lower subcaste twice removed from approved marriage circles; therefore, his wife "married down." This disparity in status caused much difficulty for Nathubhai's father-in-law, who at the time lived with his wife and daughters in Chicago. They had migrated there in 1972 from Uganda, where he was a teacher before the Asian expulsion. Nathubhai then immigrated to Chicago to be with his wife, rather than bringing her back to India where patrilocal tradition would have had her join his family. Thus, their intercaste marriage produced the possibility of migration to the United States and potentially better employment and educational opportunities for Nathubhai. These prospects, coupled with his lower caste/class status, led to a break in patrilocal tradition.

Caste-endogamous practices can also lead to breaks in marital norms in the interest of occupational and social status climbing. Jagdish was introduced to his future wife as part of an arranged marriage in Bombay. Her family had been living in Uganda, but she had returned to India for a short time when Jagdish met her. As part of the marriage discussion, it was understood that Jagdish would move to Uganda to live with his wife and her family. He had not fared badly in India, having just achieved a BSc in economics in Bombay. However, his father-in-law promised to find Jagdish a job at a prominent Indian family-owned business in Uganda where he was working. Thus, patrilocal tradition was broken in anticipation of a better occupational opportunity. The personal link to this employment opportunity lessened the risk associated with migrating and working in an unknown place, further easing the break with patrilocal tradition in this caste-endogamous marriage.

In these few cases, we can see that the breaking of marital traditions such as caste endogamy, hypergamy, and patrilocality are associated with a potential rise in social status provided by the opportunities to migrate and/or gain better employment.

Comparing Networks and Drawing Conclusions

In the life histories of Gujarati immigrants, interpersonal ties are just one kind of social tie among others that facilitated migration and mobility. Among recruits, built-in certification mechanisms that are part of educational institutions, government agencies, or firms in their organizational networks reduce the risk associated with sponsoring migration and employment. Even when immigrants recruit their colleague-friends to work overseas, those recruits must fulfill the requirements of organizations to migrate and become employed. Therefore, the organizational ties of professionals generally provide a wider and better range of opportunities than interpersonal ties, given that the requirements of the organization can be satisfied.

In contrast, trusties are characterized by composite ties. In these typically dense, multiplex networks, kin and friends are also business colleagues, suppliers, and buyers, who all belong to the same community of origin, speak the same language, and practice the same religion. The high risk of malfeasance in long-distance or transnational trade is buffered by composite ties used to sponsor network members for employment and then to monitor their behavior. Labor recruitment and monitoring primarily depend on personal relations and social obligations that are used to enforce trust between network ties.

The networks of chains can look similar to those of trusties only when interpersonal ties monitor their economic activities and sponsor their employment in ethnic economies. However, chains tend to be part of networks either that are entrepreneurial or whose members are employed in the dominant labor market. Interpersonal ties to entrepreneurs in niche industries in the host society aid newcomers to become employed and/or establish themselves in similar businesses in their ethnic economy. In contrast, workers with interpersonal ties in the host society's dominant labor market have more uncertain employment prospects because their networks tend not to dominate particular industries. The economic behavior of these chains is often not bound by social obligations to interpersonal ties. Thus, chains either become employed in occupations where their networks are dominant, such as in ethnic economies, or they must pursue opportunities through formal means. Therefore, entrepreneurship is not in the blood of Gujaratis but rather in their networks.

As shown in the preceding discussion, organizational, composite, and interpersonal ties in migrant networks lead to significantly different migration and occupational outcomes. The three types of flows of recruits, trusties, and chains illustrate that these ties play distinct roles in channeling migrants into occupations in their host societies. Local labor markets do not become linked only through historical circumstances of trade, colonialism, and foreign development. Thus, Germany's recent effort at recruiting Indian IT workers can be understood as a situation where supply networks of Indian immigrants working in the German IT sector are still few and underdeveloped. Until those networks are established, and as long as they have to compete with long-established American ones, German recruitment efforts will result in a slow trickle of those workers. In fact, the German government may have already realized the failure of its previous efforts. Recently, it has begun offering minimum annual salaries of 85,000 Euros for high-tech workers—European workers whom they have targeted for recruitment under the proposed Blue Card system (Collett 2008).

The significance of organizational and interpersonal ties in creating different migration and occupational outcomes also challenges the importance of human capital. Many chains are professionals or highly educated people. However, they cannot replicate their status on arrival in the host country without the aid of organizational ties to channel them into equivalent or better positions. Racial discrimination does not seem to play a significant role in their underemployment (especially after the 1970s) because recruits, in contrast, have organizational ties that preserve their occupational status. Trusties and chains depend on personal relations and social obligations to recruit labor (or to be recruited) and to monitor the economic behavior of those workers (or to be monitored by them). Therefore, the economic activities of these three types of migrant networks operate under different kinds of constraints that alter the role of human capital in producing migration flows and occupational outcomes.

Other signs of inequalities were apparent in the economic niches within networks dominated by the three types of ties. Most notably, coethnic solidarity did not operate as one might expect, nor as much of the migration literature would predict. Although niches were certainly formed through networks that could control labor recruitment, this process invariably excluded some coethnics and included others. Of those who were included, even they were often relegated to subordinate positions or exploited, such as Lakshmi and Harshad. Coethnicity also does not adequately predict the character of migration flows or mobility in the life stories. Gujaratis exhibit significant within-group variation in their migration flows and occupational outcomes at their destinations. Looking within Gujaratis to particular caste or other types of communities, such as the Anavils, Oswals, Patidars, or Swadhyayas, coethnicity again does not sufficiently illustrate the differences in their migration histories. All of these groups demonstrate variation within them in terms of their initial opportunities for entrepreneurship, professional work, transnational trade, public-sector employment, and so on. That variation is more reliably explained by the types of social ties migrants had at the time of their first migration. This finding exposes the weaknesses of substantialist arguments that rely on static characteristics, such as ethnicity, to predict migration processes and network theories that often also rely on such standard assumptions.

More broadly, the way that local labor markets became linked among India and East Africa and the United Kingdom and between India and the United States highlights globalization as a historical phenomenon. In the case of recruits, we can trace globalized relations back to the mid-twentieth century, when educational and philanthropic relationships were created between India and the United States, and to postcolonial relationships between India and the United Kingdom, which promoted the recruitment of medical professionals to the United States and teachers and civil servants to colonial East Africa. Neither of these examples fits the conventional discourse on globalization that would locate these relations in predominantly economic and recent forces. Links within the garment and diamond industries demonstrate much older historical *and* more recent globalized relations embedded in trade networks that promoted the migration of entrepreneurs to the United Kingdom and the United States from East Africa and India. The life histories identify not only specific processes for specific populations but also the interdependence and interconnectedness of these populations across economic, political, and social spheres of activity.

Second, that interdependence and interconnectedness expose the fallacy of the image of individual, traditional migrants in poor, developing societies looking for opportunities to reap the economic advantages of modern, developed societies via migration. Although all of these migrants certainly looked toward their own economic and social mobility, recruits and trusties, in particular, were already in secure economic positions in East Africa or in India prior to migrating. And, finally, immigrants, as with all sorts of people, are not individual, rational maximizers in their economic behavior. Their economic action is embedded in social networks that link employers with workers transnationally, often under significant constraints.

The relational approach to understanding these migration processes asks us to examine what kinds of information, resources, and influence immigrants exchanged within their social ties. By examining the configurations of different ties in these migrant networks, we have seen how different kinds of social ties link local labor markets and cause migration in the process. This process constitutes the beginning of the formation of economic niches in the host societies, which I turn to in the following chapter.

4 Networks, Niches, and Inequalities

ECONOMIC NICHES ARE A FAMILIAR SITE in New York and London. If you have ever walked down Broadway in New York City or on one of London's High Streets, you have probably encountered many Indian newsstand agents. Perhaps you have also seen Indian diamond dealers hustling about secretively in the diamond districts of Antwerp, New York City, or Hong Kong. Or you have been treated recently by an Indian physician in the United States or the United Kingdom—at least you have seen a few of them on television. Many of these shopkeepers, diamond dealers, and doctors are likely to be Gujaratis and are overrepresented in certain occupations, industries, or economic sectors, such as health services; the diamond, garment, and textile trades; hospitality; and small retail. Not all Gujaratis, however, are employed in ethnic economies.[1] Some Gujaratis have found employment outside of Gujarati or Indian niches, which leads us to question essentialist assumptions about coethnicity that are inherent in substantialist arguments. These arguments would have us think that coethnicity provides the same sorts of opportunities for immigrants. If so, then why are some Gujarati immigrants part of niches in ethnic economies while others are not? This chapter questions the role of social networks in niche and nonniche employment. It first asks what happens after labor markets become linked and Gujaratis have migrated. How do migrant networks change in the host society? More importantly, how do changes in networks and in the socioeconomic incorporation of immigrants in the host societies affect future occupational opportunities? How do occupational niches form, change, break up, or transform into new niches? How are immigrants included or excluded from these niches?

The chapter first discusses how network location affects the inclusion and exclusion of individuals as immigrants hoard opportunities in niches. Second, the formation of new social ties and the role of brokers address how ties change in the host society. Third, the chapter examines the uneven penetration of economic sectors by networks of recruits, trusties, and chains. This unevenness results in different consequences for the embeddedness of economic action in networks, which can be partial, extreme, or constrained. The chapter describes the narrative profiles of niches within migration flows of recruits, trusties, and chains to show how niches change, who is included in and excluded from these changes, and what transactions contribute to this inclusion and exclusion. While other authors have documented the importance of interpersonal ties for similar kinds of economic niches in other immigrant groups, this analysis tells us which kinds of ties result in niches that can make the difference between a dead-end job and economic mobility in an ethnic economy.

Opportunity Hoarding, Network Location, and Transactions

Niche employment involves a process that Charles Tilly called "opportunity hoarding" (Tilly 1998, 2005). The hoarding of opportunities takes place when valued resources are confined to members of an in-group. In-group members hoard economic opportunities in niches by relying on interpersonal, organizational, and composite ties in networks that span both the home and host societies. Various resources pass through these social ties to kin, community, and colleagues, which help to sustain their occupational niches. Information about jobs, recommendations to potential employers, vouchers regarding reputation and status, and financial loans and credit are among the most important. How that in-group becomes defined, however, is crucial to understanding who is included and excluded from a particular niche. Inclusion and exclusion of individuals in niche employment, or hoarding opportunities for some but not for others, does not simply follow coethnic affinities or other ascriptive characteristics.

We cannot take for granted that one's membership in a social network grants that individual access to coveted resources. The immigration literature and research on ethnic economies have gone far in documenting the role of social networks in generating advantages and disadvantages for ethnic groups' ability to locate jobs or in explaining rates of entrepreneurship among other forms of economic activity. However, we know little about how inequality is generated within a network. The resources of a network are generally treated in a homogeneous way—equally available to its members based on shared coethnicity. For example, in Light and Gold's (2000) critique of class theory as an explanation for variation in rates of entrepreneurship, they highlight the importance of ethnic group membership as a structure for generating economic resources. They argue that ethnic group membership promotes both an "ideology of solidarity" and the passing of specific forms of knowledge, skills, and norms particular to an ethnic group, which "transcend class boundaries, uniting groups marked by different class positions and interests" (Light and Gold 2000, 108). Roger Waldinger (1999) uses a similar explanation in his examination of immigrant niches in the public sector. He finds that coethnic affinities are the basis for sharing information and resources that build ethnic niches in certain occupations in New York City government. Shared ethnicity or community acts as a proxy for trust and predictability. These explanations leave us to wonder about which coethnics were excluded from this coethnic network mechanism. When one looks at the structure of migrant networks, a transcendence of class and other boundaries in favor of ethnic ones is far from clear. There are significant inequalities within a coethnic network in which class, gender, caste, and other markers of identity may be played out as part of everyday relations and transactions. An individuals' location in a network is further marked by combinations of such attributes and is manifested in the context of exchange relations or transactions with other members. That is, network location affects what types of exchange occur between two members, with influence and access to resources as two of the most indicative sources of power and inequality (Marsden 1982; Stinchcombe 1989).

Niche employment, therefore, depends, in part, on the social location of an individual in a network, which can exclude people who have the same ascriptive characteristics as most of the network members. One's location in a network affects the exchange of resources that can take place between two or more members. Put another way, network location demonstrates relative positions of power or inequality, which affect in whose favor or disfavor occupational and other opportunities will be hoarded. This hoarding, in turn, affects the formation of niches and who obtains access to niche employment and to particular positions within a niche. Niches also change. The conditions of opportunity hoarding might also change as a result of the formation of new social ties and of brokers present in networks in the host society.

The Formation of New Social Ties and the Role of Brokers

The formation of new social ties in the host country occurs in a variety of contexts, including work, neighborhood, philanthropic activity, voluntary associations, and places of religious worship. Gujarati Indian immigrants forged new network ties in two main ways. First, immigrants sponsored family members from India and other parts of the diaspora to join them in the host country. Second, they developed relations with other members of the Indian immigrant population through participation in the many and diverse Indian voluntary associations in New York and London. There is no doubt that Indians also formed friendships and ties with co-workers, neighbors, and others of non-Indian origin. These ties are described in the following narratives wherever they appear in the particular life histories of the immigrants. However, sponsoring family members for immigration and participating in Indian or coethnic voluntary associations were predominant paths for new social ties because they simultaneously reinforced immigrants' ethnic identity with other identities related to occupation, religion, residence, politics, the arts, and so on.

The priority of family reunification in the immigration policies of the United States and Britain has greatly encouraged chain migration. Therefore, kin are an integral part of migrant's networks in both the home and host countries. However, as most people know from personal experience, not all kin serve a family or network in equal or similar ways. Siblings can drop out of favor with one another or with their elders when risky undertakings arise, as often happens within the composite ties of transnational entrepreneurs. Fights can ensue over inheritance rights, dividing families. Birth order and gender can be instrumental in decisions concerning who migrates or who will assume ownership of the family business. Thus, the content or quality of kin relations affects the network location of individual family members. It cannot be taken for granted that all kin relations produce inclusive and strong relations of exchange within a network. Therefore, the family members who comprise an interpersonal network are not always structurally equivalent to each other in network terms. Some kin are favored over others for different types of economic activity. Relations of inequality often become clear on this basis. However, generally, kin play a significant if not always positive role in bridging networks between the home and host countries and in forming new social ties in the host society. In fact, given the typically large number of siblings and extended families of the majority of Indians, most of the participants have many relatives spread across India, the United States and Britain, and the Indian diaspora. Indeed, 29 percent of the London sample had at least one relative in other parts of the diaspora besides India, Britain, and East Africa, and 41 percent of the New York sample had family living outside the United States and India.

Associational Life and the Formation of New Social Ties

Apart from kin and coethnic relations, voluntary associations are an important conduit for establishing new ties in the host country. Hundreds of Indian associations exist in the United States and Britain, including numerous regional chapters within many of them. Membership or some participation in events sponsored by Indian voluntary associations is very common. Although it is difficult to establish just what proportion of Indians engage in association activities, the great majority of participants in this study (86 percent) were paid or listed members of at least one association, and some attended the activities of others. Previous studies also support the claim that Indian immigrants participate heavily in Indian voluntary associations (see Desai 1963; Fisher 1980; Helweg and Helweg 1990; Lessinger 1995; Khandelwal 2002; Rangaswamy 2000).

The sheer variety of associations in the United States and Britain is also remarkable. Many associations are culturally specific for people who share a common regional, linguistic, or caste background. These associations are especially conducive to strengthening and developing new interpersonal ties. General cultural associations are pan-Indian and open to all Indians. Typically, these associations hold cultural performances and events related to Indian art, literature, music, and dance. Also included in this category are neighborhood Indian associations, which address the local concerns of Indians living in the same neighborhoods or local jurisdictions. Religious, political, philanthropic, occupational, and umbrella organizations are also numerous. Membership and participation in these types of associations are not new experiences because many such organizations exist in India, and some were transplanted to New York and London or other parts of the diaspora. However, the content of these associations differs by addressing newly formed interests in the host countries. Whether associations are homegrown or transplanted, new network ties formed within them are organizational ties. Although it is clear that some associations foster interpersonal ties while others promote organizational or composite ties, the path to their formation is organizational, and these organizations mediate relations within them. The medium of the organization shapes the kinds of transactions that take place within these newly formed ties. For example, business contacts are made in organizations as diverse as temples and industry associations. Ties and transactions are formed among businesspeople, who meet and know each other and others in their networks as members of the same temple and will be hard pressed to adhere to the ethical strictures of their religious organization, such as not selling alcohol, in order to uphold their status and reputation. Similar business ties within other types of associations incur different kinds of constraints on the transactions and practices of their members.

Temples, places of worship, and religion-based organizations abound in both New York and London. Many represent particular sects of Hinduism and Jainism, such as the Digamber Samaj of New York, the Arya Samaj Congress in the United States and Britain, or the Sri Swaminarayan temples, also in both countries. In addition to shared religious experiences, temple activities provide a forum where some Indians meet and share common professional, business, and cultural interests. In this way, they develop new ties within the framework of a shared religious or ethical structure. In recognition of the large numbers of businesspeople who attend temple services, some Hindu sects in the diaspora have even emphasized Hindu teachings on business ethics. For example, in London the Sri Swaminarayan temple has many members who are Gujarati businesspeople. The Shiksapatri, a book of ethics written in 1826 by the first spiritual leader of the Swaminarayan sect, states that "you shall not undertake business transactions for the purchase of land—even with your son or a friend—except by a written document, attested to by a witness." Devotees should also abstain from meat and alcohol and not commit violence "for any object, be it wealth, women, or even a kingdom."[2] Thus Swaminarayan businesspeople, like most Hindu businesspeople, are discouraged from concentrating their activities in industries that require contact with meat and alcohol (although many participants reported that business*men*, especially, do not adhere to these restrictions).

Religious organizations can produce new social ties mediated by those very organizations but that have little to do with religion. Temples can serve as sites where religious and economic networks meet. Recently, the South Asia Development Partnership (SADP), a philanthropic organization, which focuses on the promotion and support of Asian business in London, held an event at the large and influential Swaminarayan temple in London. In an interview, SADP's founder recalls:

R: I held my first event there involving the business community, talking about ethics in a global context—300 businesses turned up. Now, I've not seen that number of people turn up in any other network from one community group, the Gujaratis in Neasden.[3] Now in a global business context, it was a business issue in a temple, but the temple was being used as a community hall. Now that could be tremendous. . . . It's not yet happening in a concerted, coordinated way.

MP: *And how through any of these initiatives—how do you really convince people in a sense to trust outside sources?*

R: I think this is the point. . . . I think that by building trust with the temple structure and the church structure and if the leaders establish the trust level . . . if they go to the key movers and shakers and, you know, identify 100 and build trust with ten, those ten will influence. We made contact with one guy, Mr. Lal, who came to a lecture I organized with the House of Lords. He was so encouraged by that, he said I want to do something at my temple and he brought 300 people. And it's that kind of multiple effect that's needed.

MP: *So in a sense it's creating new networks.*

R: Correct, it's identifying existing networks, but it's bridging network to network . . . moving networks and linking them.

The language of networks comes naturally to this leader of the South Asian community. He fully understands and uses his position as a broker between Indian organizational networks. Furthermore, he realizes how the act of bridging or brokering between networks can lead to more and better economic opportunities. In many ways, however, this is a top-down strategy emanating from elite members of the Indian community. Those elites are primarily concerned with raising the economic and social status of Indians through the development of mid-sized and large businesses rather than helping the family-run corner shop. Mr. Lal, incidentally, runs a "small" business and was seeking help to take the business public. To be fair, the founder of SADP recognizes the weaknesses of the top-down strategy emanating from the elite. As he expressed it, "At the moment I suspect sometimes there's not enough pull [from the top], or there is pull at the wrong places, and there's not enough push."

Most Indian voluntary associations serve multiple functions by incorporating cultural, business, and even religious and political interests on the same platform. Caste-based and regional, linguistic, or religiously based cultural associations are especially conducive to this blending of interests that promotes the formation of new interpersonal ties. They provide formal means for maintaining cultural traditions, rituals, language, and personal relationships within a specific ethnic community. They also provide a structure for contributing to philanthropic work in India and making new business or professional contacts, usually for economic advancement in the host society. The Indian Bangalorian Catholic Association in New York and New Jersey is one example of such an association. The association began when the founder advertised its first meeting through address lists obtained from a prominent Indian diaspora newspaper where he was working at the time. Two hundred families came to the first meeting in 1988 and agreed to meet for at least two main purposes, according to its founder: "to meet your own people," especially for the children to know "where their roots are"; and to send money back to India through the Roman Catholic Church to aid the education of poor children in the city of Bangalore. As an afterthought, the founder mentioned to me that

> We also thought that if there are people in different industries they will have a chance to meet each other, exchange their views, and also it might help, you know, if there is an insurance agent, maybe he will have a better chance to meet their own people and get some kind of business.

Not only are these types of associations important for facilitating economic transactions; they also imply that there are economic advantages to dealing with members of a shared community. Significantly, the organizational structure of the association provides a framework of accessibility and trust where those members can exchange valued goods, such as information, resources, and clients. Such an assumption may be misleading, however. For instance, the Patidars of Gujarat, whom we met in earlier chapters, have their own caste associations and even smaller village (*gam*) associations. (*Gams* are organized around a class hierarchy within their caste and define endogamous marriage circles or *gols*.) In the United States and Britain, Patidars have nationwide associations that unify these smaller subcaste groups. As stated in a "Grand Dinner and Dance" program publication to raise money for the construction of a building for the National Association of Patidar Samaj, United Kingdom, which was established in 1969, "you can't afford not be a member . . . if you want to triumph in unifying our sectionally and regionally divided and dismembered community." Patidars may acknowledge within-group divisiveness to each other but rarely to outsiders, such as field researchers, to whom they present a very strong ideology of unity and community solidarity.

Nevertheless, Patidar subcaste association members often interact with other associations where Patidars are generally prominent, sometimes mixing business with community interests. For instance, the Leuva Patidar Samaj of USA held a "matrimonial session" during their recent convention where an estimated 4,300 people attended. They claim that 93 percent of their community owns hotels and motels, an established Patidar niche. Although the validity of this claim is unknown, it is significant that the matrimonial session, seemingly unrelated to business interests, was addressed by the Patidar chairmen of the American Hotel and Motel Association and the Asian American Hotel Owners Association.[4]

General cultural, religious, political, and occupational associations draw a much wider cross-section of Indians in terms of regional/linguistic/caste background, although perhaps not in terms of class background. The Bharatiya Vidya Bhavan (Indian Cultural Institute) is one of the oldest Indian associations in London. It was established in 1974 and exists as a separate entity in New York (founded in 1981), Lisbon, and Mexico City. The creation of the Bhavans overseas was initiated by the original institution founded in 1938 in India. There, it is primarily educational and has more than sixty branches. In New York and London, the Bhavan offers lectures, artistic performances, and classes in Indian languages, arts, and literature to anyone interested in Indian culture.

Other general cultural associations include neighborhood Indian associations that serve the interest of Indians in a particular residential location. These are common both in New York and London. However, the London associations have become integrated with borough or council associations and share services and resources with them. For instance, the Brent Indian Association (BIA), in the borough of Brent, which contains the largest Asian population of all of the Greater London boroughs and a large Gujarati population, was established in 1965. It provides immigration, visa, and passport services and advice on welfare rights, social security benefits, housing, and legal problems. It also sponsors activities for women, youth, and the elderly. There are library, photocopying, and fax services. It offers English and Gujarati language, music, voice, and dance classes. Of the twenty-nine categorized services the BIA offers, advice over the telephone; outgoing telephone calls; assistance in filling in forms and in correspondence, visa applications, and social security benefits; legal advice; sponsorship for visitors; and language interpretation services were among the most numerous activities it performs.[5]

Occupational organizations, especially professional ones, tend to be pan-Indian and encourage a broader form of ethnic identity in favor of shared class and occupational interests. Some examples are the Indian Business and Professional Association; the Wharton India Economic Forum at the University of Pennsylvania's Wharton Business School, where Indians represent 14 percent of all international students and comprise the largest ethnic group (Haniffa 1998); the Asian Indian Chamber of Commerce; and the Jersey City Merchants Association, the latter two located in Indian small-business districts in New Jersey. Some business associations overlap with professional associations because many Indian professionals have a strong interest in entrepreneurship. In this way, distinct organizational networks come into contact with each other and create the potential for the formation of new organizational ties. For instance, an emerging Entrepreneur Conference was jointly sponsored by the Network of South Asian Professionals, the Indian American Bar Association, and the Indian CEO (chief executive officer) High Tech Council. Other professional organizations abound in New York: The American Society of Engineers of Indian Origin (ASEI), the AAPI, the Indo-American Pharmaceutical Society, the Network of Indian Professionals, and the Network of Professional and Self-Employed Women, among many others.

These professional associations are fewer and less prominent in London mainly because the two major waves of Indian migration contained more low- and semi-skilled workers and small business owners than professionals. Medical doctors remain an exception and have an association for overseas doctors in Britain's National Health Service. Other professional associations tend to be more informal and very small, such as gatherings of chemists (pharmacists), who brief each other on new developments in their industry and strategize to retain their consumer base. The Vanik Professionals Group is more formal and includes a variety of professionals who are also Jain. They provide each other with free services according to their expertise. This arrangement circumvents reliance on unknown professionals outside of their religious community and the payment of fees that would accompany that channel. Although Britain's Indians have made inroads as professional chemists, accountants, and, of course, medical professionals, the primary occupations of the first generation have been in the manufacturing and wholesale and retail sectors. Some of these workers in manufacturing and other manual employment participate in the Indian Worker's Association, which was founded by Punjabi workers in the working-class South Asian neighborhood of Southall, West London. Retailers tend to share information more informally with their interpersonal networks. The Asian Business Association, which is part of the London Chamber of Commerce and which represents 600 businesses, and the South Asian Development Partnership, which researches and supports aid to ethnic minority business through government channels such as the Training and Enterprise Councils, are recent attempts to unify the interests of the business community and to provide a forum for business growth. However, they generally do not reach out to the ubiquitous family-run corner shop.

Industry-specific associations are often comprised of individuals who work in the same industry and rely on interpersonal and composite ties to support their niche in these industries. For instance, the Asian American Hotel Owners Association, despite its pan-Asian title, consists of mostly Patidar Gujaratis. Similarly, the Indian Diamond and Colorstone Association and the Indian Natural Stone Importer's Association are also industry specific and tend to reinforce the composite ties of Jains within these industry niches. Therefore, the structure of their networks is reinforced by their participation in industry-related associations that are ostensibly open to all Indians. Occupational associations, in general, in New York and London provide the structure to develop new organizational ties, which potentially lead to better economic opportunities. Because most of these organizations are pan-Indian and are not necessarily tied to particular industries, the new organizational ties widen the sphere of opportunity for organization members.

Political organizations are few and generally have a small but vocal membership. They often use temples as platforms for reaching larger numbers of Indians, especially Hindus. The Overseas Friends of the Bharatiya Janata Party (OFBJP) (the BJP is a Hindu nationalist party that has enjoyed widespread support in Gujarat and, until recently, headed the coalition government in power in India) and the Indo-American Kashmir Forum have explicitly political aims directed at political life in India. In contrast, the Indo-American Forum for Political Education aims to incorporate the U.S. Indian population into American mainstream politics. It also works with congressional representatives to promote pro-India foreign policy statements and legislation. Another Indian political organization, the Vishwa Hindu Parishad (VHP) or the World Hindu Congress (it has independent chapters in the United States and the United Kingdom but is an offshoot of its parent organization in India), touts itself as a service, charitable, and educational association. However, it has been deeply involved in supporting explicitly Hindu nationalist political organizations and aims (Bhatt 2003; Bhatt and Mukhta 2000; Mukhta 2000; Rajagopal 2000). These political organizations, although pan-Indian, are dominated by nationalist Hindu interests and ideologies that are often contentious for the wider Indian and South Asian populations. As Prema Kurien (2007) insightfully argues, Hindu-Americans ironically want to deny freedom of religion in their home country, the very right they enjoy and insist on within the multiculturalist discourse of the United States. This could also be said for many Hindus in Britain, where such organizations are also prominent and influential (Bhatt and Mukhta 2000; Mukhta 2000).

In sum, most associations serve multiple functions by incorporating cultural, business, and even religious and political interests on the same platform. Caste-, regional-, linguistic-, and religious-based cultural associations are especially conducive to this blending of interests, which promotes the formation of new interpersonal ties. Occupational (especially professional) organizations, in contrast, tend to be pan-Indian and encourage a broader form of ethnic identity in favor of shared class and occupational interests. Occupational associations also encourage the formation of organizational ties that can lead to new and better economic opportunities. Industry-specific associations are often comprised of networks of trusties and chains who work in the same industry and rely on composite and interpersonal ties to support their niche in these industries. Therefore, the structure of their networks is reinforced by their participation in industry-related associations that are ostensibly open to all Indians.

The Role of Brokers in the Formation of New Social Ties

Brokers play a crucial role in directing new opportunities both inside and outside of niches. They are typically elite members of the community, such as the founder of SADP, and play an important role in helping to direct the opportunities of association members and linking networks at the organizational level. In the network literature, brokers are described as weak ties linking networks that otherwise do not or would not interact with each other (Granovetter 1973). Thus, brokers are a mechanism by which certain members of a network are granted advantages or disadvantages (Marsden 1982). Those who control resources in economic niches hoard opportunities for a defined group and, as such, can provide advantages to those with access to the group. Brokers are instrumental in conferring these advantages onto specific individuals or in linking networks to broaden a niche.

Different types of brokers are also prevalent in occupational niches dominated by interpersonal, organizational, and composite ties. Brokers tend to correspond to the different configurations of ties prevalent in migrant networks, but specific ties are also more dominant than others. For instance, brokers mediate many of the employment opportunities of organizational networks.

They are supervisors, teachers, or colleagues, who can link an individual from one organizational network to another, usually in the same field or industry. In composite networks, uncles are key brokers, but siblings, in-laws, parents, and spouses are also often the owners, managers, suppliers, and buyers who make transnational trade happen. Niche entry and new economic opportunities in the niche are mediated by brokers who are organizationally and interpersonally linked to different segments of their trade. Brokers in niches dominated by interpersonal networks include a wider array of interpersonal ties, such as coethnics and friends in addition to siblings, spouses, and parents.

The Irregularity of Embeddedness

Variation in network location, changing configurations of ties, and transactions within ties in interpersonal, organizational, and composite networks suggest that differences in network structure affect economic sectors differently. In Granovetter's (1985, 491) theoretical elaboration of embeddedness he has stressed that "networks of social relations penetrate irregularly and in differing degrees in different sectors of economic life thus allowing for what we already know: distrust, opportunism, and disorder are by no means absent." His statement suggests that we need to identify which areas of economic life are penetrated irregularly and what the consequences are of embeddedness in different types of social networks. For instance, do some networks perpetuate more trust or more malfeasance than others? The following narratives of Gujarati immigrants demonstrate how the economic niches of recruits, trusties, and chains are penetrated irregularly by social relations. This unevenness results in different sets of economic and other opportunities and trajectories for immigrants who are part of these different networks.

The Role of Organizational Ties in the Stability, Mobility, and Breakup of Niches of Recruits

Niche Stability and Economic Mobility for Health Professionals

Professionals recruited by the host society in many ways have occupational niches precut for them. For instance, medical doctors recruited by the American and British governments in response to labor shortages took advantage of a ready-made path for niche formation. This was made possible by the sheer numbers of coethnic doctors who found themselves together in a new labor context and the immigration policies and professional institutions that supported their employment in these niches. Recruited doctors could, in turn, aid the migration and employment of their physician-friends, -schoolmates, and -kin from India. Thus, the recruitment of professionals is a bidirectional process between the host and home societies, where the state, mediating organizations, and social networks (unwittingly) collaborate to aid immigration and occupational attainment in the host society among members of their professional networks. When one of these components constrains the process, niches can break up, as in the case of Indian civil servants in East Africa, who encountered a restrictive socioeconomic context for their labor after migrating to London.

In the previous chapter I told the story of Kishor, a medical doctor, and his wife Jamnadevi, a dentist. These professionals were able to take advantage of linked labor markets and favorable socioeconomic contexts between India and the United States. Their professional qualifications were in demand in the United States. This demand, coupled with the 1965 opening of U.S. immigration to all countries, created the possibility for their migration as doctors— not to mention the historical ties between Indian and American educational institutions prior to 1965. Both organizational ties to alumni from Kishor's medical college and interpersonal ties to his brother, who was also a practicing medical doctor in the United States, made a potential event become a reality. These ties secured Kishor with employment, housing, information, and the support he needed to migrate. He then helped his wife to do the same.

Continuing their story, both Kishor and Jamnadevi became involved in Indian and some American associations that would encourage their professional development. Kishor joined the AAPI, the New York State Medical Society, and a North America–based alumni group from his college in Gujarat. Jamnadevi joined the Indian Dental Association of New York. Together, they joined or attended events sponsored by the Indian Westchester Association and Gujarat Samaj. Of course, they also created social ties to colleagues in their workplaces. Some of these organizational ties acted as brokers for new opportunities. In fact, after Kishor had finished his residency in pediatrics, he was invited to become a partner in a private practice by a coethnic colleague, a gynecologist from his residency. Eventually, that colleague sold his practice to Kishor and another partner. It further mushroomed into a five-person practice. Jamnadevi also benefited from these weak ties to Kishor's colleagues when one of them offered her office space to set up her own practice near theirs. Together, they strategically banked on the idea that by having neighboring pediatric and dental offices, they would be able to benefit from mutual clients needing both of these health services. Some years ago, Jamnadevi's office building was bombed, and she moved to a new location just across the street. She now shares her practice in the new office with her sister's husband, another dentist. Kishor's brother, a pathologist, and his sister, a radiologist, both reside and practice in the United States; however, their strained personal relations have resulted in little exchange of information and aid in their fields of expertise.

In sum, Kishor and Jamnadevi formed new networks of kin, friends, acquaintances, and colleagues largely through Indian professional and cultural organizations and their workplaces. Many of these organizational ties among similarly situated Indian immigrants functioned primarily to enhance their lives economically and professionally. However, they were most involved in networks that included Indian colleagues in their workplaces. These organizational ties, in particular, promoted the exchange of crucial resources that shaped their occupational trajectories. The information, profession-related resources, and financial aid exchanged between these ties enabled them to become self-employed professionals in their fields.

Having firmly established themselves over the past thirty years in their respective professions and in American upper middle-class society, Kishor and Jamnadevi now find much less personal satisfaction or benefit from their memberships in Indian professional organizations. Their Indian networks have recently branched out in a different direction. On one of Jamnadevi's parents' extended stays in New York, they introduced the family to the Swadhyaya socioreligious movement, which is based in India (see Srivastava 1998). The family now devotes most of their leisure time to this movement. Many of their closest friends and relatives are also members of this movement in New York and India.

Thus, Kishor and Jamnadevi have all of the appearances of immigrant assimilation. They have professional jobs and live in a mostly white, upper-middle-class, suburban neighborhood. They have U.S. citizenship. They travel overseas often but have no plans to permanently return to India because of their American-born children. However, their closest ties, both organizational and interpersonal, are mainly Indian and Gujarati.

The Accountants: Into the Mainstream

Accountancy is a burgeoning niche among both first- and second-generation Indian immigrants in New York and London. This comes as little surprise when considering the important role of accountants in Gujarat's and East Africa's extensive commercial history and given the professionalization of the second generation in money-making fields.

Ramesh, for instance, was born into a Jain family in Kenya in 1963, the fourth son of five siblings. The first of his siblings to migrate to the United Kingdom was his eldest brother. He had gone to India to attend medical school in the early 1970s. When he returned to Kenya, well after independence, employment preference was being given to African doctors (usually trained by foreign doctors for a short period) rather than Kenya-born British citizens such as Ramesh and his siblings. Ramesh's brother, therefore, applied for a job as a physiotherapist in a British hospital and migrated in 1977. The second eldest brother followed in 1979 to attend university, and the third one stayed in Kenya, having taken over the family business previously run by their father, who is a Kenyan citizen. Ramesh, with his British passport, was considered a foreign student by Kenyan universities; therefore he would have had to pay higher fees than in a British university. As a result of this constraint and with two elder brothers already in Britain, he migrated to Birmingham in 1981. There, Ramesh lived with his brothers and finished a degree in accountancy and finance. Ramesh originally wanted to do his A-levels in physics, chemistry, and English, thinking that he might pursue chemical engineering, but he did not rank highly enough to be allowed into chemistry and physics. Thus, he opted for accountancy and economics. By the time he was ready to enter university, he had already developed an interest in accounting and had worked during summers in several accounting firms. Ultimately, however, the structure of British education kept him from pursuing his original career interest:

> I think the turning point was the fact that I didn't get to do chemistry, biology, and physics at A-level, and that like really turned me around, saying, okay, you can't do this. . . . Maybe I would have gone in that kind of area, but I think it stopped me from going into that because I mean after doing two years of A-levels in different subjects and then to go and do a degree in chemistry . . . that would have been too big a gap to carry on. I could have done it, but by that time . . . I think I just wanted to be in business or economics, or something, actuarism, accountancy, or something like that.

The choice to pursue accountancy and finance at the university level was partially a result of constraints in the British educational system. Accountancy, however, is a popular pursuit among young Indians of the second generation and among those who migrated to Britain at relatively young ages. In fact, many of Ramesh's friends from Kenya migrated "one by one," as Ramesh put it, to England to attend university, where a large number of them studied accountancy. Through Ramesh I met Hemant, a friend from university and also an accountant. Here, Hemant explains his decision to become an accountant:

> R: I generally fell into it because a lot of my friends and relatives were accountants, and it seemed a good idea at the time.
>
> MP: *And did your parents have any influence on that decision?*
>
> R: No, because they were very limited education, they don't really know what's . . . everyone wants to be a doctor or a lawyer or whatever, but I was . . . , I quite liked numbers. I was good at maths, so I fell into accountancy, really.

Hemant was born and raised outside London. His mother, born in Kenya, and father, born in Gujarat, had migrated together from East Africa to England in 1962. Many members of Hemant's and Ramesh's interpersonal network of friends from Kenya and university easily pursued a higher education in Britain as a result of having migrated at fairly young ages, when they could attend university for little or no cost, while being housed and supported by family members who were already there. Accountancy, in particular, has been developing into a popular professional niche among young first- generation and second-generation Indian immigrants because it is financially rewarding with high occupational status.

Clearly, within Ramesh's and Hemant's interpersonal network of peers, they also exerted at least some influence on each other's career decisions. Both Ramesh and Hemant, as well as a large portion of their friendship network, became certified accountants in London. Using formal means of job searching, such as employment agencies, Hemant has always been employed in the public sector, while Ramesh works in the private sector. Hemant was first an internal auditor, then a senior auditor, a management accountant, and a head accountant. Each job was better than the last, and he found every job through the referrals of agencies that place accountants. Ramesh also found his first job, as a certified accountant in a large private firm, through an agency. When he grew dissatisfied with working in such a big firm, he began searching for a new job in his field. One of his senior colleagues, a Jewish man, had left to found his own firm. Ramesh used this organizational tie to inquire about employment at that new firm, resulting in his current job. Most of the partners in the firm are Jewish, but the staff accountants are somewhat more ethnically diverse. Ramesh and Hemant are clearly well incorporated into the dominant labor market in London. Their professional degrees from an English university, facility with English culture, and organizational ties or access to formal means of pursuing employment have been instrumental to their occupational mobility and ability to contribute to the small but growing niche of Indian accountants.

Navin, a one-time accountant, tells a similar story of joining money-making professions that are deemed respectable by the wider Indian population. When I met Navin in New York, he was pursuing a master's degree in political science. He was born in Gujarat in 1971. He first migrated to New York in 1984 for only two months. His uncle, a microbiologist, had been the first to migrate to New York in 1972 on an employment preference visa. He then sponsored his wife and parents (Navin's grandparents) on family visas. When Navin's uncle died, Navin's father, the second son, became responsible for the welfare of the family and was summoned by Navin's grandmother to the United States. Navin's mother, however, did not want him and his siblings to be raised in the "openness" of U.S. society, so the family went back to India until 1988, when they returned again to New York. Navin finished high school in New York and attended college for two years pursuing an engineering degree:

> I wanted to pursue a degree in engineering because all the Indians, there is a stereotype of Indians that they go into medicine or engineering or computer science . . . because basically the reason why you came here is to make money, and you go into [those fields].

After an inspirational class in political science, however, Navin changed disciplines and colleges. When he graduated in 1995, he found a job in the accounting department of an air-freight company. He then moved into paralegal work at several law firms. Simultaneously, he began pursuing a master's degree in political science, in which he hopes to make a career. Much like Ramesh and Hemant, Navin had migrated to New York at a young age and was well integrated into the American higher educational system and culture. This helped him to successfully use formal means of obtaining his positions as an accountant and paralegal, means that tend to be more difficult for less-educated and less-well-integrated immigrants.

The stories of Kishor, Jamnadevi, and the young accountants represent the stability of employment and mobility in well-established and burgeoning professional niches. In each case, organizational ties created through occupational associations, university colleagues, or workplaces aided the mobility of these immigrants in their occupations. When organizational ties were not strong, formal means of obtaining professional employment, such as using employment agencies or advertisement, were sufficient to achieve parity and desired occupational status, especially, however, with English or American credentials. But this is not always the case. In the next section, we will see how the rupture of organizational ties that accompanied migration and a new labor market resulted in the breakup of a prior niche of recruits.

The Makeup and Breakup of a Teaching Niche in East Africa and Britain

Migration, even from a developing to a developed country, does not always lead to mobility. As we saw in Chapter 3, organizational ties make the difference between those immigrants who become employed in positions equivalent to their human capital and those who do not. This was the case for teachers recruited from India to work in schools developed by the British during colonial rule in the East African protectorates. Their organizational ties channeled them into jobs that matched their human capital qualifications. However, those immigrants who were not tied organizationally often faced underemployment relative to their human capital qualifications. Economic action is partially embedded in organizational networks because organizations control and select recruits based on more universal requirements, especially human capital criteria. The example of the teaching niche in East Africa and Britain demonstrates this partial embeddedness and how niches structured by organizational networks can quickly break up under new organizational requirements.

During the first half of the twentieth century, the British began recruiting civil servants, including teachers, administrators, clerks, and lawyers, from India to the East African Protectorates of Uganda, Kenya, and Tanzania (see Gregory 1993). In addition to their development of transportation and commerce, the British had begun developing an administrative infrastructure and a formal educational system for the native African populations and the large Asian population. To fill these positions, representatives of the Ugandan, Kenyan, and Tanzanian High Commissions made regular trips to India to recruit directly from a small, educated middle class. When we met the Anavils in the previous chapter, they were part of an occupational niche of teachers. Organizational ties to personnel in recruiting institutions or formal means of recruitment such as advertisement aided these Anavils and others like them to form a teaching niche in Asian schools in East Africa. Some Indian teachers were also recruited from within East Africa, as in the case of Radhika.

Radhika is not from the Anavil caste community. Although she belongs to a much lower caste community, where teaching is not a traditional occupation, her family comes from the same region of Gujarat as the Anavils. Radhika was born in Kampala, Uganda, in 1934 and was educated there. After finishing her A-levels, she qualified to be a teacher and was hired to teach the primary grades at an Asian school in Kampala. She held this position until the Asian expulsion by Idi Amin in 1972, at which time she left for London. Most civil servants were permitted to stay in Uganda beyond the expulsion date to keep the country running. Nevertheless, Radhika and her husband, Suresh, a lawyer in Kampala, strategically split up during that time. Radhika migrated to London as a refugee, and Suresh stayed behind in Uganda. At the time, they thought that the political situation might improve so that Radhika could eventually rejoin Suresh in Uganda. Instead, as the political environment for Asians worsened, Suresh was forced to join her in London in 1973.

Migration to London for Radhika and other Gujarati teachers resulted in downgraded employment opportunities or underemployment. Their human capital qualifications were reevaluated in this new socioeconomic environment. It was precisely because the British held lower standards for the Asian teachers and their schools in East Africa that they would not accept their qualifications in British schools that taught British children.

For many teachers in the British colonies and protectorates, good A-level scores, bachelor's degrees, or teaching certifications obtained in India or Africa were sufficient to build a career as a professional teacher. After all, the British had imposed their own educational system on these countries. These qualifications were deemed sufficient by the British because they were just beginning to develop formal education for mostly African and Asian children. The segregation of children into African, Asian, and European schools promoted different standards in the curriculum and in teacher qualifications. The European schools were, of course, held to a higher standard closer to their countries of origin. Therefore, the transfer of qualifications from the East African to the British context was not recognized unless Indian teachers had a postgraduate degree. Few had such a degree because it was not required for teaching in British India or East Africa. Furthermore, these Indian civil servants did not migrate to London voluntarily. Especially in the case of Ugandan refugees, they were politically and economically forced out of the country. These difficult circumstances surrounding their migration hindered their ability to form strong organizational ties with British educational institutions or organizations that might have helped them retain their teaching niche. In fact, most of their organizational ties were broken in East Africa by the shift in power from the British to the Africans. During and after this political upheaval, Britain only reluctantly accepted the Indian economic and political refugees. Therefore, the breakup of the teaching niche resulted from a changed socioeconomic environment in East Africa and in the receiving context of these migrants in Britain. But that is not all. These circumstances also led to a break in organizational ties among teachers and other civil servants. The following profiles from two networks of teachers demonstrate the effect that changes in migration and socioeconomic environments have on sustaining niches. This evidence also has wider implications for what happens to organizational networks, generally, when organizational ties become weak or nonexistent in a new socioeconomic context.

Pravin, Uma and Kanti migrated to East Africa in the 1950s after being hired to become teachers there. Pravin taught in a small school in Tanzania until 1968, when the political situation in the country pushed him to migrate to London with his British passport. He migrated to London alone. His wife and three children had already returned to India so that his son could pursue a college education there. By 1970, when Pravin had found suitable accommodations for his wife and children, they joined him in London. Pravin went to the employment department to find his first job in London. On learning that his college education and experience as a teacher were not sufficient qualifications to continue at that job in Britain, he took his first job as an estimator in the sanitary department of a builder merchants (construction) firm. Pravin survived in this same position for twenty years, under five different managing companies, until his retirement.

Pravin, Uma, and Kanti are all members of the Gujarat Welfare Association in their working-class London neighborhood, where they met. Uma and Kanti, whom I introduced in Chapter 3, worked in the same jobs in London for about fifteen years until they retired. Kanti was formerly a headmaster at an Asian school in Uganda, and his wife, Uma, was a teacher at that same school. In London, Kanti took a job as a clerk. Uma worked as a machinist in a garment factory. They, too, could not transfer their teaching experience and secondary- and bachelor's-level education to teach in London. The post–World War II Indian migrants from India to the United Kingdom, recruited to fill Britain's labor shortage as it reconstructed its economy, and the Indian women migrants from East Africa, such as Uma, who migrated in the 1960s and 1970s, were probably those most affected by London's large losses in manufacturing jobs in subsequent years. These segments of the Indian population had little education, often only matriculation, and had found work as assembly workers or, in the case of women, in garment factories and as homeworkers who were paid piece-rate. Nonetheless, Uma's experience as a teacher seemed to have no place in this history of "labor migration" to London.

Pravin, Uma, and Kanti were all nearing middle age when they were politically forced to migrate to London. Their financial capacity was also very limited. In the case of Uma and Kanti, they were allowed to take only £150 each when they left Uganda, even though they had been a modest middle-class family. Both families also had children to support. Therefore, with almost no capital to invest in obtaining British teaching qualifications, they had little choice but to accept inferior employment opportunities in their new country of immigration.

Radhika and Suresh had similar experiences. Radhika was a teacher, and Suresh was a lawyer and a government magistrate in Uganda. He had a bachelor's degree in law from Bombay, good A-levels, and teaching certification in Kampala. They were nearing middle age when they were forced from Kampala to Uganda as refugees. Although they did not have children to support, they both felt that it was too late in their lives to pursue further education. As refugees, they also lacked the capital to do so. Thus, Radhika became a clerk in a motor company and later took a low administrative post in government. Suresh was downgraded to the post of a magistrate's clerk in government. Radhika and Suresh's work and educational qualifications were also not sufficient in their new socioeconomic environment.

Two important counterexamples suggest that the field of teaching was not closed to Indians as a result of direct racial discrimination but rather because of a changed socioeconomic context and changes in their social ties. Bharat, from the Anavil network of teachers, held a postgraduate degree from a college in Bombay. He was the headmaster of a prestigious European school in Kampala. Through this position he met an official of the Ugandan High Commission, who recommended him for an educational post in London that involved the development of multiracial schools. Bharat was given the choice to teach or to become an officer for the project. He chose the latter position. Fortunately, he arrived in London the day before Idi Amin issued his "fatwah," as Bharat put it to me, on the Asians in Uganda. Bharat continued in this position until retirement. Not only did he have the educational qualifications required in the British context, but he was also strategically located in a high position at a European school in Uganda, where he developed the organizational ties that enabled his recruitment. Even if Radhika, Pravin, Uma, and Kanti had developed similar organizational ties, these probably would have been of little use to them because their educational qualifications were still too low to become teachers in Britain. Nevertheless, they had little opportunity to develop those types of organizational ties with British educational officers and institutions because of their network location. They were teaching in small Asian schools during a time of declining British power. Neither did they seek Bharat's help to find jobs once they befriended him in London.

The second counterexample is the case of Nandini, who, with Radhika and Suresh, is part of the Mandhata network. The Mandhatas are from the Koli caste of south Guajrat, many of whom raised their caste status through migration to East Africa. Nandini was born in India, but she migrated to London at a young age. She finished her A-levels in London in biology and chemistry and completed a technical degree in pharmacology. Her first job was as a researcher in a London university. Later, she qualified to be a teacher and has held teaching positions since then. Native qualifications and formal means of obtaining employment, through employment agencies, have been the key to her ability to pursue her career.

The breakup of the Indian teaching niche in East Africa, therefore, occurred in the context of an involuntary migration to a new socioeconomic environment that did not recognize the experience and qualifications of migrants from the sending region. A break in organizational ties, which first aided Indians' employment in this niche, also occurred as a result of the political circumstances surrounding their migration. This was common for many other civil servants and professionals in East Africa, who relied on the host governments for jobs. Downgraded employment opportunities for immigrants in a new host society are not original findings in migration research. However, the irony of the situation is significant. The British held different and lower standards of education for different racial groups of people in the overseas colonial context. This, in fact, helped to create the Indian occupational niches in East Africa that would later be broken in Britain using the same logic. The predominance of newly formed interpersonal ties in the teachers' networks also constrained access to the necessary resources to overcome the poorer employment opportunities they faced in London. Capital to pursue further education and ties to network members in organizations and, therefore, to better positions were sorely missing.

Niche Stability and the Extreme Embeddedness of Trusties
Diamond Dealing in Our Blood

The structure of social networks in the transnational diamond trade is exceptional in many ways. In such a high-stakes business, social ties are closely guarded and controlled more than most other businesses. The trade is well known for its insularity, which guards against risk and the possibility of malfeasance (Westwood 2000). The high risk of malfeasance in the trade stems from the transfer of such tiny and valuable goods across the world's diamond trading centers on what seems to be no more than a handshake or a phone call. One diamond dealer reflected on her role selling diamonds in the American market:

> It has become very risky, very competitive trade . . . It's a lot of sleepless nights and a lot of money you lend out . . . your life is on the line all the time because you're taking millions of dollars of goods with you in your hands and selling to people, walking from door to door. And you're a target once they identify you.

That handshake or phone call is buttressed by huge portions of enforceable trust, which lubricate the trade. These relations of trust are unsurprisingly found in the dense network ties of Gujarati Jains in the trade. Their composite ties to family members, who have been trained and have worked in the trade across many generations, offer real and perceived security. One participant told me a story of malfeasance in the community:

> R: [Some time ago], one of the Indian merchants . . . borrowed goods from other diamond, jewelry Indians, you know. About $25 million worth of it. Went and sold it for $11 million and pocketed the money. Until last week somebody caught him when he was not paying his bills back. And you know, that's how the business has become. Luckily, we were not hurt by it because we didn't sell to this guy. But there are at least another forty Indians who had been selling to this guy who are now fighting for their money. And that's how risky it has become, the business. And that's how business is done. Like once I know you, and I've dealt with you for a while, I don't mind giving you any amount of goods, the truth. It's like a handshake. I have to just know you, and I'll come give you goods.
>
> MP: *But they had never sold to this guy before?*
>
> R: They had all been selling to him before. And he had a good reputation. And he used that . . . You know, it's all from the community, people, he's this one's this, or that one's brother, or that one's nephew, and it's quite frightening.

And how can you get the lawyers involved, and you know, the lawyers get half the money, and there are forty people, and you know, it's tough . . . It's a very good community. As I was saying, this man went bankrupt. But, you know, in a year or two, they were forgiven. They'll again give him goods, and he'll again be accepted back into the community. It's not [as] if he did all this and so many people were hurt, and that he's totally ostracized, no. That doesn't happen. People forgive him. They'll again get him back. That's the nice part.

How smooth the process of regaining trust in a dense network such as these diamond traders is arguable. However the idea or ideal that the community always envelops its members even when they do harm attests to the extreme embeddedness of economic activities in those networks. This kind of embeddedness enables those within the network, many of whom are born into it, to become employed in the niche very easily. Even the dealer described in the previous paragraph, who betrayed his business partners and customers, will be contained within the community because it would be too risky to ostracize him completely, given the secretive nature of business information. This extreme embeddedness can also prevent network members from exiting the niche when they find it in their interest to leave. It also keeps outsiders, those without generations of family linked to the trade, far away from niche opportunities and activities.

One diamond-dealing couple, Lakshmi and Narendra, who were pioneers on the American market, migrated to the United States in 1970. Their immigration visas were sponsored by the headquarters of their firm in Antwerp. They had few contacts, but they joined the India Diamond and Colorstone Association and forged new ties with other Indian pioneers in the American diamond market. Among the first Indian families to break into this market, they had to make contacts with buyers from scratch:

For two years we were here just setting up the business, making contacts, going on the road a lot . . . We stayed in Queens in a one-bedroom apartment . . . And even I knew very few people from the community . . . Even those ten people [other Indians who pioneered the industry], because being the youngest in the family I was never out there in the community, I didn't get married into the community . . . But we had a lot of fun . . . There was very little money, we earned $1300 a month at that point . . . We had this Red Book in the diamond community of all the jewelers in America—it's called the Red Book . . . which gives you the name of all the merchants in every county and city in America.

Then they give the ratings and everything. So according to these ratings we decide [to] which customer we want to sell. You go to those cities, those states. Then we stay there for a week or fifteen days, meet every customer there, and keep in touch continuously.

Soon after these initial forays into the American market, and with the help of their sponsor firm in Antwerp, their business made great profits, and they expanded into the manufacturing and sale of jewelry. They had a series of partnerships with other Jain traders. Finally, their firm became independent while still selling diamonds and jewelry polished and manufactured in India. Their composite ties to other traders in New York and Antwerp and to their exporters in India helped the firm to grow, which fed back into economic expansion in India:

> When we came into the country all we did was sell diamonds, no jewelry . . . loose diamonds to the Jewish people and the retailers . . . Then as we learnt the trade, we saw how jewelry was being made over here, and it was very expensive, and labor back home was very cheap. That's when we started developing factories. And now we've got one of the largest factories in India, many factories in India . . . Our laborers, I mean artisans, in India, they are so good at copying anything. You know, because they don't have machines and all that, and they just know how to copy it with their hands.

Their first partner ran the Indian side of the business, exporting diamonds to their New York branch, which Lakshmi and her husband managed. Later, they became partners with two other firms to enter the jewelry trade, which required greater amounts of capital. Conflict with one of those partners, a leading diamond merchant with a $150 to $200 million business, led to their decision to become independent.

By most standards, their business has been a success, and Lakshmi proclaims that she loves the diamond trade. However, her role in their network of Jain diamond dealers, particularly as a female member, produces severe constraints on her ability to pursue new opportunities. Lakshmi's generation was the third generation of Jains in the trade but the first for women. Many women from diamond families were never taught the trade. They were instead encouraged to marry within the diamond community and to become mothers and caretakers. Although Lakshmi was born into the trade and has been learning the trade ever since she was young, she holds a subordinate position to her husband in their firm. Her husband, as mentioned in the previous chapter, was an outsider from a prominent Hindu business family and was taught the trade by Lakshmi's uncle. Here, Lakshmi describes the bounds of their relationship:

> Though my husband is modern . . . if I'm there in the office, he wants to make sure that I never speak back to him. If I do, we will have major fights, if I say anything in front of anybody else in the office . . . Everything I can say, we're modern and everything, but if today he says you can't do this, I cannot do it.

Lakshmi's husband controls their firm, and he controls her role in it. As Lakshmi later explained to me, she wanted some capital to start a jewelry firm of her own. Her husband, however, would not provide her with the necessary start-up capital. To consider other employment options was out of the question. The high prestige, status, and extreme embeddedness of the diamond trade have an almost prohibitive effect on exiting the niche. Lakshmi felt not only that her husband would not permit her to leave the trade for another industry but also that the community would ridicule them. Social pressures within the trade are onerous:

> People come in from India, visit us all the time. So when they come to visit us, we have to be with them. We take them out shopping, we'll do everything, whether we like it or not. Because if we don't, we'll be talked about, mocked upon. So we're very much all traditions still.

Exiting an economic niche is not impossible for differently located members of this network of diamond traders, such as Chandrika and Madhu. Continuing their story, Chandrika, a friend of Lakshmi, was also born and raised in a diamond family. Like most women in their community, she was not expected to work in the trade. Instead, she was expected to marry and to become a mother and caretaker. Her marriage was arranged to Madhu, a Jain from their community who lived in New York. Although he also comes from a diamond family, his father had entered the garment manufacturing industry in Bombay. Madhu ran the New York branch of this transnational firm. After their marriage, Chandrika moved from Antwerp to New York, where she took an informal job in the New York office of her parent's diamond firm:

> Well, when I got here, I wasn't allowed to work, so I didn't have a valid working permit, so I worked, my family had an office here at that time, so I worked

there as a sorting person for diamonds . . . [then] I switched from being a sorting person to being a counting person.

Afterwards, Chandrika attended college and received an associate degree in business management. She worked for another diamond company, which left her dissatisfied. Later she had a child and began working in her husband's firm because she did not want to stay at home all day, but she needed flexible hours. Although she was raised in a diamond family, Chandrika had never been extensively trained in the diamond business. She held low positions as a counter and a sorter. Her marginal network location in the niche allowed her more flexibility to exit niche employment, especially because her husband was not active in the trade. His involvement in the garment industry, instead, created an easy link to the possibility for employment in his firm. As a result of this tie, exit from the diamond niche did not result in ridicule or social pressure by other members of their network. Thus, Chandrika was able to switch her employment from one niche industry to another with some ease. However, we should not forget that because Chandrika and Madhu are from diamond families they are still closely tied to the extremely dense networks of Jain diamond traders active in this industry niche.

The Transnational Garment Trade

Trading and manufacturing of textiles has been occurring in Western India for centuries. Factory industrialization in the textile industry in Bombay emerged in the 1800s and as a purely Indian enterprise in Ahmedabad. Jains have long dominated the Indian cotton-mill industry in Ahmedabad and Bombay, the two leading textile centers in India up until the 1930s (Leadbeater 1993). In Leadbeater's description of the origins of the cotton-mill industry, he profiles several pioneer mill-owning families, from the Nagar Brahmin, Shrimali Jain, Oswal Jain, and Vaishnava Vaniya communities. He explains how the Nagar Brahmin family was never able to sustain and develop a dominant position among mill-owning families in the industry because of the lack of acceptance and status associated with business enterprise in the Brahmin community and the failure of the founder's sons to successfully develop the business in later years. His analysis implies that these Brahmin mill owners could not gather up the necessary social ties to create a niche in the industry within members of their network, other family, and friends in their caste community, who mostly looked down on trading activities. In contrast, the Jain and Vaniya families, positively sanctioned by their communities to engage in such enterprises, readily formed a dominant position and niche in the cotton-mill industry. In a clear case of opportunity hoarding, the management and development of these mill companies was put in the hands of kin (usually sons or adopted sons, such as nephews, grandsons, sons in-law, and the like) and members of the community who were also involved in the industry. This recalls the common practice of the "adoption" of nephews, grandsons, or sons-in-law by their uncles, usually for economic purposes, such as for family firms. This practice is codified and sanctioned in the idea of the Hindu Undivided Family (see Goody 1996 and Chapter 2). These are exactly the composite interpersonal and organizational ties that characterize transnational entrepreneurship in these and many other transnational firms today.

By the time Madhu's father entered the garment industry in Bombay during the 1950s, the stage had been set by earlier generations of other Jain communities. Madhu, the eldest of two sons, was sent by his father to New York to study fashion design in the late 1970s. At that time, his father already had a New York branch of his garment firm, which was run by an Indian partner. However, when that partner incurred a $300,000 debt, the partnership folded, and Madhu took over management of the branch. While managing his father's branch, he started his own company in 1982. The firm is a vertical organization. It has factories in southern India, where cottons are spun and then sent to their factories in Bombay, where the manufacturing is done. The same process takes place in their factories in Kenya, and they also contract out work to factories in Pakistan and Bangladesh. These goods are then exported for sale in the United States, Canada, and Western Europe. Madhu has two wholesale businesses today, a private label business for smaller retail stores and a business for mid-range and high-end garment firms that put their own labels on the goods. The success of the company clearly benefited from the preexisting organizational ties to suppliers and buyers established by Madhu's father. Chandrika, who knows all aspects of the business, explains:

> It's a little easier if you already have a setup in India or wherever you're manufacturing because you can count on somebody to do the manufacturing for you. You know where it's coming from, you know who is in charge, you know you can yell at them if you have to. It's easier to monitor everything, but I mean we still come across problems . . . Some problems are seasonal, meaning that if it's in the monsoons and we are having shipments coming here, sometimes they are in transit before they get on the plane, and once they've

left the factory they're not covered properly, so they get damaged. We just got a shipment here of sweaters that got damaged by rains. It was soaking wet when it arrived here.

Although Madhu shuns involvement in formal associations and organizations, he spends much of his time traveling overseas in search of new designs and contacts for the business. The size and reach of this transnational firm makes it difficult to employ people only from their community; however, they do employ numerous Indians in their New York office. But, like most transnational entrepreneurs, the top management in their business is mostly run by family members.

Chandrika, who deals with almost every level of the firms' transactions, however, has more independence and freedom than Lakshmi, even though Lakshmi has a higher occupational position. The success and high status Madhu and Chandrika enjoy as transnational entrepreneurs make it unlikely that they will exit this niche. Although they do not experience the extreme embeddedness of diamond dealers, they are very densely tied to the composite organizational and interpersonal relations of others in their community and the garment industry, which has so far enhanced their economic opportunities and business success.

Movement in and out of Flexible Niches

Not all Gujarati immigrants in transnational trades stay employed in niche industries. Neither are they only entrepreneurs or salaried workers throughout their work histories. Fluidity of movement in and out of niches and entrepreneurial activity suggest that some Gujaratis are well integrated into the host economies and have access to social ties that help them to make strategic occupational moves. Harshad and Dinesh represent two cases where niche employment was strategically used at different turning points in their work histories. In both cases, niche employment was one option among several in the dominant labor market in London. Niche employment, therefore, was not always the result of constrained interpersonal networks or extreme embeddedness. Rather, it was a good option at the time (although sometimes obligatory), which was facilitated by institutional access to the formal labor market or by brokers in networks linked to that market.

Harshad, whom we met in previous chapters, was born in Kenya. In 1968, at the age of twelve, he was the last of his siblings to migrate to London. Thus, he finished his secondary schooling there and entered university. Harshad first entered the garment business when his eldest brother summoned Harshad to work for him. They had a transnational business in the wholesale garment industry with factories in London and India. Through their close connections with the factory in India, they also secured jobs for several maternal cousins. After the market became flooded with Indian cottons, they began to import fabrics from Europe. As a result of this market saturation, Harshad's brother sold the business, and Harshad was left unemployed. As a transitory job, Harshad helped a friend from Kenya launch a business manufacturing towels in Ireland for export to Kenya. After "helping" that friend, and with plenty experience of his own in transnational businesses, Harshad decided to start an independent business. He opened a high-end boutique in a coastal English town. Harshad's entrepreneurial and transnational business activities were made possible through composite ties with other Oswal family and friends in the garment and other industries. Harshad, however, had solid A-levels and an unfinished bachelor's degree. He was by no means unsuccessful in his business ventures, but he was frustrated with the instability of entrepreneurial work. He wanted more economic stability for his young family. To achieve this, he enrolled in a six-month training program in computer technologies, where he learned programming and analysis. Interpersonal ties helped him land his next job in the primary labor market using his new skills. However, this time, the interpersonal tie was his wife. More importantly, it was not her but rather her organizational ties to a colleague, an acquaintance or weak tie (Granovetter 1973), that provided the crucial information about this opportunity. This colleague-friend of Harshad's wife had a position in the human resources department of a large telecommunications firm, where they both worked. She passed on the inside information Harshad needed to apply and obtain a temporary position at that firm. That friend was not a member of their Oswal Jain community. She was a weak tie in an organization, wholly different from the composite ties Harshad used to become employed in transnational trade.

Harshad's life history shows that he had the capacity to gain access to the resources necessary to enter and exit niche employment, to further his training or education, and to enter the primary labor market. That capacity was largely a result of his strategic location in a network of family and friends with ties to transnational trades on the one hand and jobs in the primary labor market on the other. In addition to these important ties, Harshad was able to take advantage of his native English educational qualifications and available financial capital to further his education and training when needed.

Dinesh represents a reverse movement from work in the primary labor market to niche employment in the garment industry as a wholesale and retail trader. Dinesh wanted to attend university in London, where his younger brother lived, after completing his A-levels in maths and accountancy in Kenya. However, he lacked the three-year residency requirement to gain free entry into a London university. So he set out to find a job. His first job, which he found through an employment agency, was as an insurance evaluator in an English firm. He then became an accounts clerk and later a supervisor in a different London firm—jobs that he also found through an agency. The death of Dinesh's father had changed his work trajectory at the time I interviewed him in his East London shop. When his father died in Kenya, Dinesh's elder brother, a medical doctor there, summoned him to Kenya to manage their father's wholesale business. Dinesh uprooted his wife (also from their Oswal community) and children to do this for five years. After those five years, Dinesh and his wife sold the business and moved back to London so that their children could be educated there. Dinesh was then faced with finding employment again in London. (His wife was fortunate to be rehired by her prior employer, Inland Revenue, as an inspector.) Dinesh's newly acquired experience in Kenya and an opening in wholesale and retail for many immigrants in London in the 1980s helped him to become a market trader in London. Equally significant, Dinesh's cousin, also a market trader in the garment industry in East London, helped him to join this entry point of wholesaling and retailing. Eventually, with savings and a loan from a building society, he opened his own retail clothing shop. In Kenya, members of the Oswal community rarely borrowed money from formal institutions. The community served as a major source of financial support and information. At that time, however, the Oswals were still a modestly wealthy community. Dinesh confirmed that, as the community achieved greater wealth in Kenya and later in the United Kingdom, they gave up their old economic practices based on trust. Dinesh himself admitted that he would trust only one or two members of his family with knowledge about the financial status of his small business. He described the changed ways in which people from his community help each other:

> They help each other, not as much as in Kenya . . . if they want to put in a reference to—like if I want another label, then I know my friend down the road in Ilford. I know a few people in our community sell shirts, so we tell each other what's happening or what labels are doing better. We give each other information that way. Nowadays people don't help when it comes to money. I mean it's so easy for me to get help from a bank or something—and plus I keep that very

confidential, you know I don't want people to know I'm struggling because it's, you know, they'll probably go and tell every[body], so I'm scared of that. So if I'm struggling, I wouldn't tell them. I wouldn't ask help from them. I would go to my brother, or, if I really want a loan, banks. I've got good credit with banks, so financially I don't have that much of a problem.

His business today is in a larger, double-front shop. He employs one English sales clerk, and his son and nephew help out on Saturdays. When I interviewed him, Dinesh expressed anxiety about the future of his shop and small retailers like himself. These small shops are slowly being pushed out of business by what is often referred to as the superstore revolution in Britain (see Barrett, Jones, McEvoy, and McGoldrick 2002; Cowe 1999). The commercial vitality of entire High Streets is deteriorating as a result of competition produced by superstores offering lower prices and convenient parking. Dinesh even justified giving me his home address and phone number in case he went out of business soon. I asked him, "What will you do then?" He replied, "I don't know—get a regular job."

Dinesh's experience in the dominant labor market in London was generally at parity with his educational attainment and skills. He used formal means to learn about and obtain these jobs. Composite ties to family and friends in the garment industry, on the other hand, were necessary for him to establish himself in the wholesale and retail trade of London's garment industry and in transnational trade in Kenya. Although he does not seem to have the financial means to easily further his education and training, as does his friend Harshad, Dinesh gives the impression of ease of movement in and out of niche employment in London. The changing culture of trust in the composite ties of his Oswal network and the wider Oswal community, ironically, has allowed him more flexibility to move in and out of niches and in and out of the ethnic economy. Thus, Dinesh is constrained much more by the poor economic prospects for small retailers brought on by London's changing economic structure than by the economic opportunities presented by his interpersonal ties with family and friends in the Oswal community.

Constrained Embeddedness and the Niches of Chains

An Indian at Every Newsstand

Gujaratis have been quite successful in establishing themselves in industries in New York and London in which they had no prior experience either in India or East Africa. Two economic sectors with prominent Gujarati niches in New

York and London are retail trade and services. In retail trade, common industry niches in both cities include CTN, groceries/food, and stationery.

Small retail trade in London is overwhelmingly dominated by South Asians. Hindus make up approximately 70 percent of newsagents in London, most of whom belong to the Patidar caste community (Lyon and West 1995). Of the 576 Patel (usually Patidar) small businesses surveyed by Lyon and West, 67 percent were in the CTN industry. A further 23 percent owned groceries, general stores, off-license (liquor) stores, and post office outlets. Fewer were self-employed professionals (12 percent); dentists, doctors, and pharmacists topped the list. These figures are fairly consistent with employment statistics for Indians in the United Kingdom, generally in the 1990s. Indian and "African Asian" men comprised 25 and 30 percent, respectively, of professionals, managers, and employers (Mason 2003, 74). Employers of small establishments, however, constituted the largest portion (11 percent and 14 percent) of this socioeconomic group (74). Retail businesses are geographically dispersed across central and Greater London in an ethnic ownership economy that caters to a broad mix of clients to maximize profits. Many small retail businesses in commercial and residential Indian enclaves (in both New York and London) sell goods that cater to a coethnic and larger South Asian community. These are ethnic enclave economies. However, most Indian retailers are able to pursue the economic advantages of serving the mainstream market.

In New York, Logan, Alba, Dill, and Zhou (2000) reported that 22 percent of Indians were owners in retail and wholesale in 1990. They also show that new niches in New York have been growing in food stores, eating places, and social services. For instance, Gujaratis in the United States have been forming a niche in particular food franchise outlets, notable in Dunkin' Donuts franchises (Sun 1998). In the service sector, Gujaratis are a significant part of the hospitality industry in the United States, owning close to 50 percent of mid-size motels, according to the Asian American Hotel Owners Association, but they have no such niche in the United Kingdom (see Dhingra 2009; McDowell 1996; Varadarajan 1999). These motel franchises are concentrated in the southern and midwestern states of the United States. In these entrepreneurial niches, owners often employ kin and others from their community. Therefore, the owners and employees in these niches form an ethnic ownership economy but not an ethnic enclave economy (Light and Gold 2000). The clientele whom they serve are part of the general population. Thus, Indian businesses are located in predominantly native, white, commercial and residential areas.

Typically, Gujaratis cite cultural reasons for pioneering or entering a new industry in the host country. Industries that are not polluting (that is, that do not require handling food) are especially desirable, as are those that offer immediate cash flow and housing. As vegetarians, Gujaratis are keen not to enter industries where they must handle meat, fish, or alcohol. Thus, the ubiquitous curry house in the United Kingdom is actually a Bangladeshi niche, among whom meat, fish, and alcohol restrictions are not always as strong. Vegetarianism, immediate cash flow, and housing, often located above one's business, are the same reasons Gujaratis give for starting CTN shops, postal service outlets, stationery stores, and small groceries that sell only fruits, vegetables, and packaged frozen and dry goods. The overarching reason for starting small businesses in these industries is that they require a small amount of capital, and these owners already have interpersonal ties that can help them to navigate the industry. Furthermore, Gujaratis are able to quickly mobilize this necessary capital and labor from within their interpersonal networks.

In addition to the cultural aspects of pioneer niches, the socioeconomic and institutional context of the host country must be open to such entrepreneurial activities for immigrants (Barrett et al. 2002; Kloosterman and Rath 2001). In the case of Gujarati niches in both New York and London, the strategy was the same. Gujaratis looked for shops to lease or buy in declining commercial areas and sometimes in declining industries. Many relied on interpersonal ties to find these empty shops and neighborhoods. Zimmer and Aldrich (1987) found that choosing a geographical site for a business depended on either formal methods or interpersonal ties. For example, a little over half of the shopkeepers in the Ealing borough of West London used formal channels, such as newspapers, to locate available shops for sale. Many shopkeepers told me that newspapers, such as *Exchange and Mart* and *Dalton's Weekly*, are the most popular sources of formal advertisement for the sale of London shops. These advertisements also describe the location and turnover of shops. The other 50 percent used information from family, or they knew the owner.

Gujarati small business owners have also introduced innovative practices to their businesses, thus giving them a competitive advantage over native owners in the same industries. One notable example is parallel trading. A leader of the Asian Business Association at the London Chamber of Commerce explained this phenomenon to me. In parallel trading, a retailer may buy products that are manufactured in the United Kingdom but that are destined for sale in Kenya or some other country. One day, for instance, I bought a tube of

toothpaste in the South Asian neighborhood of Wembley that had authorization from the dental associations of several African countries. Often, these
products are exported to foreign countries for sale at a much cheaper price
and then reimported back into the original country for sale at the more expensive price. Thus, even small local retailers can operate with transnational
advantages.

Other advantages were related to how Indian families ran their shops and
the relations or transactions within these interpersonal ties composed of shop-
owners and employees. One leader in the South Asian community described
how his family first entered the retail business in London in the 1970s:

> Oh, it wasn't difficult because we had cash, even though it was small cash, a
> few, a few hundred pounds. We pooled it because these shops were really be-
> ing underutilized. They were opening at 7 a.m. and closing at five or six in the
> evening, so the volume of turnover was, and there was a formula . . . So we
> then went in, and we added firepower of people for free, so we had an edge.
> We made our margins. We opened longer, right. We brought in niche goods
> like Irish goods . . . and that immediately boosted our turnover . . . Techni-
> cally, we were three families. But, we said, look, we'll all be together; we've
> got no choice; we are brothers, sisters, nephews, all together, so fifteen [people
> staying in] four bedrooms, you buy your first shop. You really get a go, and six
> months later you can buy another shop because you've made the money, and
> you've really not spent as much . . . You're generating capital, which spawns
> the second shop. You've now got two . . . so literally one became two, became
> three, became six. And in the second shop, for example, there, the brother
> wanted to outdo this brother. So, he said, look, I've got a clever idea. I'll go to
> Covent Garden Market, buy fresh fruits and vegetables or ethnic goods, which
> come in, and bring them here. And that's got even more margin, but it means
> getting up at four in the morning. It means going to the market at five, and
> coming back at six, and offering everybody cassava and plantain and corian-
> der that you couldn't get otherwise.

Many aspects of this story were echoed by other shopkeepers I interviewed
in New York and London: the introduction of ethnic goods; the long, hard
hours family members worked behind cash registers and stocking shelves, wak-
ing up before dawn to buy goods at wholesale cash-and-carry stores or farmer's
markets; and the subordination of one's personal interests and desires for the
collective goal of making the shop profitable. Most shopkeepers, however, did

not have such an enormous amount of labor power to put to work in these shops as in the story of Ram's family above. Many shopkeepers sufficed with only three or four family members in one shop over the course of many years, even decades. Less labor power to exploit, "firepower of people for free" as Ram put it, has kept these shops from growing and kept the workers within them from opportunities to exit the niche. More importantly, interpersonal ties, which on the one hand made these niches possible and profitable, on the other hand constrained mobility. In other words, both the networks of actors within these niches and the set of businesses representing the niche were constrained in their embeddedness within the niche and the wider economy. Even when new ties were made in temple organizations or industry associations, these organizational ties reinforced the occupational status of owners and employees in the niche. In some cases, one's status in a temple organization, such as the Swaminarayan Hindu sect, could become intimately linked with one's status as a shopkeeper. Therefore, exiting the niche would be akin to exiting one's community or at least risking giving up the practices associated with representing one's social status.

This intertwined relationship between business and community keeps some college-educated shopkeepers from pursuing other lines of employment. Although these network processes include in-group members, albeit in a constrained way, out-group members will be excluded from the niche because of a lack of old and new interpersonal ties to small businesses such as CTN shops. This constraint is less than the extreme embeddedness of composite networks in much riskier economic activities such as the global diamond trade. Thus, interpersonal networks behave differently in different economic sectors and industries, allowing easier but constrained niche entry and exit in small, less risky businesses such as CTN shops.

"Patel Motels": The Hospitality Industry in the United States

"Patel Motels" illustrate another case of constrained embeddedness. According to the Asian American Hotel Owners Association (AAHOA), Asian Americans currently own about 50 per cent of the economy lodging sector and 37 percent of all hotels in the United States. Although the association calls itself Asian American, the overwhelming majority of its hotel-owning members are Indian. Even more astounding is that, among Indians, about 70 percent of the hotel owners who dominate this niche are members of the Patidar caste community from Gujarat (Varadarajan 1999), hence the well-known title, "Patel motel." In fact, many of these Gujaratis are twice and thrice migrants from East Africa and/or the United Kingdom (McDowell 1996; Varadarajan 1999). The AAHOA has about 9,000 members. Collectively, they own an estimated 13,500 franchised hotels, worth $36.6 billion, and 8,500 independent hotels, worth $23.4 billion. The franchised hotels employ about 625,000 people, and the independent hotels employ 175,000 in this ethnic ownership economy.[6]

David Mumford, president of a hotel brokerage firm in Virginia, tells the story of how Indians and Gujaratis entered the hotel industry (Varadarajan 1999). It runs something like this: In the 1960s, there were perhaps sixty or seventy Indian-owned motels in the United States, mostly in California. Usha Jain (1989), for instance, describes the Gujaratis who pioneered the hotel business in San Francisco. The immigration of Indians to the United States rose sharply after 1965. During the 1960s through the mid-1970s, American motel owners were aging, and their grandchildren were not succeeding them in the business. A depressed economy at the time, which resulted in less profit, discouraged people from investing in the industry. In response, property prices decreased. By the early 1980s, hundreds of motels went up for sale.

The sale of these motels could not have been more timely for the new wave of nonprofessional Indians immigrating to the country via India or East Africa and the United Kingdom. These future motel owners bought their motels in the South and the Midwest, where properties were less expensive than on the coasts. Other keys to the story can be found in the weak social ties developed by Indian pioneers in the industry. These organizational ties included a vice president at United Insurance Agencies, which insures hotel businesses. In the early days, before there was a niche, his company helped convince underwriters that Indian immigrants were "outstanding risks" (McDowell 1996, 1). Other franchisers were strong supporters of the early days of the AAHOA. Pioneers of this Indian niche thus developed organizational ties with key American insurers and franchisers to secure their ability to invest in the hotel industry. These important weak ties also helped to ensure the future development of this niche for the interpersonal networks of Gujaratis. Today, there is no question that Indian hoteliers exert influence on the industry. As one Gujarati independent hotelier put it, "Now we are the establishment" (Varadarajan 1999, 40). Gujaratis have made significant gains in the organizational hierarchy of the American Hotel and Lodging Association (previously the American Hotel and Motel Association) as past chairpersons and present members of the board of directors.

Despite the common Gujarati cultural myths that business is in their blood, that hospitality is inherently Indian, that Indians work harder than other groups, and that Gujaratis do not like working for others, some cultural aspects do bear on why Gujaratis found the hotel industry desirable. The AAHOA notes that "the hospitality industry was a popular career choice because it offered immediate housing and cash flow, as well as the opportunity to 'blend in' despite any cultural differences."[7] Another important reason was that most of these Gujaratis were vegetarians. Owning a small or mid-size motel did not require the handling of food, especially meat, fish, and alcohol. Motels served as businesses and homes, which eliminated the costs of buying a separate home. Owners also saved costs by employing family labor. Most important, however, was the low start-up capital, which could be quickly mobilized through interpersonal networks to buy a motel. Mira Nair poignantly depicts the racial and class tensions in the lives of these Gujarati motel owners from Uganda in the film *Mississippi Masala*. In the film, Mina, the "darkie daughter," and her parents become refugees in 1972. Forced to leave their upper-class home in the lush landscape of Uganda, where Mina's father was a lawyer, they first migrate to England and then to Greenwood, Mississippi, where Mina cleans rooms at the Monte Cristo Hotel owned by Gujarati relatives. Her mother is chastised by their community for owning a liquor store in a poor, run-down, African American part of town. The family is also ridiculed for being in debt and for her father's constant petitioning of the Ugandan government for the restoration of his property as he pines to go back "home." Interpersonal ties, although crucial, only reach a short distance for this family as they try to remake their lives.

Another factor favoring the use of interpersonal ties to hoard motel-owning opportunities is that franchisers give preference to existing franchisees (Sun 1998). When those existing franchisees are Gujaratis, the likelihood that new franchisees will also be Gujarati increases. Because Gujaratis employ family labor in their businesses, similar to chains in the retail sector, those members learn all aspects of the business and become primed to become owners themselves. Thus, interpersonal ties are a key aspect of both ownership and employee status in this industry (see also Dhingra 2009). Organizational ties are important only insofar as owners need access to franchisers to buy and insure their businesses. Today, organizational ties exist not only to natives in American firms but also within the composite and interpersonal ties of Indians via organizations such as the AAHOA and the American Hotel and Lodging Association.

Comparing Networks and Niches

The economic niches composed of the organizational, composite, and interpersonal ties of recruits, trusties, and chains described above illustrate how the extent and mode of embeddedness of economic behavior in distinct networks of relations varies. Network location, new social ties and brokers, and the relations of exchange within ties contribute to inclusion and exclusion in economic niches, which illustrate various differences in economic niches and the immigrants who work in them: upward mobility, niche breakup and downward mobility, extreme embeddedness, niche flexibility, and constrained mobility.

The addition of new ties to old ones in most ways reinforces the initial ties that led to distinct flows of migration. Generally, recruits become involved in professional organizations related to their occupation, trusties are members in industry associations dominated by composite ties in their economic niches, and chains belong to many associations that develop new interpersonal ties on the basis of common religion, caste, region of origin, and language. Certainly some recruits also take part in the latter kinds of associations, but these are not central to their economic activity. Therefore, organizational ties within recruits, composite ties within trusties, and both composite (in the case of entrepreneurs) and interpersonal ties within chains are reinforced by their new network ties in host countries.

In addition to new network ties, the location of individual immigrants in a network has significant consequences for the types of economic transactions that take place in the new context of the host society. For example, Lakshmi is extremely central to her network of diamond traders but in a relationally subordinate position to her husband. She is severely constrained in her ability to work independently, even though she and her husband are co-owners of a very successful firm within a lucrative industry niche dominated by members of their coethnic community. Contrast her position with Chandrika. Chandrika's low position in the diamond trade and legitimate access to the garment trade allowed her to easily exit the diamond trade and enter the garment trade, where her husband is an owner of a profitable wholesale business. Thus, the network location and the resulting transactions within those ties— Lakshmi's ability to act with authority in business matters, and Chandrika's ability to avoid ridicule and the social pressures of their network—led to quite different outcomes for each of them. This was true even though both could be considered upwardly mobile (surely an understatement) in lucrative niches dominated by members of their Gujarati Jain communities.

The example of Harshad and his brother Mahesh also revealed how transactions within ties create or reinforce relative positions of power and inequality within networks. In a common strategy among eldest sons in Gujarati families, Harshad was summoned out of university by his eldest brother Mahesh to join him in his wholesale garment business. Although not a bad economic opportunity for Harshad, he had very little decision-making power or freedom to act independently of his brother, the owner of that firm. And when the firm began to falter, Mahesh sold it, leaving Harshad to seek employment elsewhere.

These kinds of transactions are less evident in the stories of recruits. Niches that are formed through organizational networks are monitored by external organizations, such as educational and certifying institutions or states. These organizations are very exclusive and selective in terms of human capital and organizational requirements. Once organizational criteria are met, transactions within these ties are less risky than within interpersonal and composite tie networks. This was evident in the story of Bharat, who met the human capital requirements to continue as a teacher in Britain but who was also strategically located in a network that included British brokers in the education industry, who could connect him to a job in education in Britain. This partial embeddedness of economic behavior is shaped and regulated by organizations and network ties, allowing for niche change on this basis. In composite networks, however, the dense network ties based on trust do the work of regulating and sorting individual and network level economic behavior such that embeddedness is extreme and niche exit and entry are more difficult. The embeddedness of economic behavior in interpersonal networks is typically constrained because interpersonal ties offer few new opportunities for exiting a niche or for mobility within it. Where there is a lack of brokers in one's interpersonal networks, as is the case with many small shopkeepers, niche employment can constrain individual mobility. Similarly, the absence of interpersonal ties or brokers, who can connect coethnics to industry niches, excludes some individuals from these opportunities altogether.

In these narratives, we also see that different configurations of ties and their transactions penetrate economic sectors irregularly. Despite heaps of trust, which are inherent in the composite ties needed to run the diamond trade, the risk of malfeasance always looms, quite unlike niches dominated by organizational networks. Interpersonal networks also regulate economic sectors such as retail trade and services through the network ties that select labor and monitor behavior.

There are broader implications here that are related to the role of the social origins of migrants and niche employment and ownership and to the broader diversity of workers in different industries or economic sectors. The narratives show that social processes, that is, the network processes that include and exclude immigrants from particular economic opportunities, are more important than social origins. In other words, coethnicity operates on many different levels and very unevenly in networks such that it is not the overriding mechanism for the cooperation necessary to sustain niche employment. Individuals with very similar attributes, such as gender, caste, ethnicity, and class status, are presented with very different kinds of opportunities for niche employment as a result of their network location and transactions within their social ties, rather than based on those individual attributes. Coethnicity does not afford similar opportunities within networks of trusties and chains, especially, and is even much less relevant in networks of recruits. Thus, examining processes of inequality within and even between different immigrant groups by focusing on coethnicity seems likely to be a misguided approach. These findings and implications about the structure of migrant networks, their role and meaning, the importance of transactions within network ties, and how coethnicity operates within those ties are elaborated in the next chapter as we have seen in the case of Gujarati immigrants and for migration research more generally.

5 Migrant Networks as Webs of Relations and Flows

Networks migrate; categories stay put.
—Charles Tilly (1990, 84)

THE FOREGOING CHAPTERS ILLUSTRATE Gujarati migration flows to New York and London and the social networks of these migrants. They have shown how those flows have various historical origins, which resulted in different sorts of social ties that migrants used to move to destinations in East Africa and to New York and London. They have also shown how those flows have been selective based on the types of social ties migrants had in their countries of origin and where those ties connected them. Those ties channeled Gujaratis into particular occupations, which linked local labor markets across international borders and established some migrants in various occupational niches. As Gujaratis migrated and settled into their new destinations, new social ties created at their destinations often consolidated those niches but also demonstrated inequalities within Gujarati migrant networks that limited some Gujaratis, especially those with predominantly interpersonal ties, from further mobility. The life histories of Gujarati immigrants in these various types of networks revealed inequalities within the Gujarati immigrant sample as a whole and within particular networks, as central actors within those networks were able to command the resources of the network or as various migrants were positioned differently within them. The mechanisms of migration and mobility—configurations of social ties in migrant social networks and the relations of exchange or transactions within those ties—seem rather clear for these Gujaratis. Can we also explain the migration of people from other regions and countries around the world in terms of the same sorts of social ties and transactions? Obviously, we cannot generalize the case of Gujaratis to all sorts of other migrants given the limits of qualitative research and of this study. However, owing to their long history of migration and wide diversity of flows, Gujaratis are a critical case that we can learn from by comparison to other migration flows that we know about in studies of migration.

This chapter aims to do that by first elaborating theoretically on a relational account of migration and migrant networks, which focuses on network ties and transactions as the causes of migration and related aspects of mobility in the lives of migrants. It then discusses the relational account as compared to competing substantialist approaches, some of which are perpetuated in social network accounts of migration in problematic ways. Specifically, I criticize substantialist assumptions in those network accounts of migration in terms of their definition of the network, their treatment of coethnicity and coethnic solidarity in migrant networks, and the problem of how boundaries, particularly ethnic boundaries, are constructed in these networks of relations. The chapter also suggests some implications for the historical role of globalization and ideas about modernity in thinking about migration flows. Finally, it considers what an entirely network account of migration might look like for many different groups of migrants from different parts of the world and how we might read other studies in terms of such a network-oriented or relational approach.

Migrant Relations and Networks

Migrant relations exist within social networks made up of social ties. In other words, migrants, as with all kinds of people, are part of larger social networks that connect them to other individuals but also to families, households, communities, organizations, institutions, and states. We are all part of different kinds of networks that include family members, neighbors, friends, co-workers, coethnics and coreligionists, teachers, community leaders, politicians, government bureaucrats, and the like. Of course, not everyone is equally connected to each of these sorts of people in our communities and institutions. Some connections are stronger than others; some are more distant than others, for instance. Thus, in various ways the strength and quality of these network ties matters a lot for our everyday ability to get things done, for example, to secure important information or resources that can better our lives—in short, to provide us with mobility. So it is with migrant networks when potential migrants face the prospect of moving their lives across international borders to better them economically, politically, or socially. Although networks themselves do not cause migration, the relations within network ties have been instrumental

in causing migration flows to particular destinations over others and in causing different prospects and outcomes in the social and economic mobility of
migrants. Migration flows are "selective" in this way. In other words, those
who emigrate from a particular country are rarely if ever representative of
the population from which they come. Instead, particular kinds of migrants
constitute various types of flows. These might be selective flows based on gender, class status, age, and the like, so that women dominate some flows from
certain countries; however, they are often more complex than that. Migrant
flows are also selective in that they direct migrants to particular destinations
resulting in large concentrations of immigrants in particular cities and neighborhoods who share the same regional or local origins in their home countries.[1] The structure of social ties in a network or set of networks and the
transactions that take place within ties—often negotiated exchanges of money,
information, resources, influence, and status—continuously change and can
cause very different outcomes for immigrants. Broadly, as we have seen in the
previous chapters, at least three types of social ties or relations have dominated
the social networks of the immigrants who, as a whole, make up today's large
diaspora of Gujaratis. They are interpersonal, organizational, and a composite
of the two types:

1. Interpersonal ties, which are commonly cited in studies of immigrant
    and native populations, include relationships to kin, friends, and com-
    munity. These are strong ties that often, but not as a rule, generate
    trust and cooperation. They include parents, spouses, siblings, cous-
    ins, friends, and coethnics. Although many of these ties contain the
    strongest of bonds, most of us are all too familiar with the kinds of
    rivalries, tensions, and inequalities that can also arise within family
    and interpersonal relations. I have referred to migrant networks made
    up mostly of interpersonal ties as *chains* because they most resemble
    chain migration. Chain migration is the most common form of migra-
    tion from virtually every historical era that has been documented by
    migration researchers (for example, Massey et al. 1987; Portes and Bach
    1985; Smith 2006; Thomas and Znaniecki 1918–1920; Tilly 1978, 1990;
    Tilly and Brown 1967). In this type of migration, sets of individuals
    move with the encouragement and aid of their families and communi-
    ties, who, in turn, help and encourage others from their sending region
    not only to migrate but also to find jobs and adjust in other ways. Thus,
    as chains of migrants move, a considerable proportion settle near each

other at their destination. The immigration policies of many countries, which favor sponsorship of potential immigrants based on family ties, also promote (sometimes inadvertently) chain migration. Other types of migrant flows, such as recruits (for example, professionals, recruited workers, students) and trusties (such as transnational entrepreneurs), often become chains.

2. Organizational ties, which are typically thought of as weak ties (Granovetter 1973), exist when individuals are connected or relate to each other through the same organizations and institutions, for instance ties to co-workers, employers, bureaucrats, or community leaders. Organizations of all kinds, such as schools, government agencies, businesses, voluntary associations, professional organizations, labor unions, places of employment, religious institutions, and the like, mediate relations within these social ties. I have referred to these migrant networks as *recruits* because their organizational ties facilitate their recruitment into particular jobs and to particular destinations rather than their interpersonal ties.

3. Composite ties are made up of both interpersonal and organizational ties. They are distinct from the two types above because the relations within composite ties are mediated by the organization and the family or community together as a single entity. These relations coexist in such a way that they are inseparable and indistinguishable from each other, for instance in family firms. They are also relatively rare compared to interpersonal and organizational ties. I have referred to these migrant networks as *trusties* because the high-risk nature of their relationships and economic activities requires that they continuously place valued goods and activities into the hands of others—often outside any formal means of policing or enforcement. In other words, their transactions require loads of trust.

The fourth possibility contains the smallest proportion of migrants among these flows. That possibility holds that some migrants may migrate without any ties at all. I have referred to them as *solitaries* even though, in this study's sample of Gujarati immigrants, I found no solitaries. Typically, we think of these migrants as pioneers—mavericks, adventurers, explorers, even accidental migrants. More migrants seem to claim to be pioneers than those who really do migrate without ties (therefore I refer to them as solitaries to highlight their lack of ties). And our accounts of pioneers are always very rare because they are so few in number and their stories are often told in biographies, legends, or as oral histories. Nevertheless, some solitaries do (and should) exist.

Setting aside the absence of ties among solitaries, the three types of ties or relations—interpersonal, organizational, and composite—can dominate networks, regulate them differently, and affect the mobility of individual immigrants both within a network and across networks. We see these effects, for instance, in the example of the Halari Oswal Jains, such as the fathers of Harshad, Mahesh, and Dinesh, who migrated to East Africa at the turn of the twentieth century and established small and large centers for local and transnational trade and industry until those countries gained independence from Britain. Their interpersonal ties, relations among family, friends, and community members, provided the necessary links to encourage the migration of particular Gujaratis to particular places in East Africa. Interpersonal ties, such as the relatives in Kenya who enabled Harshad's father to risk crossing the Indian Ocean on an Arab dhow and later to send for his wife from Gujarat, channel migrants to very specific destinations, such as the tiny town of Fort Thomson, where Harshad was born. These ties also allowed families and community members to hoard economic opportunities such as in the retail trade occupied by many Oswal families, including the families of Harshad, Mahesh, and Dinesh. However, they also limited future access to different opportunities outside those network ties and industry niches.

Organizational ties, on the other hand, create different circumstances for migration prospects and destinations. In the example of recruited physicians and medical professionals to the United States and United Kingdom, we saw that American foundations and higher education institutions supported the development of a set of elite Indian universities specializing in science, technology, and management just after India's independence from Britain in 1947. Prominent foundations and universities, such as Ford, Rockefeller, Harvard, and the Massachusetts Institute of Technology (MIT), created transnational ties by sponsoring faculty exchanges and spreading influence through curriculum development among other activities. Even though these efforts were designed, at least in part, to stem the influence of the Soviet Union, this aid prompted significant streams of highly educated Indian immigrants (primarily scientists and engineers) to the United States after 1965 (among whom many physicians had been recruited to Britain first) when U.S. immigration law abolished national-origins quotas. They were recruited by the government and businesses to fulfill labor shortages. In this history, globalization was at work through institutional ties between foundations and universities in the United States and India even during an era typically described as national or protectionist. For these immigrant professionals, such as Jamnadevi and Kishor, organizational ties created better economic opportunities and monitored their behavior through licensing, education, and certification requirements, sharply limiting but not eliminating the need and use of their interpersonal networks.

Composite ties contain elements of both interpersonal and organizational ties, which cannot be disentangled. Transnational entrepreneurs in risky businesses, such as the diamond trade, illustrate how transactions in these networks operate. Among diamond dealers, ties to members of one's family or community are simultaneously ties to one's business partner, employer, supplier, and producer in the trade, as in the families of Lakshmi and Narendra and Arun and Sadvati. The density of these ties is extreme, thus limiting opportunities to those within the trade as these merchants must protect their very lucrative and risky economic interests by engaging only those whom they trust and can monitor closely through social relations. Transnational entrepreneurial families or networks can be found in far-reaching diasporas located in destinations where they pursue commerce (for example, diamond centers such as Antwerp, Bangkok, Hong Kong, and New York City) and are clearly linked to global economic processes. Surat, as a center of the diamond and gemstone trade at least since the 1600s, shows that these links are historical. They are also contemporary, as when U.S. diamond markets opened up in the 1970s, establishing free-trade zones and prompting an expansion of generations-old diamond businesses (and some of their owners and workers) to move to this new consumer market.

We can see in these historical instances and in the life histories of immigrants, which have been elaborated in this book, how different types of ties produce different kinds of migration flows. These flows are part of globalization from earlier eras in that they have historical origins in Britain's colonization of East Africa and India or global commercial ties in the diamond and garment industries, for instance, and in transnational institutional ties between India and the United States. Thus, global migration is hardly a new phenomenon, nor is it simply the result of today's faster transportation and communication. Although the form and speed of trade relations that once connected Gujaratis to distant places in Eastern and Southern Africa, the Mediterranean, and north into the Caucasus Mountains were different, the relations that drove their mobility were global in very similar ways. In other words, globalization has been part of the context of these migrant's collective histories for many centuries. Here, *globalization* refers not only to economic globalization, especially the capitalist varieties, but rather, more generally, to the interdependence and interconnectedness of the world through trade, politics, economy, culture, and, of course, migration. Mercantile cities such as Surat, trade, colonial ties, institutional links between states, and extensive diasporas hold complex economic and social relations that organize global migration. Neither are Gujaratis and other Indians who make up these flows "traditional" people moving into modern worlds across unknown borders. Rather, their migrations are modern; their worlds have been connected or integrated in specific ways across borders for many years. Moreover, these examples of global networks and the economic niches that they form are tied together not by the fact that they are present within the Gujarati population or in the culture of Gujaratis. Nor did they result primarily from rational economic action where individual migrants or households weighed the costs and benefits of migrating to different countries or in which their employers searched and found the best-skilled person for the job. The way that they have moved within these worlds and made lives for themselves, economically, has often relied on "nonrational" processes—the use of different sorts of ties in their networks to secure jobs, housing, and the like and to mitigate risk. In short, these examples of migration flows and mobility are tied together by the relations found in the migrants' social networks. We might also find similar kinds of networks and relations within many different populations. Gujaratis, however, are a strategic research site because they help us to see these network processes more clearly and to provide a meaningful point of comparison with other groups and historical eras. They also represent extremely diverse types of migrants, which offer a unique view of the variety of social ties that migrants use to move and secure resources, how migrant social networks are structured, and what takes place within them.

Substantialist and Relational Explanations

The case of Gujarati migration to New York and London is also important because it speaks to a newly revived debate in sociology about how to understand and study social processes in the world. This debate is between the relational and substantialist approaches to understanding social action. The relational approach is prevalent in the classical works of sociology, such as in

Karl Marx's and Georg Simmel's theories. For Marx, the capitalist and working classes were never independent, static entities that could exist apart from each other, for instance. They have always been in a dynamic social relationship with each other (Marx [1844] 1975). Simmel's (1955, 1971) thought is even closer as a precursor to contemporary network theory as he was concerned with the relationship between the individual and the group, which exhibited tensions between the self and society within a "web of group-affiliations." Erving Goffman (1967) and Frederik Barth (1969) were later proponents of relational approaches to understanding social life. However, relational sociology has been lost to the substantialist approach, which has dominated thinking in contemporary sociology as positivism gained more influence in sociological studies. Recently, however, a number of scholars have argued for a return to the relational approach to understanding social life because they believe that it offers a more accurate view of social realities than the reductionist tendencies of positivist, substantialist approaches (for example, Abbott 2001; Brubaker 2004; Emirbayer 1997; and Tilly 1999).

The central idea behind the relational approach is that social life is about processes and relations that are always changing rather than substances or entities that remain static and fixed. In other words, when we think about social life and, for instance, an individual's place in history or position in the social order of a society, many individual attributes of that person appear important in obvious ways—level of education in a class-based society or race and sex in a race- and sex-stratified society. These attributes, class, race, and sex, are substances that are assumed to have a fixed meaning in much of social science analysis. These substances, however, cannot be entirely fixed categories. Societies change; they are dynamic. The meaning of these categories also changes. Everyday relations between people who command different resources in societies change and shift as people use these categories to distribute valuable resources. In the contemporary world, there is never a clear, unchanging line between one's various sorts of attributes and one's place in society, although surely these attributes matter. The relational approach seeks to take account of these changes that are sometimes minuscule and other times huge, rather than to assume that they never change at all. Furthermore, if the relational idea is correct, then social scientists must also develop analytical tools and concepts that can explain the dynamic character of social life (Abbott 2001).

Relational analyses, therefore, focus our attention on networks as sets of relations that continually change. This is a process that we can see by looking at the patterns of social ties in these relations and the types of exchange or trans-actions that take place within ties, such as the passing of money, information, status, and resources. The relational approach rejects the tools of positivism, which focus on static, categorical attributes that have become so commonplace in sociological analyses—for instance, gender, race, ethnicity, class status, and the like. This is not to say that these largely ascribed characteristics do not matter. They do. However, they matter as part of the process in which relations between actors occur and change. On their own, as fixed characteristics of individuals in variable-based analyses, they hold little explanatory power for all sorts of social action. In other words, the substantialist approach assumes that the basic units of social action or phenomena are relatively stable and independent entities, es-pecially individuals. It also claims that attributes of these entities explain their behavior. Therefore, it expresses these attributes as individual-level variables, such as class, gender, race, ethnicity, and the like and explains all outcomes or behavior as a result of variation in these individual-level variables. In doing so, it ignores the processes that actually form relations between and within ethnic groups, the working and capitalist classes, or men and women. The attributes are meant to substitute for the real relations that make up all of social, economic, political, and cultural life. At best, however, these static attributes demonstrate strong correlations among variables to explain some phenomenon. The explana-tion of how those variables cause various phenomena, however, is far weaker and requires that we understand some sort of mechanism that connects the re-lationship between variables. It requires that we understand some kind of causal process that is taking place. Understanding processes is the strength of the rela-tional approach.

To correct for the weak explanations provided by the substantialist approach, relational accounts of social behavior or action have shifted attention to net-works as a way of taking into account relations rather than simply individual-level attributes. However, network analyses, too, often treat nodes or locations in networks as attributes of individuals or whatever unit of analysis is represented by the node, such as households, organizations, states, and the like. For example, a household of undocumented immigrants might be one node in a network of households. Or a democratic state among different kinds of states describes the characteristics of the network node but also reproduces it as an attribute that is unchanging when analyzing the network. Thus, network researchers often transmit the problem of the substantialist approach onto network studies that are meant to be relational analyses, especially in highly quantitative studies.

Most network studies of migration repeat the same problem as discussed below. In a different sort of problem that combines substantialist with relational arguments, Alba and Nee's (2003) prominent study of immigrant assimilation argues that causal mechanisms, such as context-bound individual action, *exchange in social networks*, various forms of capital, and the structure of institutional incentives need to be identified to understand contemporary assimilation or the incorporation of immigrants (italics my emphasis). In their relational approach, boundary crossing, blurring, and shifting are also important mechanisms of change that affect assimilation processes. However, the authors then gather and present evidence from U.S. census data that is static and fixed, such as race and ancestry categories, often conflating different categories along the way (see Poros 2004 for a more detailed review). Static, fixed categories are unlikely to be able to explain dynamic processes; however, the authors do not have the appropriate data on hand. Indeed, these data are hard to come by.

Thus, many network studies, including those about migration, often lack accounts of negotiated transactions that occur within networks. They do not tell us about the mechanisms or processes that occur as actors (individuals, communities, organizations, states) exchange information, money, resources, influence, persuasion, and power. To correct these problems, this study calls for three theoretical and related methodological shifts to: (1) relational accounts of social life from substantialist ones, (2) the study of relations and transactions within network analyses, and (3) a focus on relations and transactions in studies of migration. This last shift is addressed in the following section.

Social Network Theories of Migration

The sociological literature on international migration has identified social networks as a crucial aspect of migration flows and processes of economic incorporation and mobility, such as finding employment. We have known for a long time—at least since the 1918–1920 work of W. I. Thomas and Florian Znaniecki in *The Polish Peasant in Europe and America*—that migrant networks are important to the formation of chain migration flows and economic activities. Since their now classic work, network studies of migration have offered the most accurate explanations of migration flows (see Boyd 1989; Gurak and Caces 1992; Massey et al. 1987, 1998; Portes and Bach 1985; Portes and Rumbaut 1996; Tilly 1990, 1998; Tilly and Brown 1967).

The empirical evidence that has documented the effect of social networks on migration flows solves many problems with economic models of migration, which have been most prevalent in the policy arena of migration studies. The role of human capital in causing migration flows and in labor market incorporation, the issue of selectivity, and the question of migrants' destinations have been debated widely by economists and sociologists. The substantialist approaches of economists have proposed economic models that generally view migrants as rational individuals who are trying to maximize their economic prospects. Therefore, they suggest that individuals migrate to secure a higher income in a labor market that will evaluate them based on their human capital characteristics (Borjas 1990, 1999; also see Massey et al. 1998 for a review and evaluation of these theories). Following this logic, we would expect to see large flows of migrants moving from capital-poor countries to capital-rich ones. The human capital characteristics of these flows would presumably be similar in this economic account even though migrants may be, on the whole, more favorably selected than nonmigrants (Chiswick 2000). Instead, just a few developing countries send a substantial proportion of the world's immigrants to a few developed countries (Castles 2001; Faist 2000; Massey et al. 1998; Portes and Rumbaut 1996). Global migration flows, therefore, exhibit a very particular set of destinations, not simply a movement of people from poor to rich countries (Faist 2000; Sassen 1999). Network studies of migration have explained these particularities of migration flows better by showing that the destinations of immigrants most often depend on whether they have family and friends or social networks already residing in the country of immigration (Donato, Durand, and Massey 1992; Massey and Espinosa 1997). This factor then encourages the process of further chain migration. Networks become the locus not only for the ability to migrate but also for the process of adjustment to and economic incorporation in a foreign society. International migration flows are, furthermore, enormously diverse in terms of human capital across different destinations and to the same ones.

Massey and his colleagues (1998) maintain some of these criticisms of economic models in their extensive and valuable undertaking to review and evaluate the theories and empirical evidence for global systems of international migration. They criticize theories that offer solely historical-structural or individual-atomistic accounts of the causes of migration. Instead, they favor an amalgam of theories that, in combination, explain different historical cases. This amalgam, in general, begins with substantialist explanations that attempt to explain how migration begins, such as neoclassical and new economics models, dual labor market theory, and world systems theory (the latter of which Massey and his colleagues argue best explains the initiation of contemporary mass migration). For example, neoclassical models of migration contend that migration is a matter of rational, individualistic behavior. As such, migration should occur between countries with large wage differentials, and people who live in low-wage countries will find it in their interest to migrate to places where they can obtain higher wages. Or, in the view of Massey and his colleagues, world systems theories of migration have provided more empirical evidence for migration flows than neoclassical models. These theories argue that a new geography of production brought on by economic globalization has resulted in a demand for cheap labor in low-skilled service jobs that are often filled by low-skilled laborers migrating from developing countries (for example, Sassen 2001). In these theories, globalization is considered to be a fairly recent phenomenon defined by changes in economic production around the world since about the 1970s.

Massey and his colleagues (1998) then use relational accounts to explain how migration is perpetuated over time through social networks (that is, social capital theory and cumulative causation). The term *cumulative causation*, for instance, refers to the argument that international migration reproduces itself over time through the expansion of networks and a culture of migration, among other mechanisms. Each time someone migrates, the social context of subsequent migration decisions changes, so that further migration becomes more likely as the network expands, and so on. In these explanations, the authors define social networks as interpersonal relations among kin, friends, and community. In their theoretical synthesis, which combines substantialist explanations of migration that focus on the individual-level attributes of immigrants or their sending countries (as found in neoclassical and world systems theories), with relational explanations (social network theories), Massey and his colleagues do not identify causal mechanisms for the *initiation* of migration flows—only for their continuation. In fact, they say that "immigration may begin for a variety of reasons, but the forces that initiate international movement are quite different from those that perpetuate it" (Massey, Durand, and Malone 2002, 18). Their theoretical approach adds historically relevant parts of different causal models for particular sending regions or national-origin groups resulting in amalgamated explanations.

For instance, Massey and his colleagues (1998) point out that ideological links tying former colonial powers to their once-colonial subjects, such as those between the United Kingdom and India, create populations in peripheral or developing countries who already speak English, are acquainted with English customs, and are educated in English-style schools, just as we have seen with many Gujarati immigrants who migrated to East Africa and the United Kingdom. The diffusion of these ideological links then encourages migration from the peripheral, once-colonized countries to core countries. The causal mechanism identifying how this might happen, however, is missing from their example. Surely ideological links are important. They are also present in specific organizational ties that are formed between "core" and "periphery" states, as in the educated Gujaratis who were recruited by the East African High Commissions to become teachers and other kinds of civil servants. Thus, the notion of organizational ties provides a causal mechanism for thinking about how historical-structural forces actually create ties to particular migrants. Hernández-León (2008, 70) makes a similar argument in his study of the Monterey-Houston circuit of Mexican immigrants:

> Economic crisis and restructuring may be the *efficient* causes that explain the migration of these urbanites but not necessarily the *sufficient* factors that account for why and when a border-crossing move is undertaken. Individuals and families might endure declining real wages, blocked mobility opportunities, shrinking or no access to credit and insurance markets . . . But even under these circumstances, people may not resort to migration. Recruitment, the presence of pioneer migrants, the availability of facilitating networks, and the pressures of an expanding household are often necessary for migration to occur.

Furthermore, both economic and world systems models focus solely on labor migrants and have yet to show how extensive is the relationship between migration and economic globalization because virtually everyone is assumed to be first and foremost a labor migrant. More importantly, neither has provided adequate evidence to explain the selectivity of migration flows, especially for professional or high skilled migrants. In other words, although it seems quite obvious that migrants take into account and even prioritize the potential for economic gain through migration, why is it that more people with similar characteristics to migrants do not migrate? Neither of these theories also accounts for the complexity of political, social, and cultural forces that interact with economic ones, such as in the migration of refugees and asylum-seekers or social obligations to family so commonly cited as reasons for migration.

A fully relational approach can instead incorporate historical context into its explanation of migration and locate causal mechanisms of migration that can better explain migrant selectivity for many different migration flows. In other words, a relational approach shows how historical, geographical, political, and economic context can affect the formation of certain types of social ties that in turn encourage migration and different types of migrant streams. In this way, relational explanations can also account for the ways in which states, for instance, fail or succeed in their intended regulation of migration flows through policy making.[2] Organizational ties link the state and its agents to particular migrants, initiating flows that can be traced historically. The immigration literature has recently renewed its awareness of such organizational ties, though most often as community-based organizations (CBOs) and other associations formed or dominated by immigrants (for example, Chung 2005; Cordero-Guzmán 2005; Schrover and Vermeulen 2005). The concept of organizational ties explicated in this book, in contrast, includes ties to native and host state organizations or agencies in addition to immigrant organization ties.

Therefore, although network theories of migration have offered the most empirical evidence to explain migration flows, they have still conceptualized networks in a fairly narrow way. The role and meaning of networks as they affect migration have been taken for granted, in part because migration flows have often been conceptualized in terms of the character of time and space inherent in the flow. Different "types" of migrants have been identified on this basis—often indicating multiple kinds of characteristics and motivations. For example, the terms *sojourner* and *settler* describe the permanence (time) of migration. Sojourners temporarily migrate to a new destination, while settlers move more permanently. Circular, chain, and transnational highlight the spatial characteristics of migration flows. Circular migration is often used to describe migrants who may move to several different destinations before returning "home" to begin the cycle again. This type of movement is common among some agricultural or seasonal workers, for instance, who move in accordance with the demands of their work—for example, Mexicans who move up the Pacific Coast from California to Washington state and even Canada and back down again (Basok 2003; Massey et al. 2002). Historically, circular migration was also common within Europe among young female domestic workers, male artisans, and agricultural workers from the 1600s to the 1800s (Moch 1992). Chain migration, as already discussed, is the movement of people from one destination to another "one by one" or as part of a chain of connected interpersonal others (Massey et al. 1987; Tilly 1990). Finally, transnational migration refers to the movement, activity, and often settlement of migrants across two or more places, suggesting multiple lives across international borders (Glick-Schiller 1992; Levitt 2001; Portes, Guarnizo, and Haller 2002; Smith 2006; Vertovec 2009).

Still other studies emphasize one aspect of migrants—labor migrants, asylum-seekers, high-tech workers, low-skill, or high-skill. Even though social networks have been clearly established as an important mechanism that encourages migration for all these "types," the network characteristics, or the quality of the network ties that actually drive migrant streams, are not typically used to conceptualize those streams.[3] This reluctance in the literature is a result of the combination of relational and substantialist explanations used to explain migration flows as network theories become problematic when they revert to substantialist assumptions.

Several theoretical and methodological problems with social network theories of migration illustrate more strongly why the combination of substantialist and relational approaches is insufficient as a theoretical model. Current theories tend to have at least one of three problems: the definition of the network; the assumption of coethnic solidarity in migrant networks; and the specification of boundaries, particularly of ethnic ones, within networks. In the following pages, I consider the sociological literature on migration and social network theory to discuss each in turn.

What Is a Network?

Massey and his colleagues (1998, 42) define migrant networks as "sets of interpersonal ties that connect migrants, former migrants, and non-migrants in origin and destination areas through ties of kinship, friendship, and shared community of origin." In research studies on social networks, social ties are typically defined in terms of similar interpersonal labels, such as friend, relative, or neighbor, and/or by the frequency and quality of contact.[4] For instance, Krackhardt (1992) defines these strong "philos" types of ties by interaction, affection, and time. These labels and measures can be ambiguous, however. Not all "friends" are the same. For instance, a workplace friend might be a quite different kind of tie from a childhood friend. Furthermore, if my childhood friend lives in India and I live in New York, frequency of contact is probably not a sufficient measure for the strength of this tie because the quality of the ties might not be affected by physical distance even if the frequency of contact may be. For migrant networks, this measure is especially faulty because migrants, by definition, are very likely to have networks that span at least two countries.

Distinguishing ties based on the channel through which the two nodes of a tie are related, for example the way that two people meet or the organizational context of a relationship, helps to correct for some of these ambiguities. Krissman (2005), for instance, argues that the "migrant network" fails to explain international migration. However, his criticism rests on a conventional definition of networks that is made up solely of interpersonal ties. Recognition of organizational and composite ties can account for the actors he complains have been ignored in migration studies. Distinguishing ties based on the organizational context of a relationship also clarifies why some ties are strong (and tend to generate trust) while others are weak (and generate new information) (Granovetter 1973). The channels through which people know and relate to each other, at least initially, organize social ties in terms of mutual relations or interests, for example a mother and daughter, a supervisor and workers, or a university department faculty. Using this logic, I have crudely distinguished these ties as interpersonal and organizational ties. Obviously, interpersonal ties of friendship and family exist within organizations (Heimer 1992). However, I am arguing here that organizational ties are distinctive in that they refer to the mediating structure of the organization, where colleagues, co-workers, supervisors, government bureaucrats, and even friends, family, and acquaintances relate to each other. For instance, the relationship between two friends, who are respectively a secretary and a paralegal in a law firm, is shaped by their differential status in that organizational hierarchy—quite unlike two friends who meet and associate as neighbors. Thus, neighbors are more like interpersonal ties whereas workplace "friends" are organizational ties.

Examples of organizational ties, therefore, are to others in firms, schools or universities, cultural institutes, and government or state agencies.[5] Ties to people in these organizations encourage migration in various ways. Organizations actively recruit their own members and outsiders to work, live, or study abroad. Individuals pursue overseas opportunities that become known to them through organizations. Meyer and Brown (1999), for instance, identified at least forty knowledge networks, much like the professional organizations of Indians discussed in Chapter 4, in over thirty countries that link countries to their high-skill nationals in the diaspora. Formal aids to labor recruitment that exist within organizations, such as interviewing for overseas jobs or taking professional certification exams in sending countries, are also common. In fact, entire industries have recently sprung up to facilitate the international circulation of labor in the form of "body shopping." These agencies arrange for employment contracts, visas and work permits, travel, and even housing to supply Western countries with high-tech labor, much of it from India (Aneesh 2000; Biao 2006). They are just one example of a larger migration industry, which includes entrepreneurs who provide a variety of services to many types of migrants, that has developed to capitalize on large-scale migration flows (Castles 2007; Hernández-León 2008).

In other cases, such as family businesses, these interpersonal and organizational relations overlap in such a way that they are indistinguishable or inseparable from each other. For example, the president of a family firm might have his or her children or other relatives each manage separate branches of the firm. A married couple may own and operate a business together. These are composite types of ties that are distinct from interpersonal or organizational ties alone because the relations within composite ties are mediated by the organization and family or community together as a single entity. Such distinctions have significant and differential consequences for migration flows because interpersonal, organizational, and composite ties regulate network relations differently. These distinctions also give meaning to networks. They ask us to look at what kinds of relationships make up social ties and what kinds of transactions pass through those ties in migrant networks.

The Problem of Ethnicity and Coethnic Solidarity

In addition to the differences discussed in the preceding section in networks characterized by interpersonal, organizational, and composite ties, we still face the question of ethnicity in shaping solidary networks and the opportunities and constraints created by those relations. Network theories of migration have generally viewed networks as a form of social capital—"the ability of actors to secure benefits by virtue of membership in social networks or other social structures" (Portes 1998, 6; also see Portes 2000)—or as the embodiment of social capital (Bashi 2007; Faist 2000; Massey et al. 1998). Such migrant networks are often based on coethnicity. Thus, membership by virtue of coethnicity is thought to grant one access to the tangible and intangible benefits of network-mediated social capital, which can aid socioeconomic incorporation in the host country. In particular, social capital can be converted into other (positive) forms of capital, such as economic capital in the form of migrant remittances (Massey et al. 1998). Although some migration researchers have acknowledged and documented the constraints of belonging to such networks (see Faist 2000 on "negative" social capital; Kyle 2000; Levitt 2001;

Mahler 1995, Menjívar 2000; Portes 1998; Portes and Sensenbrenner 1993), the question of whether and how these networks become solidary is open to further investigation.

In most migration studies, the concept of social capital essentially substitutes for network dynamics. The dominant view is that coethnicity is an ideology of solidarity. For instance, in their comprehensive work on ethnic economies Light and Gold (2000, 108) argue that "ethnic solidarity transcend[s] class boundaries, uniting groups marked by different class positions and interests." Similarly, Waldinger, in his earlier work (1995, 1996), viewed coethnicity as a proxy for mutual trust and predictability. Thus, in his illuminating studies of ethnic industrial niches in New York City, he argues that niches are built on coethnic solidarity. In later work, Waldinger and Lichter (2003) introduce the notions of social closure and exclusionary closure to illustrate how outsiders are excluded from economic exchanges among members of an in-group. The more dense the ethnic or migrant network, the more likely outsiders will be excluded.

Coethnicity, of course, can and frequently does provide a form of solidarity. After all, the entire phenomenon of ethnic economies is the outcome of more or less cooperative relations between coethnics (see Light and Gold 2000), relations that often include positive and negative interactions involving generosity, affection, social obligations, negotiation, conflict, resistance, and even capitulation. Korean grocers and Indian newsagents, for example, create and reproduce ethnic ownership economies, where they are self-employed and employ other coethnics, while serving a wider consumer base (for example, Min 2008). Ethnic enclave economies are another example. In these cases, ownership, employment, and a consumer base are integrated on the basis of coethnicity. Think of Little Havana in Miami, the Chinatowns of San Francisco and London, or New York's Little Italy.

Less apparent in these accounts of how migrant networks aid or hurt economic incorporation are the relations that contribute to unequal status *within* coethnic networks where in-groups may not only be defined by broad notions of ethnicity. Inequalities that are played out within migrant networks have important consequences for the distribution of power, influence, and important tangible resources, especially money and information. Studies that document economic behavior based on an ideology of solidarity held by coethnics leave us to wonder about which coethnics were excluded from the network mechanisms that aided employment in ethnic economies or in ethnic niche employment. Why and how were they excluded? We cannot assume that co-ethnic resources are equally accessible or equally distributed to members of a network—resources that can make the difference between migrating or not and in deciding whether to open a business, get a job, or marry into a particular family. In fact, throughout this book we have found much evidence to the contrary that will allow us to answer the question of how inequality is expressed in a network based on coethnicity.

One might look to network research in economic sociology to address this problem. From economic sociology we know that economic action is embedded in larger social structures, with social networks among the most significant of those structures (Granovetter 1985, 1995; Smelser and Swedberg 1994). Landing a job, borrowing money to start a business, and similar types of economic behavior often depend on one's social ties (often consisting of friends and family) rather than institutionalized mechanisms (Granovetter 1974; Grieco 1987; Tilly and Tilly 1998). Network studies have focused on measures of network structure, such as density, range, prominence, multiplexity, structural equivalence, cliques, brokerage, and the like (see Burt 1982; Burt and Minor 1983; and Emirbayer and Goodwin 1994 for a glossary of those terms) to illustrate the unequal positions of actors within a network. They have described networks with stunning complexity to show, for instance, where the most central actors are located or how extensive the reach of those actors is. These studies, however, have paid less attention to the content of network ties (transactions) that shows us what that inequality is made of. For instance, what resources, information, or influence is exchanged between these unequal positions in a given network, and what are the consequences? As Stinchcombe (1989, 125–126) persuasively argues, we need to integrate

> our theories of the macro-structure of networks with the causal processes ensuing in the micro-structure of those networks that fuel social relations. People's rationality and sentiments are likely to be mobilized by social relations that are close and intense. If we have a network science that ignores that fact it will be largely a mathematical and statistical exercise, rather than social science.

Or, in Emirbayer's (1997, 305) words, network analysis "too often privileges spatiality (or topological location) over temporality and narrative unfolding."

Thomas Faist (2000) recognizes the problems of what networks mean and of the absence of transactions in network studies of migration. He argues that network theory uses circuitous reasoning in its claim that networks are the crucial mechanism causing migration. Instead, Faist contends that networks are formed by a process in which transactions form clusters of social and symbolic ties, which develop into networks. Although social ties involve continuous transactions, the resources that arise from both social and symbolic ties represent social capital embodied in networks. This focus on transactions within ties improves our understanding of what networks are made of and how they are activated for different types of action. However, Faist (2001, 101) also emphasizes the interpersonal dimension of social ties as a "continuing series of interpersonal transactions to which participants attach shared interests, obligations, expectations, and norms."

Thus, network studies of migration need to reach beyond identifying instances where networks are seen as enabling or constraining for migration prospects or for particular opportunities for mobility. We need to begin to understand how social ties and the transactions within those ties shape and change unequal relations that can, for example, affect migrant selectivity, result in different migration streams, or affect labor market outcomes over time. Although the language of networks (as a metaphor, for instance) is an effective way of expressing and examining these relations, in themselves, networks do not cause migration or mobility, as is so often expressed in the migration literature. Ties and transactions give meaning to networks. Different configurations of relations among people shape migration and social and economic mobility. Categories such as ethnicity are relational and call out to be treated as empirical questions rather than assumed to be stable and fixed much of the time.

The Problem of Boundaries

Concurrent with the problem of coethnic networks as networks of solidarity is the problem of boundaries (Barth 1969; Brubaker 2004). In Barth's now-classic work on *Ethnic Groups and Boundaries*, he calls for a shift in the study of ethnicity to examining not what is inside the box of ethnicity—for example, customs, rituals, language, food, symbols, and so on—that makes up differences between ethnic groups but rather to study how the boundaries around a group are formed and therefore differentiate one group from another. In other words, he asks that we understand how boundaries are made and how they change, thus making our study of ethnicity acknowledge the dynamic processes inherent in ethnic groups. Reflecting on Barth, where do we draw analytical boundaries around networks or observable relations? All social science analysis creates categories or boundaries in order to produce measurable variables. Age cohorts, race and ethnic groups, gender, and class status are typical of these kinds of variables. However, we need to know the validity of those boundaries that represent static realities and to capture how those boundaries change if we are to obtain valid data on migration or any other social phenomenon. Many studies of migration treat coethnicity at the level of national or sometimes regional identities. Further analysis then leads migration researchers to describe other internal divisions, such as class, gender, religion, language and even ethnicity. Bozorgmehr's (1997) concept of internal ethnicity, for instance, has been important in demonstrating that nationality groups are not monolithic but are divided internally. However, even these divisions are often then treated as static categories. Similarly, in network analysis, drawing boundaries around networks reifies categories or individual attributes. One solution to this problem from social network analysis has been proposed by Breiger, who suggests that researchers make reflexive the problem of boundary specification within the frame of relational analysis. "Boundaries are [then] played off against boundaries defined by relations" (in Emirbayer 1997, 303). This approach makes the existence of boundaries an empirical question rather than a given essence, category, substance, or variable. I have adopted this approach by labeling and analyzing networks according to the boundaries that the participants indicated to me but also by examining how those boundaries really operate in the narratives of the participants and the narratives of their networks. At what level do they result in solidarity? At what level and for what purposes do people identify with the boundaries/networks that they are part of?

For example, Raj, whom we met along with his wife Parvati in previous chapters, experiences many levels of ethnic affiliation. At the level of the nation-state, Raj was born in Uganda as a British subject and holds British citizenship. His ancestry is Indian. At the regional level, his family hails from the Kheda district of Gujarat state in western India. He is Hindu. He speaks Gujarati and practices Gujarati Hindu customs. He belongs to the Patidar caste. Within Patidars, he is from the Panch gam circle of villages that define endogamous relations. He is married to a woman from the Cha gam marriage circle, an intermarriage because Cha gam females are not permitted to "marry down" without suffering a loss in status. He lives with his wife, two children, and mother in a working-class East London neighborhood. His next immediate kin live in India, Britain, the United States, and Canada.

Citizenship, residence, region of origin, religion, language, caste, subcaste, and kinship describe different levels of Raj's ethnicity and access to different kinds of networks. Where should I draw the lines around Raj's networks? Raj describes himself at all of these different levels, but mostly he identifies himself with the Patidar caste. However, Raj does not have real relations with all Patidars, although Patidars do maintain a collective imagination around their caste group, what we might call symbolic ties. My answer to the problem, then, had to consider all of these many levels of ethnicity that describe Raj's identity and simultaneously the actual relations or social ties that Raj uses as a basis for action in his life. This distinction allows us to understand how coethnicity operates in Raj's networks of social ties.

If we consider two major events in Raj's life, migration as a refugee from Uganda to London and owning a business, Raj's life history shows that the British government and close and extended kin provided tangible resources related to these events. Raj and his family migrated with the help of the Uganda Resettlement Board of the British government (organizational tie), which accepted their refugee status and placed them in refugee camps that were established after the expulsion of Asians by Idi Amin in 1972. A cousin (interpersonal tie) then housed Raj and his family after only one week's stay in those camps. Some years later, after his father's death, Raj also inherited his father's shop. Raj's more symbolic relations with Patidars, Hindus, Gujaratis, and Indians did not manifest themselves in the transactions that resulted in Raj's migration or business ownership. Therefore, in these two specific events, we can know that kinship ties and organizational ties based on citizenship status were the most significant determinants of Raj's mobility, rather than assuming an instrumental or positive role for his many levels of coethnic relations.

Models that use individual attributes, such as class, gender, caste, region of origin, religion, human capital, and the like, to predict migration, therefore, misspecify the causal mechanisms of migration. Although these markers do connect people to particular interpersonal networks, they obscure the structure of relationships within ties that drives migration. For example, among Gujaratis, who make strong claims to network solidarity based on one or more of the previously listed markers (such as Raj, depicted in the preceding paragraphs), we can see very unequal transactions between ties that affect selectivity and that may lead to inferior job opportunities, forced social obligations, and so on. Because the types of social ties and transactions within those ties vary across similar networks and similarly categorized people within networks, inequalities are more likely to be produced through configurations of relations rather than static characteristics. This is apparent even between kin relations, for instance in the case of Jagdish and Pravin, who are cousins.

Jagdish and Pravin migrated within eight years of each other in the 1950s to East Africa (Jagdish to Uganda and Pravin to Tanzania) after finishing their college educations in India. Pravin migrated first after he answered an advertisement that was placed by a representative of the Tanzanian High Commission for a teaching job in Tanzania (organizational tie). Jagdish migrated via an arranged marriage (interpersonal tie) to a woman whose family lived in Uganda. Her uncle worked for a prominent Indian industrial firm, where Jagdish was given an entry-level job. During the movement for African political independence in both countries, Pravin migrated for a second time—to London—with only a few interpersonal ties to some friends from Tanzania. Four years later, Jagdish also migrated to London as a result of a promotion and the transfer of a part of his firm's operations to London. Jagdish's organizational ties to that firm helped him to establish himself and his family in a stable, middle-class, London suburb. In contrast, the rupture of Pravin's organizational ties and his few interpersonal ties in London afforded him only an inferior job (relative to his human capital qualifications) and a modest home in a working-class South Asian neighborhood in East London. Although Jagdish and Pravin are part of the same kinship network and hold similar levels of human capital, their markedly different status in London (formed through the different configurations of ties in their migration and work histories) has deeply affected the conditions of their transactions and their differential socioeconomic incorporation.[6]

The relational approach to networks, then, provides a framework for explaining how power and inequality are expressed within social ties in coethnic networks.

A Relational Account of Migration and Migrant Networks

A relational approach to migration and migrant networks can account for the three major weaknesses of network theories of migration described above: the problems of network definition, coethnic solidarity, and boundary specification. By examining and redefining networks as (1) configurations of social ties or relations and (2) transactions within those ties, we can understand the elements that give meaning to networks as they shape migration. We can further see how relations change in the process of negotiation over crucial resources or positions of power and status.

Migration, therefore, is a relational act. It shapes networks; it creates possibilities for new networks, and it changes relations within old and new social ties. The interaction between configurations of social ties and migration, then, is a reciprocal causal process. Configurations of ties cause certain types of migration, and migration streams produce and reproduce networks that affect migrant's physical, social, and economic mobility. Constraints on mobility are ironically set by existing network ties, more so than *but not instead of* human capital, individual attributes, wage differentials between countries, immigration policies, socioeconomic contexts of receiving countries, racial discrimination, and so on. This claim extends prior theories of migration that emphasize networks and relations and that can be read as implicitly or partially relational. See, for example, studies by Bashi (2007), Grieco (1987), Hernández-León (2008), Julca (1997), Kyle (2000), Levitt (2001), Massey et al. (1987), Portes (1995), Smith (2006), and Werbner (1989). It also builds on those theories by providing an account and a method for how individual attributes and historical context are part of the process of shaping network ties that encourage migration, rather than adding variables to account for historical particularities of specific cases.

To rid us of substantialist assumptions and explanations in network theories of migration and to specify what a relational migration looks like, it seems useful to develop a typology of migration streams based on social ties. We can then use the typology to think about how configurations of social ties (interpersonal, organizational, and composite) can explain variation within and between migrant networks among other immigrant groups in the world.

Types of Migration Streams

Roughly four ideal types of migration streams can be distinguished according to their different configurations of ties: solitaries, chains, recruits, and trusties (see Table 5.1).[7] These types of flows are not mutually exclusive. For example, as network ties change, flows of recruits and trusties can become chains. Some chains can also become trusties. These ideal types, then, can work together, as they can be represented simultaneously in different configurations within households or larger networks or in sequence when networks change from one type to another. Although these four types are admittedly crude categories, we can see regularities within each type in terms of migrant selectivity and, in some instances, for socioeconomic outcomes in the host society.

Table 5.1 Typology of migration flows.

Migration flow	Social tie type	Examples
Solitaries	None	Rare (e.g., first two Oswal Jains migrated to Kenya in 1899)
Chains	Interpersonal (e.g., kin, friends, community affiliations)	Formal sponsorship by kin via family visas; informal sponsorship of kin, friends, and community members
Recruits	Organizational; ties to individuals in firms, schools or universities, cultural institutes, government agencies, employment agencies, non-governmental organizations, refugee organizations	Transnational corporations (TNC) employee transfers; labor recruitment (e.g., software engineers, teachers, low-skilled workers, guestworkers, domestic workers); students; asylees/refugees
Trusties	Composite; interpersonal and organizational ties overlap (e.g., in family firms and businesses)	Transnational traders (e.g., diamond trade, garment industry; import/export trades)

Solitaries

Solitaries have no prior ties. A lack of ties leads to little or no migration because international migration is costly and risky. Accounts of individuals migrating without the help of interpersonal, organizational, or composite ties in the home or host countries are rare. Accounts of solitaries are typically narrated through oral histories, written and oral biographies, and other materials that are difficult to corroborate with additional sources of evidence. For instance, Banks (1994) reports that the first two Oswal Jains migrated to Kenya in 1899 after the onset of a devastating drought and famine in their region of Gujarat. These two Oswals were probably solitary migrants. They may have, therefore, provided ties to Kenya as the famine became severe for many agricultural families and as they began to migrate out of the Jamnagar region. Because we often lack reliable evidence on solitaries, it is difficult to know with certainty how rare they are relative to the other types described below. Theoretically, however, they should exist.

Solitaries should not be confused with pioneers. That is, not all pioneers are solitaries as commonly assumed. Although pioneers are often thought to have migrated without ties, they often have weak ties to organizations such as universities or governmental agencies and thus resemble recruits. For instance, students commonly report using organizations, such as the U.S.

Agency for International Development and other U.S. governmental representatives to obtain information and aid on migrating and applying to American universities. Those universities then provide an immediate basis for new organizational ties in the host society. Even refugees are directed to particular destinations by governmental and nongovernmental organizations. These types of migrants are not solitaries because they migrate with some ties to their destination. Therefore, the migration of solitaries, those with no ties, is very rare.

Chains

Chains have interpersonal ties. Chains represent the most common form of migration. Chains are formed through interpersonal ties that control the process of migrant selection according to personal relations and social obligations to kin and community, not according to the formal requirements of organizations. Thus, chains typically migrate with the help of family, friends, and coethnics who already reside in the host country. Many of these individuals migrate on a family visa, under immigration provisions for the spouses and children of permanent residents, the most numerous and common visa category in many countries. Some chains also migrate illegally or with temporary visas, such as tourist visas, with the expectation of informal sponsorship by kin, friends, and community members, who promise aid with jobs, housing, and social support. Examples of migrations to the United States that are generally dominated by formal and informal chains are Azuayan Ecuadorans (Kyle 2000), Peruvians (Julca 1997), Mexicans and some Cubans (Massey et al. 1987; Portes and Bach 1985), Salvadorans (Mahler 1995), and West Indians (Bashi 2007).[8] In Europe, (as guest worker systems become chains of family reunification) portions of Turkish migration to Germany and the Netherlands (Musterd and Ostendorf 1996; Soysal 1994; van Amersfoort 1995), Albanians to Italy and Greece (King 2005), and Sylheti Bangladeshis to Britain (Ballard 2001) are dominated by these formal and informal chain mechanisms.[9]

Recruits

Recruits have organizational ties. Those ties generally lead to the migration of professionals, students, and recruited low-skilled labor. However, recruited professionals depend more heavily on organizational ties than do most other recruits. Organizational ties play a critical role in controlling the process of selectivity for recruits, especially for recruited professionals. The migration of recruited professionals is dependent on organizational requirements, such as educational degrees, certification, and licensing (see also Waldinger 1999). The help of friends or family is secondary to these requirements for migration except where those friends or family can broker the organizational ties between destinations.

In Bashi's (2007, 81) study of West Indians in New York and London, for instance, one participant, Taran, migrated to New York "as a nurse when she was recruited from her Trinidadian nursing school to a first job at a hospital in Brooklyn." She then helped to sponsor a childhood friend when she asked a doctor in her hospital if he needed a maid. He did not, but his doctor-friend did, thus assuring Taran's friend a job on arrival. Another participant, Randall, explained how his wife was also sponsored by the hospital that hired her, and then she subsequently sponsored him: "When my wife came I think she went straight to the hospital that sponsored her. They didn't have a relative or anything like that" (103). Bashi describes Taran and Randall's wife as typical hubs in her study—central actors who play crucial roles in selecting and sponsoring others for migration. She also describes them as "pioneers—that is, persons who arrive without the help of a network" (103). However, they are clearly not solitaries. They had organizational ties to schools and workplaces that facilitated their migration. They then used their position to sponsor interpersonal others (those that Bashi calls spokes), such as Taran's friend and Randall. Multiplied dozens of times, these initial flows of recruits become chains.

Students often follow a similar path as recruited professionals by using organizational ties to faculty and classmates in their universities to pursue advanced degrees or to seek employment after finishing their degrees. Although students enter most countries as temporary migrants (that is, they are expected to return to their home countries after completing their degree), many stay in the host country by changing their visa status or by overstaying their student visas (see U.S. Department of Education 1997). Changing visa status has also been a recent trend in Germany, as about 21 percent of foreign students in German universities were granted green cards as IT specialists in 2000.[10]

Flows of recruited low-skilled labor (such as guest worker systems), which initially resemble recruited professionals, quickly begin to resemble chains because human capital requirements for their recruitment are low. Once employers recruit some low-skilled labor from a foreign country, they can lower their transaction costs by relying on those migrants to then informally recruit family, friends, and community members to live and work with them.

Pierette Hondagneu-Sotelo, in her 2001 study of Latina immigrant domestic workers in Los Angeles, draws a contrast in the way that different states have recruited these workers. Canada, for instance, put into place a formal recruitment mechanism since 1981 in which it recruited women, mostly from the Caribbean and the Philippines, to work as live-in domestics for two years to qualify for "landed" or permanent immigrant status. Since the 1970s, Hong Kong has had a similar recruitment process for live-in domestics, again mostly from the Philippines but also from other parts of Asia. Its program regulated the workers through formal employment agencies, employers, and government policies. Hondagneu-Sotelo tells us that many fewer Latina women have been recruited to work as domestics in the United States this way. Although initially some private employers, such as diplomatic families or others vacationing or working in Central and Latin America, personally recruited women by sponsoring their immigration and labor certification, many came to the United States via other routes and were then informally "recruited" to work as domestics by other migrant domestic workers. Thus, while Canada and Hong Kong seem to have had formal flows of recruits that lasted longer, in the United States such flows quickly became chains.

Asylees/refugees and smuggled migrants also roughly belong in this category. Although they are not recruited in the same sense as labor, they do migrate through networks of organizational ties (governmental and nongovernmental agencies) that are often set up to aid their flight from their home countries and resettlement into new host societies. Many refugees and smuggled migrants have interpersonal ties that also aid their migration, but those interpersonal ties will not suffice in the case of recruits. Organizational ties are necessary for their migration. For instance, in some cases of human smuggling across borders, friends or family in the destination country will send money to a broker, who pays the coyote who will guide potential migrants across borders. Because some migrants know that they cannot obtain a legal visa or claim asylum successfully, they are at the mercy of smuggling organizations composed of coyotes and usurious middlemen until they reach their destination. At their destination, they are aided by kin or friends, often those same individuals who lent them money for their perilous journey. Kyle and Koslowski (2001), for example, provide an analysis of different organizational networks that operate such global human smuggling operations in their book *Global Human Smuggling*. In that volume, David Spener documents four different types of smugglers: (1) *pateros*, who linger around the U.S.–Mexico border, waiting to usher migrants across it; (2) local-interior coyotes, who are usually known by those in the sending region and may lead migrants from the start to end point of their journey; (3) friends and kin, who also may lead migrants across the border and who are waiting on the U.S. side to help with assistance; and (4) border commercial smugglers, who may range from kin and community relations and who may move small groups of migrants from their hometowns, to large-scale commercial smugglers unknown to the migrants. In all of these cases, whether friends and family are involved in the smuggling process or not—and they often are, Spener tells us—smugglers are a kind of organizational tie. A potential migrant needs to get connected to a *patero*, coyote, or smuggling organization, whether through friends or in some other manner, to cross the U.S.–Mexico border without authorization. However, obviously not just any friend or relative can provide this link.

Asylum seekers are often subject to human smuggling when they cannot claim political refugee status through formal organizations, such as the International Rescue Committee or the International Red Cross. Crisp (1999) notes that refugees often migrate to countries where they have interpersonal ties to help them settle and to pay for their journey. In contrast, de facto political refugees (asylees) are relocated and resettled with the formal assistance of international nongovernmental and governmental bodies.

Trusties

Trusties have composite (interpersonal overlapping with organizational) ties, as in dense multiplex networks (see Portes 1995). Composite ties lead to entrepreneurial migration and are very few compared to chains and recruits. Portes and his colleagues (2002), for instance, estimate that transnational entrepreneurs make up less than 10 percent of their sample of Dominican, Colombian, and Salvadoran migrants. The lack of external mechanisms for monitoring and enforcement in these networks (such as those that exist for recruits) makes economic activities riskier for trusties. For instance, in high-stakes activities such as the transnational diamond trade, the selectivity of migrants and the monitoring of their behavior occur within dense networks of composite ties, some of which control the recruitment of labor through social obligations between network members, not according to human capital characteristics (Poros 2001 and Chapters 3 and 4). Many Chinese networks of transnational traders and businesspeople resemble trusties (see Ong 1997, 1999). For instance, Aiwha Ong describes the strategies of elite Hong Kong Chinese as families who participate in decades-long itineraries shaped by a mix of strategies that stagger the departures of children, expand entrepreneurial activities overseas, and relocate members and homes in choice locations abroad . . . thus strategies of Chinese emigration are driven by a mix of economic and political reasons that express not merely entrepreneurial savvy but also the professional and cultural competence to maneuver in global settings. (Ong 1997, 93, 95)

These Chinese entrepreneurs involve *guanxi* networks and regimes that emphasize gender and age hierarchies, interpersonal dependence, and other practices that organize transnational trade and industries in which they are invested. In a very different example, Kyle (2000) describes the networks of Otavalan Ecuadorans, who tour the world playing and selling their authenticated native music. Their composite ties as entrepreneurial musicians who are also friends and, sometimes, family members from the region of Otavalo, overlap producing dense networks that control who migrates as part of their entrepreneurial endeavor.

I have described these four ideal types (solitaries, chains, recruits, and trusties) as a first attempt at establishing a relational account of migration, which describes migration streams according to the various elements of social ties that drive those streams. While social networks cause migration in a reciprocal causal process, the typology tells us about which specific social ties cause specific kinds of migration flows. Relational mechanisms within those social ties bring about differences in mobility, for instance, and other kinds of inequalities. These relational mechanisms have not been specified very systematically in this study; however, future research using the relational approach as a foundation for understanding migrant network processes may go further in doing so. The methodological implications for adopting this approach are considerable. We need a method that will illuminate configurations of social ties and transactions within ties. Those implications have been discussed in Chapter 1.

Conclusion

These comparative illustrations of migrant streams point to the importance of configurations of social ties and transactions within ties in explaining international migration. It is only when relations between individuals, sets of individuals (for example, households, families) and organizations are put into play with each other through transactions that migration occurs. Although much of the migration scholarship implicitly suggests that migration occurs in this relational way, those studies still hold on to many aspects of individual-level, substance-over-transaction sorts of analyses that are concretized in variables such as gender, class, race, ethnicity, religion, and the like. Here, I have tried to make explicit the significance of a relational account of migration, a process that unfolds within the relations and transactions of actors, not because of individual-level characteristics or entities. The relational approach addresses some of the problems inherent in past theories of migration. The role and meaning of networks becomes clearer by defining and analyzing networks in terms of different types of social ties, their configurations, and the transactions that occur within them. In this way, we can actually see relations change in the process of negotiation over crucial resources or positions of power and status. A relational account of migration and migrant networks also addresses the problem of coethnicity as an ideology of solidarity. By comparing the categorical boundaries of coethnicity with the relations and transactions that occur within those boundaries, we can identify the contours and practices of solidarity and, of course, inclusion in and exclusion from opportunities for mobility.

Equally compelling, the relational approach to migration can explain similar patterns in migration streams across geographic sites and time periods. Thus, we can see how guest worker programs in mid- to late-twentieth-century Europe, for example, resemble indentured labor migrants in the mid- to late nineteenth century as those streams of recruits became chains. Or we can understand how the underdevelopment of organizational ties between Indian IT workers and English and German firms has resulted in a slow trickle of those workers to Britain and Germany, while the United States has a backlog of Indian IT workers waiting for high-skill H1-B visas. And we can explain why some Korean, Cuban, or Lebanese immigrants are stuck in low positions in ethnic enclaves despite the apparent benefits of working in those ethnic economies or why some of those immigrants never make it at all into such entrepreneurial positions.

Fortunately, much of the evidence for a relational account of migration and migrant networks is already present in existing migration research. A small leap toward the relational approach could rid us of the patchwork theory and lack of consensus that presently characterize the field of international migration.

6 Immigration in a New Century

Implications of the Relational Approach to Migration

In today's context of globalization, governments and corporations both import immigrants for specific types of work and export jobs overseas in search of cheaper labor. This seeming contradiction creates a contentious popular discourse in which immigrants of all kinds are often scapegoated when native workers no longer find it easy to reap the benefits of a capitalist economy. The picture is far more complex than this apparently zero-sum game. As in the research of other sociologists, such as Roger Waldinger, we see that Indians occupy significant economic niches or concentrations in a relatively small number of industries or occupations. In some cases, this phenomenon does mean that Indians have taken native jobs. However, they have also filled labor shortages in response to recruitment by the American and British governments. And they have stimulated economic growth by creating jobs and revitalizing urban neighborhoods as part of their ethnic economies. Migrating to New York and London and hoarding opportunities in economic niches occur when Indians mobilize their social networks for these activities. Even then, such hoarding comes with exclusion and inequalities *within* networks and immigrant groups, not only between them.

The relational approach allows us to see these inequalities because it focuses on transactions and exchange within social ties rather than static categories. More generally, the life histories documented in Chapters 3 and 4 challenge assumptions about the economic basis of migration and free labor markets, a point worth reemphasizing in the persistent debate between economics and sociology. Economic theories and more broadly substantialist theories of migration and migrant employment in both economics and sociology assume the rationality of both individual migrants and the markets within which they work. They do so even though they portray immigrants from less developed countries as rooted in traditional societies and practices and as struggling to become modernized as immigrants in developed countries. These ideas about modernity also portray Western societies as somehow fully modern and thus absent of "irrational" practices, unlike traditional societies. These ideas are common for instance in the Orientalist literatures about the East (Masuzawa 2005; Said 1979). The life histories of Gujarati Indians presented in this book, however, illustrate that no great chasm exists between developed and developing countries. Immigrants do not simply imagine abstractly where in the world they might like to migrate in search of a better life based on differences in wages or economic advantages, as in most economic theories of migration. Network ties form across developed and developing countries to create migration flows. Migration is also not simply or only a result of the economic and political dependency of developing countries in the world capitalist system. Possibilities for migration are shaped by preexisting historical ties that have been formed through specific relations that account for the multifaceted nature of migration as an economic, political, historical, and sociocultural phenomenon. These social networks produce highly selective flows of migrants to New York and London. They are made up of ties not only to family, kin, and community, but also to institutions, organizations, and states. Migrants' relations within these network ties drive migration flows, the linking of local labor markets, and the formation of and change in economic niches.

Globalized relations within these networks are not always a new phenomenon brought on by modern capitalist relations, although surely modern capitalism has its place in these relations and migrant flows. Globalization is apparent in historical trade relations, as with the centuries-old diamond trade. The garment trade has been centered in India for several hundred years and still prevails today, even though it lost much of its primacy to the British during and after Britain's colonial conquest of India. Even after World War II and India's independence, a time when globalization is thought to have contracted in much of the world, educated Indians were being recruited as civil servants in Britain's East African colonies and as low-skilled labor in Britain, and, eventually in the 1960s and 1970s, as scientists and engineers in the United States and as physicians and other health care providers in the United States and Britain. More recent globalized relations have resulted in the exchange of students, high-tech labor, and so-called knowledge workers. Of course, many Indians have migrated outside of any global labor relations, for instance as refugees from Uganda and most prominently as family reunification migrants. Nevertheless, "labor migration" dominates the discourse of migration everywhere because even family reunification migrants, asylum seekers, and refugees must eventually work to sustain themselves and their families in a new society.

These globalized relations should not be viewed (simply or at all) as a one-way street in which India provides labor to capital-rich economies because of its dependency on these core economies, as in world systems theory. This substantialist view of the world system masks the complexity of relations between India and the United Kingdom and between India and the United States, both historically and today. It overgeneralizes the primacy of core economies in all historical periods and for all areas of economic life. For instance, we have clearly seen, in the diamond and garment trades, that India dominated those relations and markets for hundred of years. "Core" countries, that is, the modern industrialized economies of the "First World," were initially dependent on India for these kinds of goods. Even the more recent migration of Indians as part of these trades is a result of Indian commercial and market expansion and not as a dependent labor supply.

In contrast, flows of recruited labor (both low- and high-skill) during Britain's colonization of East Africa and the development of its and the U.S. economy after WWII certainly reflect dependency relations of a capital-poor, labor-rich country, such as newly independent India, on capital-rich countries such as the United Kingdom and the United States. However, it would be wrong to think that these sorts of dependency relations persist simply on their own momentum. Today, for instance, these dependency relations are beginning to turn upside down. Six of the Global Fortune 500 companies are from India (Rudiger 2008). Although this is still considerably fewer than the number of U.K. or U.S. companies, India seems to be making significant strides. The number of Indian companies on the London Stock Exchange is expected to rise, and, perhaps more telling, Indian foreign direct investment into the United Kingdom has also increased significantly. In the United Kingdom, 580 Indian companies now operate totaling almost £800 million in 2006–2007 (Rudiger 2008, 18). According to UNCTAD's (the U.N. Conference on Trade and Development's) World Investment Report, India's outward foreign direct investment (FDI) rose significantly, to $20.4 billion in 2007, most of which is directed at North America and Europe (India Brand Equity Foundation 2008); some $6 billion is directed to the United States alone. India has begun investing heavily in Europe too, especially in Germany. However, "when it comes to UK investment Indian companies rely increasingly on existing ties and there are already many Indian companies here" (Rudiger 2008, 25). The United Kingdom is also the largest foreign investor in India, and a high number of mergers and acquisitions are also taking place between India and the United Kingdom, not only between India and the United States. Little by little, trade and investment relations between India and other developed countries are becoming more of a two-way street that turns the assumptions of modernization theory (and migration) on their heads. The relational approach allows us to see the complexity of these flows of globalized relations through trade, investment, and migration because it asks us to continually look at these relations as social ties rather than to assume static categories of developed and developing, traditional and modern, and so on. Slowly, the United Kingdom and other developed countries are beginning to wake up to the realization of India's new role, too.

The Future of Migration Flows: Policy versus Reality

Immigration debates in many countries focus on the problem of how many immigrants to accept, from which parts of the world to accept them, and how to integrate them into society after they arrive. These concerns of nation-states are no exception for the United States and the United Kingdom. According to the Migration Policy Institute, the foreign born made up 12.6 percent of the population in the United States in 2007 and 9.7 percent in the United Kingdom in 2005. Indians now comprise the third largest foreign-born population in both countries. The policy histories of both countries have differed somewhat over the last fifty years, with the United States generally liberalizing, but retrenching periodically, and the United Kingdom generally restricting immigration since decolonization in the 1960s. Both countries, however, have encouraged migration either explicitly through labor recruitment programs, or by fairly liberal family reunification and asylum policies, or, especially in the U.S. case, by looking the other way at unauthorized immigrants. The schizophrenia of migration policies that seek at the same time to limit and to attract immigration demands that we understand the contradictions of the power and authority of states and the social mechanisms that encourage migration. These mechanisms lie not in the problem of economic supply and demand so much as the social networks that allow specific people to migrate to specific destinations. These ties are formed out of communities of people linked by colonial relations, trade, educational and professional exchange, war, religion, and a host of other globalized relations between countries. Indian immigrants in the United Kingdom and the United States provide a particularly interesting lens on the future of immigration because their population includes virtually every type of migrant, from refugees; temporary high-skill IT workers; students; recruited doctors, scientists, and engineers; entrepreneurs in various trades; and, finally, family reunification migrants. The huge range of migrants in this population gives us an unexpected view on directing future policy efforts.

Policy versus Reality in the United States

Perhaps ironically, however, most policy efforts have neglected to take into account the network mechanisms inherent in the migration process. Instead, they persist in viewing migration as an economic matter of supply and demand. Even when such assumptions come up empty, policy makers still fail to account for continued immigration in a comprehensive way. For instance, recently, the Migration Policy Institute, a very respected and highly informative nonpartisan think tank in Washington, D.C., published a report on immigration and the current financial crisis specifying the effects of the crisis on various types of migrants by legal entry and on the unauthorized population (Papademetriou and Terrazas 2009). The report discusses the possible effects of the financial crisis on legal categories of immigration: legal permanent residents (LPRs), those who have entered by employment preference, those who are part of a family reunification, those who have refugee or asylum status, temporary residents, and unauthorized migrants. It finds that only unauthorized migrants seem to be vulnerable to the volatility of capitalism. Each of the other categories responds to quite different logics or is likely to experience a delayed effect because of the backlog in immigration processing at the Department of Homeland Security (DHS). The lack of a strong correlation between legal categories of migration governed by immigration policy and shifts in the economy suggests that other mechanisms may be more important in the formation and continuation of migration flows. Yet many policy makers persist in thinking that policies themselves drive migration flows rather than social mechanisms such as networks. This position is not true only now in a time of economic crisis but is also a persistent feature of policy discourse. Policy makers struggle with alternative explanations when the data do not support their expectations.

For instance, it seems obvious that humanitarian (refugee and asylum) flows are produced by political upheaval in other parts of the world. Even then, networks matter. Refugees are evacuated and linked to new countries of residence through organizational ties to international governmental and nongovernmental organizations. Refugees and especially asylum seekers look for help from their interpersonal ties to reduce the extraordinary risks they take in fleeing to another country (Crisp 1999). These ties can include smugglers as well (Kyle and Koslowski 2001). Family reunification flows depend on social relations inherent in interpersonal ties among relatives. Through these ties, immigrants in host countries sponsor their relatives for immigration, as in chain migration. Such processes often continue in spite of economic supply and demand, financial crises, and so on.

Papademetriou and Terrazas (2009) expect employment preference migration to continue because of a backlog in economic demand. They also apply this logic to temporary economic migrants, such as those who migrate under the high-skill H-1B visa, for seasonal employment, or as students. Here, again, organizational ties are critical to the migration process linking specific people with educational opportunities and jobs through organizational and sometimes interpersonal ties. According to the analysis of the authors, only unauthorized immigrants are subject to the purely economic logics inherent in financial crises because they are the most vulnerable workers during such periods. They tend to be younger and less educated and have usually entered the labor market more recently than other economic migrants. They are also overrepresented in vulnerable economic sectors and industries such as manufacturing and construction. However, this substantialist approach still ignores the significance of social ties, even for the unauthorized, who rely heavily on interpersonal ties to make their way into a new society but whose migration has often been closely correlated with economic patterns, especially in the case of unauthorized Mexican migration (see Massey et al. 2002). Unsurprisingly, this oversight was also common during the attempts at bipartisan immigration reform in the latter part of George W. Bush's administration. During those debates, the unauthorized migrants were the target of the most contentious discussions about how to control immigration to the United States given that so many policies of the past simply failed to control the estimated 11.6 million unauthorized migrants now resident in the United States (Hoefer, Rytina, and Baker 2009; see also Passel 2006).

The explanations put forth in the authors' report are surely relevant ways of understanding migration flows. However, because they highlight the international political aspects of those flows embedded in legal categories of migration, they mask clear network processes that can go far in explaining why and how migration persists (even unauthorized migration) despite economic downturns and other fluctuations in supply and demand. The distinction between different types of social ties—interpersonal, organizational, and composite—allows us to explain how all of these kinds of flows persist (see also Table 5.1 in Chapter 5). Furthermore, we need to understand how such ties are formed historically and how they form from specific relations of exchange in the social networks of migrants.

Policy versus Reality in the United Kingdom

Over the last ten years, the United Kingdom has changed its immigration position and legislation rather dramatically. Until the late 1990s, its immigration policies could be summed up as allowing no immigration and some asylum. Yet there, too, migration flows persisted over the three decades that the United Kingdom held this position. In the past decade or so, the number of permanent immigrants entering the United Kingdom every year has risen even more, to about 185,000, and unauthorized immigrants have reached a total of about 470,000, according to the government (Somerville 2007). Beginning in the late 1990s, with the election of Tony Blair as prime minister, immigration and asylum became central policy issues. Blair was largely responsible for changing the course of immigration and asylum policy over the last ten years by introducing multiple policy strategies and parliamentary acts to try to better control asylum and to open Britain to more economic migration. These acts included the Immigration and Asylum Acts of 1999 and 2002, the Asylum and Immigration Act of 2004, and the Immigration, Asylum, and Nationality Act of 2006. The trend in all of these acts has been that asylum has become far more restrictive, and immigration has become more open, especially for so-called economic migrants who qualified under the new points system, which favored both high- and low-skill migrants, those with job offers, and students.

In a pattern similar to those of the United States and many other liberal immigration countries, immigration policy rarely corresponds well to actual flows of migrants (Durand, Massey, and Parrado 1999). Despite concerted attempts to control their borders, both countries have a substantial number of unauthorized immigrants entering and living within their borders. The continued migration of unauthorized persons into the United States and the United Kingdom, coupled with increasing threats from foreign terrorists and terrorist groups, has linked migration to problems of national security, certainly since September 11, 2001, but also before that time.

The Securitization of Immigration

A dangerous trend in both countries has been the securitization of immigration. The United States and the United Kingdom have increasingly focused their policy efforts on securitizing their borders and the persons who cross them. They have done so by building walls on their borders, as on the U.S.–Mexico border; using biometric tools in their databases and on passports; deporting more and more immigrants at faster rates; and reconfiguring the government institutional apparatus responsible for regulating immigration. Although security is important for any state, these trends are dangerous because they have begun to treat immigration as a potential crime (and immigrants as potential criminals) along with terrorism and other criminal activity, rather than a result of real political, economic, and social relations that take place between two countries in a world in which global interdependency and interconnectedness is increasing, ironically, as a result of state activity itself.

The USA PATRIOT Act (Uniting and Strengthening America by Providing Appropriate Tools Required to Intercept and Obstruct Terrorism) was signed into law on October 26, 2001, in the wake of the terrorist attacks of September 11, 2001. Remarkably, the U.S. Congress passed the act with overwhelming (but not unanimous) support and almost no debate a little over one month after the attacks of September 11. The PATRIOT Act represents the unprecedented expansion of executive powers to interfere with the civil liberties of both foreign and native-born residents of the United States. Many of these powers are not even required to be related to terrorism. Its provisions related to immigration, for instance, include many powers that are not required to substantiate a link between suspected terrorism and immigration. For instance, Section 213 eliminates the requirement that law enforcement officials provide contemporaneous notice of a search warrant to a person subject to a search. Surveillance devices can be installed anywhere in the United States under the authorization of a court, according to Sections 216 and 219. The act further allows government authorities access to personal financial information and student information without any suspicion of criminal activity. A portion of the PATRIOT Act applies specifically to immigrants by extending government authority to detain noncitizens indefinitely, even when they have not been charged with any criminal wrongdoing but have violated the terms of their immigration status in some way. In essence, many provisions of the PATRIOT Act have granted unprecedented and extraordinary authority to law enforcement officials to limit the civil liberties of both citizens and noncitizens, even when there are no charges of wrongdoing or suspected terrorist activity. Bakalian and Bozorgmehr (2009), for instance, have carefully documented the negative consequences of these powers on the Middle Eastern and Arab American population in the United States. These powers related to immigration have been enacted most significantly within the new Department of Homeland Security, created in 2002, which replaced the former Immigration and Naturalization Service.

In particular, the National Fugitive Operations Program led by the U.S. Immigration and Customs Enforcement (ICE) now operates with a $218 million annual budget and 1,300 percent growth in personnel since it began in 2003 (Mendelson, Strom, and Wishnie 2009). Although the original intent of the program was to arrest dangerous fugitive aliens (individuals with outstanding removal/deportation orders) by making a priority of those who come from countries with Al Qaeda presence or activity, the program increasingly arrests ordinary status violators (individuals without any outstanding removal order but who are believed to have violated some aspect of their immigration status and who have not yet been adjudicated by a judge). Those arrests rose to 40 percent of all arrests in 2007. In addition to these statistics, only 9 percent of arrested fugitive aliens had criminal convictions. According to the Migration Policy Institute's analysis of the program, the original mandate of the program has been eroded significantly to focus on only the easiest targets rather than on the most dangerous fugitives (Mendelson et al. 2009). Its authority, granted by changes made possible through the PATRIOT Act, has been used not to combat terrorism but rather to target noncriminal noncitizens. Overall, according to the Detention Watch Network (2008), the United States has deported about 349,000 immigrants in 2008 and 2.2 million since 1994.

Similarly, the United Kingdom has passed a number of measures related to immigration focused on border security and antiterrorism. The Antiterrorism, Crime, and Security Act of 2001 stated that suspected terrorists who were immigrants could be interned indefinitely. The U.K. Borders Bill of 2007 gives police powers to immigration officers and requires that foreign nationals have a Biometric Immigration Document (BID). A number of reform and policy strategies were also enacted by the Blair administration. A plan in 2005 entitled "Controlling Our Borders: Making Migration Work for Britain" focused on gaining control of borders and managing migration through a new points system, which was enacted the following year. In 2006, "Enforcing the Rules" integrated biometric visas into its border controls.

In 2006, the reform plan called "Fair, Effective, Transparent, and Trusted: Rebuilding Confidence in Our Immigration System" created the Border and Immigration Agency, which replaced the Immigration and Nationality Directorate. In 2007, the government announced its plans to divide the Home Office into two departments, the Ministry of Justice and a new Home Office that focuses on crime, immigration, and terrorism. The Border and Immigration Agency, previously part of the Home Office, now has even greater independence to operate apart from it (Somerville 2007). This was one of the most important initiatives of the Blair government because it created new institutional arrangements that linked immigration and crime, including terrorism.

Unlike in the United States, the nature of the debate around unauthorized immigrants and immigrant links to crime and terrorism has been more directly related to the problem of asylum and asylum seekers in the United Kingdom. For instance, in a damning report by the House of Commons Committee of Public Accounts (2006), the committee criticizes the government for both the inaccurate record and high number of failed asylum seekers who are released from custody without consideration for deportation. It also severely criticizes the government for not considering released foreign nationals for deportation after serving their sentences in U.K. prisons. The report recommends that the government centralize the databases of the U.K. Prison Service and of the Immigration and Nationality Directorate to accurately track and systematically deport convicted foreign national criminals and failed asylum seekers. In fact, the Blair government made substantial efforts at reforming asylum procedures to enable the government to process asylum cases more quickly, deport failed asylum seekers, reduce asylum appeal rights, and so on. Nonetheless, more and more noncitizen immigrants and asylum seekers are being associated generally with crime and even terrorism. Institutional changes in the U.K. Home Office and Border and Immigration Agency reflect this trend.

Rising deportations, the development of new border controls, biometric technologies, and surveillance for tracing the lives and movement of immigrants, and most importantly the criminalization of immigration through new institutional and legal arrangements all point to the increasing securitization of immigration and society in the United States and the United Kingdom. Although these strategies will do much to frighten immigrants who may come to the United States or the United Kingdom and those who are already there, they will have little effect on the persistence of migration flows overall because migration relies fundamentally on networks to reduce the risk of migrating even under the most unwelcoming legal conditions. Policy makers incorrectly locate the cause of migration flows when they focus solely on laws that govern border crossing or when they grossly overstate the relationship between immigration and criminality or terrorism. Therefore, it comes as no surprise to so many migration researchers that all sorts of migration flows still persist (especially unauthorized migration) and that, generally, such policies fail to manage migration effectively and humanely (Durand et al. 1999)

Modern Migrations

Migration is a network phenomenon. With his usual efficiency and elegance, Charles Tilly (1990, 84) summed up the relational approach to migration when he said: "Networks migrate. Categories stay put." Networks are dynamic, changing, moving phenomena. Categories are static, essentialist phenomena. When we view the world through static categories, we miss processes or how things change all around us. Yet it is difficult not to create and use categories. We can overcome this tendency not by denying categories but rather by treating them as empirical and historical questions to be investigated. For instance, we can question just how a nation-state, ethnic identity, class, or gender creates various boundaries; what those boundaries are really made of; and how they change. The power of the relational approach is that it allows us to better explain the causal mechanisms that drive various processes rather than using categories or attributes to substitute for the real relations that we know make up everyday social life. Therefore, this book has called for three theoretical and related methodological shifts. First, it has suggested that we move from substantialist accounts of social life to relational ones, in other words, from categories to networks. Second, it has asked us to focus on relations and transactions within network analyses of social life. Third, it has extended that focus on relations and transactions to studies of migration.

I have tried to illustrate the advantages of making these theoretical and methodological shifts through this investigation of the migration and mobility of Gujarati Indians in New York and London. Gujaratis are part of a long history of migration from a region that has been shaped by early modern and modern economic relations in trade, production, labor, and education between India and the United States and between India and the United Kingdom. This is not to speak of the political and cultural transactions that often accompany such economic relations. It is insufficient to attribute these relations solely to a legacy of colonialism, dependency, or economic differences in wages. A closer look at the historical formation of different social ties that set migration flows in motion uncovers the complexities behind such simplistic assumptions. The advantage of the relational approach to understanding social action is that it allows us to see these complexities because it focuses our attention on social networks. The social ties that are instrumental in migrant networks go beyond just the interpersonal ties that are so familiar to migration researchers and that have gone far in explaining migration processes. The organizational and composite ties that I have identified in this book are equally significant for our understanding of how particular individuals and networks migrate as part of a selective process.

The relational approach, which focuses on the transactions that take place within network ties, also demonstrates the weaknesses of viewing ethnicity in categorical, substantialist ways. In fact, as Gujarati migrant networks move across borders, linking local labor markets and forming economic niches in New York and London, coethnicity, whether we speak of Indians, Gujaratis, Hindus, Jains, or Patidars, and the like, fails to explain the significant within-group inequalities that are posed by these categories and that are evident in the kinds of exclusion that many Gujaratis experience within their networks. The nonrational network mechanisms through which economic action occurs is a persistent feature of modern societies, not one limited to migrants and their networks or to a traditional past. In this sense, immigrants are modern. Migrations are modern. Dichotomies such as traditional/modern, developing/developed do little to describe and everything to hide the integration and interconnectivity of India and the United States and of India and the United Kingdom historically and today. They also hide the integrated worlds of which migrants are very much a part. The life history narratives of Gujaratis in New York and London instead illuminate these dynamic relations as part of the ongoing search for mobility by immigrants.

Notes

Chapter 1

1. Pseudonyms replace all personal names to protect the anonymity of the participants whom I interviewed for this study.

2. Oswals practice the Jain religion, which dates back to the fifth century BCE. The close interrelationship between Hinduism and Jainism has a long history in India (Dundas 2002) and has continued to change in different ways in the diaspora and for different communities within Jainism, only some of which are found in the United States and the United Kingdom (see Jain and Forest 2004 for the U.S. case). As discussed in Chapter 2, Jains are one of the most prominent religious groups in Gujarat, largely because of their trading history there. They have been economically influential in India, and, even though they are a tiny minority there, they are three times as numerous in Gujarat (1.03 percent), and in Maharashtra (1.34 percent, especially Bombay) (Census of India 2001).

3. The earliest migration of Indians to the United States occurred around the turn of the twentieth century, primarily between 1900 and 1917. Although they were called "Hindus," these immigrants consisted mostly of Sikhs from the Punjab region of India who had been recruited by the British colonial government to serve in army stations and police forces in other parts of the British Empire, such as Canada. There, they were recruited to work on the railroads and in the lumber mills and quickly moved into agriculture and lumbering in California and the Pacific Northwest as a result of the racist, exclusionary policies of the "White Canada" movement. Students from India, among them many from the Bengal region, also came to U.S. universities, such as University of California, Berkeley, to study. Many were radical intellectuals who were motivated by anticolonial resistance and believed that the revolutionary history of the United States would create sympathy for their cause. However, Indians of all sorts ex-

perienced legal and institutional discrimination in the United States. By 1960 there were only about 12,300 foreign-born Indians in the United States, according to the U.S. Census Bureau. See Poros (forthcoming) for a more detailed review of the early history of Indians in the United States and the brief discussion in Chapter 2. See also Jensen (1988) and LaBrack (1988) on this early history, Leonard (1992) on the community created from Punjabi–Mexican marriages and unions that developed in the agricultural areas of California, and Takaki (1998) for a general history of Asian Americans.

4. Some of the most important studies and discussions of network approaches to migration that have been used to challenge economic and macroaccounts of migration include Thomas and Znaniecki (1918–1920); Tilly and Brown (1967); Portes and Bach (1985); Massey et al. (1987); Boyd (1989); Tilly (1990, 1998); Gurak and Caces (1992); Portes and Rumbaut (1996); Massey et al. (1998); Faist (2000). Although Castles and Miller (2003) also include social networks in their causal explanations of migration, macroeconomic and macrosocial forces dominate their account of migration.

5. Some of these stories exist as autobiographies and personal histories written by Gujarati immigrants to East Africa or by the children of those early migrants. For instance, Kotecha (1994) and Mehta (1987) are well-known examples. Although they are often gripping and poignant tales of life in East Africa, these stories often provide little historical evidence for flows of solitaries as many of them seek primarily to influence how the immigrants themselves will be portrayed in the collective memory of their families and communities. I am grateful for the generosity of two participants in London, who gave me personal copies of these rare books as gifts.

6. Numerous books on Indian immigration since 1965 to the United States and since the 1950s to the United Kingdom have been published; some of these also include Gujaratis in their studies, as they have been a significant part of these flows. In the United States, the first generation of these studies published in the 1980s and early 1990s provided important demographic profiles of what was then a new migration stream and rightly focused on the high education and skill level of those migrants, like Kishor, who were recruited as scientists, engineers, physicians, and the like and migrated under employment preferences. Those studies addressed Indians from all backgrounds, religions, and regions of origin, especially because, as a whole, they constituted a fairly small population at the time (for example, Bhardwaj and Rao 1990; Chandrashekar 1982; Helweg and Helweg 1990; Jain 1989; Jensen 1988; Saran 1985; Saran and Eames 1980). Subsequent studies from the mid-1990s through the present reflect how the diversity of the Indian population has grown as have many of its concerns. For instance, many of these studies focus on various aspects of incorporation having to do with race, identity, and assimilation (Bacon 1996; Bhatia 2007; Joshi 2006; Kurien 2007; Prashad 2000; Shankar and Srikanth 1998), gender (Abraham 2000; Dasgupta 1998; Khare 1997; Narayan and Purkayastha 2000; Purkayastha 2005b; Sicar 2000), the second generation (Joshi 2006; Maira 2009; Purkayastha

2005a), politics (Das Gupta 2006; Kanjilal 2000; Khagram, Desai and Varughese 2001; Lal 2008), communities (Khandelwal 2002; Leonard 1992; Lessinger 1995; Ranga-swamy 2000; Rudrappa 2004) and culture (Maira 1999, 2000; Mukhi 2000).

Studies of London's Indian immigrants have also followed a pattern that reflects the history of Indian immigration to the United Kingdom shortly after WWII, al-though usually as part of broader flows of South Asians and African Caribbeans who were lumped together as "Black British." The first generation of such studies, published from the 1960s through the 1980s, tended to focus on how immigration from the new Commonwealth countries, such as Jamaica and India, led to pronounced demographic changes and cultural challenges for immigrants and the native British population (for example, Allen 1971; Bhat, Carr-Hill, and Ohri, 1988; Desai 1963; Ellis and Appleton 1989; Hiro 1973; Jackson and Smith 1981; Peach 1984; Robinson 1979, 1986, 1996). Later studies, which began to differentiate between British Asians and black British follow-ing the U.K. Census in 1991, have focused on growing concerns about labor (Barrett and McEvoy 2005; Clark and Drinkwater 2007; Kalra 2000; Metcalf, Modood, and Virdee 1996; Ram and Jones 2005; Srinivasan 1995) gender (Bakrania 2008; Herbert 2008; Hussain 2005; Hussain and Bagguley 2007; Wilson 2006) religion—mainly con-cerning Muslim South Asians (Abbas 2005; Barot 1993; Lewis 2007), youth and the sec-ond generation (Anwar 1998; Bhatti 1999; Hall 2002; Lau 2000); and race, identity, and culture (Baumann 1996; Hyder 2004; Sharma, Hutnyk and Sharma 1996). These studies of Indians in the United States and the United Kingdom, which seek either to explain the causes of migration or to discuss those causes as background for other issues, such as the adaptation or incorporation of Indians in American and British society, tend to reproduce the standard narrative that Indian migration was led by changes in policy, rather than to question it anew.

7. See Mistry (1994) for a discussion of Gujarati names and Gandhi (1992) for the meanings of personal names.

8. The surnames and subcaste names are withheld to preserve the anonymity of participants. The practice of caste has been associated with Hinduism and other re-ligious and social groups in South Asia for thousands of years. Although today its formal practice is illegal as a system of stratification, it operates informally to various degrees in rural and urban areas, for instance, and in all aspects of Indian society, especially social ones, such as eating and marriage. Varna refers to hierarchical status distinctions based largely on ritual purity whereas jati defines endogamous relations. In the broad varna system, Brahmins represent teachers, scholars and priests; Ksha-triyas, kings, warriors, and military personnel; Vaisyas represent merchants, traders, and agriculturalists; and Sudras include artisans and servants. Many outside the caste system are considered "untouchable" or Dalits. In contrast to the emphasis on caste hi-erarchy in the varna system, Shah emphasizes caste division as part of his larger argu-ment elaborated in Shah and Desai (1988), which opposes Louis Dumont's well-known

Homo Hierarchicus (1972). Shah contends that Dumont and others who have studied Indian castes did so largely in the context of rural India rather than contemporary urban India. Shah stresses that the principle of division is more important than the principle of hierarchy when understanding modern, urban conceptions and uses of caste. This is clearly evident in Gujarat, where caste divisions number in the hundreds and where caste relations have been significantly influenced by the prominence of merchants and traders in the region. Most notable, Vaniyas in Gujarat, part of the Vaisya caste, which is third in the varna hierarchy, have higher status than Kshatriyas (discussed in Chapter 2). See also Beteille (1996), who discusses the historical ambivalence and fluidity surrounding contemporary practices and meanings of caste in India.

9. Muslims can generally be recognized by their first names. Therefore, they were easily removed from the New York sample, which initially came from public phonebooks that were used to contact potential participants by mail (discussed in the following section). This was not possible in London because its telephone directories list only first initials. Therefore, the participants had to be screened over the phone for inclusion in the sample.

10. In this study of Gujaratis, a higher response occurred in New York than in London for at least three reasons: better recognition of my affiliation with Columbia University, less suspicion about the protection of confidentiality, and the higher number of shopkeepers in London, who had less free time to volunteer for the study.

11. The secondary school certification mechanisms of the United Kingdom and many of the Commonwealth and new Commonwealth countries, which include India, are somewhat different from those of the United States. In the United States, a high school diploma typically certifies students who have completed the requirements for secondary school education. This diploma or its equivalent is necessary for entry into a postsecondary college or university degree program. In the United Kingdom, the General Certificate of Education certifies the completion of secondary schooling and is achieved by taking a set of examinations in the final years of secondary school. Those examinations consist of O-levels, the "ordinary level" subject-based qualifications, and A-levels, the "advanced level" subject-based qualifications. The latter prepare students for entry to university. Matriculation in the Indian educational system refers to completing the tenth standard (grade) and passing the state exams required for the qualification.

12. One such quantitative study of immigrants in the United States is Alba and Nee's (2003) *Remaking the American Mainstream*, which proposes a new institutionalist understanding of migration that incorporates a relational approach into its theoretical framework. Its argument is, however, weakened by the fact that it uses nonrelational, that is, categorical, data to support its thesis. See Poros (2004) for a detailed review of Alba and Nee's book.

13. The life history interviews were audiotaped and lasted from one to four hours. They were unstructured to flow naturally as in a conversation. Borrowing a method

from Jean Bacon's (1996) study of Indian immigrant families in Chicago, the life history interviews began with a request to state when and where the participant was born and what they remembered about growing up. If the participants seemed to need probing for subjects to discuss, they were asked to describe elements of family life, neighborhood, education, friends, and so on. Most respondents, however, needed little probing. In fact, some had an active agenda of issues that they wished to share with me. The telling of these life histories was guided in a chronological way covering experiences of natal family life, education, migration, work, marriage and marital family life, associational activity, and general cultural, economic, and political activities. The purpose of the interviews was to obtain as complete a picture as possible of the life experiences of the participants in relation to broader concerns about how the participants migrated, found jobs, and responded to new environments. This relatively unstructured interviewing method can bring to light many variables that are previously unknown. Thus, it removes the blinders with which interviewers approach their subjects.

14. Leaders of associations were asked to give an account of the history and mission of the organization (when it was founded, by whom, with what resources, and for what purposes), current activities and the population served by those activities, formal membership statistics, if available, and financial and other requirements for membership.

15. I also benefited greatly from a specialized library containing "grey literature"—pamphlets, reports, historical periodicals, ethnic newspapers, and print media—located at the Centre for Research in Ethnic Relations at the University of Warwick in Coventry, England.

16. Throughout this book, *London* refers to Greater London, which is the area surrounding Inner London within a metropolitan Green Belt established in 1938, including Inner London. Its population and size (about 610 square miles) is comparable to New York City's regional core (as defined by Hughes and Sternlieb [1989] in Fainstein and Harloe [1992]), which includes the five New York City boroughs and parts of eastern New Jersey. New York's and London's Indian populations have high concentrations in the suburbs of both cities, that is, Greater London and the New York metropolitan area outside of New York City's regional core. *New York* refers to the greater New York metropolitan area defined as a metropolitan statistical area by the U.S. Census Bureau, which includes New York City and the surrounding region, northern New Jersey, and Long Island. That geographical area is significantly larger than Greater London and contains a population size that is about 2.5 times greater than London's.

17. Population statistics for New York and London and their foreign-born populations come from the 2005 American Community Survey of the U.S. Census Bureau, retrieved on June 21, 2009, from http://gstudynet.org/gum/US2005ACS/NYC2005 .htm, and the 2001 U.K. Census of the Office of National Statistics (cited by the Migration Policy Institute and retrieved on June 21, 2009, from http://www.migration information.org/datahub/gcmm.cfm). This discussion does not include the growing

populations of Indians born in other countries in the Indian diaspora, for example, Fiji, Guyana, Trinidad, Pakistan, Bangladesh, and so on, and the large second-generation population born in the United States and the United Kingdom, as they are not the main focus of this study.

18. See Peter Gowan's article "Crisis in the Heartland" (2009) in the *New Left Review* for a cogent argument about the current crisis of capitalism emanating from the United States.

Chapter 2

1. Evora was an ancient city of significance under the Romans and Moors and a court city during the fifteenth- and sixteenth-century Portuguese Christian dynasties.

2. As early as the second millennium BCE Mesopotamian ships had been trading along the Indian Ocean. By the time Greeks learned to exploit the monsoon winds, around 116 BCE, the ocean trade was burgeoning. The *Periplus Maris Erythraei*, a first-century guidebook for merchants, which was written in Greek by an Egyptian Greek merchant, describes some of the earliest trade between the Mediterranean and the Indian Ocean. Mainly, however, it was written to give traders valuable information, such as the different products to buy and sell in various ports, ranks and names of local rulers, and relevant socioeconomic and political realities that merchants might encounter (Casson 1989).

3. In 1573, Gujarat was conquered by the Mughals, who protected trade routes and encouraged merchants (Hardiman 1996). Surat was the most important city in India until the 1620s and remained a significant center of trade for centuries later (Braudel 1981a). See Commissariat (1957) for a history of Gujarat and Richards (1993) on the Mughal period of Indian history.

4. In fact, Indians dominated Europeans in shipping until the advent of the steamship in the mid-nineteenth century. The Surat Castle (1791–1792), for instance, weighed 1,000 tons, far more than any European ships at the time (Braudel 1981a).

5. Fernand Braudel argued that the three huge world economies of Islam, China, and India were indeed capitalist and were far ahead of their European counterparts in trade, exports, and industry from about 1500–1800. His view of capitalism and modernity does not entail the required extraction of surplus value as in Marxist theory. From a Marxist perspective, India (and China and Islam) was not capitalist (or modern) during this period; therefore, from this perspective, a fully capitalist economy may not have existed in this period of India's history. However, contrary to Marx's Eurocentric viewpoint about "traditional," or premodern, Asian economies, the historiography on India shows that India did contain an early capitalist economy, most prominently in its dominant textile industry, even if it was uneven geographically and across industries (see Washbrook 2007). At the very least, India's merchant capitalism and manufacturing were in a transition phase to modern capitalism, according to Washbrook.

This new historiography of world economic history, which places Asia, particularly India and China, at the center of the world economy over the course of most of the last millennium, has been explicated most importantly by members of the so-called California School (Goldstone 2001), including authors such as Andre Gunder Frank, Jack Goldstone, Jack Goody, and Kenneth Pomeranz and by other world historians such as Giovanni Arrighi. These authors have also challenged Max Weber, whose notion of modernity was not explicitly linked to the extraction of surplus value from the capitalist mode of production but rather to an impersonal order and rational forms of economic and organizational practice. They argue that Weber was wrong in thinking that Asian societies and economies were "traditional" and not able to become modern.

These debates about the origins and nature of "modern" capitalism speak to common assumptions about the circulation of laborers and others, such as merchants and seamen from India to other parts of the world. In this respect, the historiography on India shows that from about the 1500s (if not earlier) until the 1800s India participated as a dominant player in a very strong merchant or trade capitalist system in which migration across empires was linked to trade not to labor. Only after India became "underdeveloped," to use Frank's (1998) words, by the ascendance of Europeans in the world system around the 1800s do we see international labor migration of Indians become more prominent than trade migration. In other words, early capitalist production (often using bonded or servile labor) in India up until the 1800s kept most Indians working at home in agriculture and manufacturing (although workers migrated within India), while merchants and traders of much higher status sought new markets for their raw and manufactured goods within India and abroad. This changed as Britain "deindustrialized" India under colonialism (see Braudel 1981b; Frank 1998; Richards 1993).

6. The purported absence of modern capitalist organization and practices in India is often compared to the presence of those business firms and practices in the West. The West, here, however, refers completely to "lazy southern Europe," primarily Italy and Iberia (Braudel 1981a, 569), not Western Europe, where modern capitalism was thought to have flourished first and then spread to the rest of the world. Recent historical scholarship has shown that "modern" forms of capitalist businesses and financial practices in India developed separately from southern Europe and were, indeed, present in India and other non-European parts of the world (Goody 1996). These included bills of exchange, banking, stock exchanges, joint-stock companies, and the like. Also see Birla (2009) on the Hindu Undivided Family (HUF) and Goody (1996) on the HUF and *commenda* forms of business organization and on early financial instruments of capital. See Molly Greene (2002) on the use of the *commenda* in the interaction between Venetian and Ottoman traders in the Mediterranean.

7. The Parsis of India have Persian origins dating back to their migration to India more than 1,000 years ago.

8. As with almost all Asians in Uganda, the Madhvani family had to leave their business capital, technologies, and estates behind after the expulsion of Asians by Idi Amin in 1972. However, recently they and other Asian business families have been able to reclaim some of their business interests to operate in Uganda again. The Madhvanis' firm headquarters, however, are still in London.

9. USEFI has become the U.S.–India Educational Foundation (USIEF) under the 2008 Fulbright agreement, which will include equal contributions to the program by the Indian government.

10. The first generation of the prestigious Indian Institutes of Science, Technology, and Management were created following India's independence. They include the Indian Institutes of Management (IIMs) at Ahmedabad and Calcutta (1961); Indian Institutes of Technology (IITs) at Kharagpur (1951), Bombay (1958), Madras (1959), Kanpur (1959), and Delhi (1963); and the Indian Institute of Science at Banglaore (1909), which, unlike the others, predates independence.

11. On a personal note, when my own parents migrated to Boston for postgraduate study in the late 1950s, they were marginally part of an interdisciplinary group of Greek intellectuals who were making plans and connections to institute economic and social reforms in Greece. When leaders of that group, students at MIT and future Greek politicians, approached MIT's administration to secure support and financing for those reforms, they were told that the university was instead concentrating their investments in other countries, notably India.

12. These more recent Institutes are part of a new educational trend that also includes new Indian Institutes of Management and Indian Institutes of Science Education and Research (IISERs). The proliferation of these schools and universities has also raised questions about their quality (see Overdorf 2008).

13. The Northwest Punjab region was divided into independent India and Pakistan during the partition of the Indian subcontinent in 1947. It is considered the homeland of Sikhs and has the highest concentration of Sikhs both in India and Pakistan. The Sikh religion was founded in the mid-fifteenth century; its theology is derived from elements found in both Islam and Hinduism.

14. For an excellent treatment of early Asian immigration and exclusion see Mae Ngai's *Impossible Subjects* (2004).

15. The 1965 Act is frequently touted as a "liberalization" of immigration policy because it lifted national origins quotas. However, viewed over the long run, it can be seen as continuing a history of racist policies toward nonwhite immigrants since the first naturalization Act in 1790, which restricted naturalization to "free white persons." The meaning of "white" has had a highly contested history since that time and has been reflected in immigration policies (see Jacobson 1999). For instance, the 1924 Immigration Act sought to severely limit any new immigration by "probationary whites," to use Jacobson's phrase, for example, Eastern and Central Europeans, Italians, Jews, Slavs, and the like, so that existing immigrants might assimilate and con-

tribute to a more racially homogeneous culture. The 1965 Act continued this ideological thread as Eastern and Southern Europeans by that time had become consolidated into the "white" race and could now be admitted more readily to the United States. The creators of the act, among them prominent antiracist opponents of the national origins quotas, did not anticipate, however, that so many new non-European immigrants would seek immigration to the United States.

16. The New Commonwealth countries include former African and Caribbean colonies, Bangladesh, India, Pakistan, Sri Lanka, and Hong Kong. The Old Commonwealth includes Australia, Canada, and New Zealand (Coleman 1994).

17. Anti-immigrant rallies were carried out from 1962 through 1966 by the British National Front and the Southall Residents' Association. Southall in West London was then becoming, and now is, a major area of South Asian residential and commercial settlement. Enoch Powell's famous, racist "rivers of blood" speech in 1968 further ignited and legitimized racist attitudes and discrimination (Malik 1997).

Chapter 3

Portions of this chapter are related to a previously published article: Poros, Maritsa V. 2001. "The Role of Networks in Linking Local Labour Markets: The Case of Asian Indian Migration to New York and London." *Global Networks*, 1, 3: 243–259.

1. Although Indians were a fairly low proportion of all applicants, they had been granted green cards at a high rate. By July 2001, they had received 20 percent of green cards given to foreign workers; Russia, Ukraine, and the Baltic States followed close behind (personal communication with Central Placement Office of the Federal Employment Service, Press Office, Bonn, Germany [Zentralstelle fur Arbeitsvermittlung der Bundesanstalt fur Arbeit (ZAV), Pressestelle.]) Since 2004, when the program ended, the German government has looked more closely within Europe to recruit high-tech workers.

2. The AAPI, which was founded in 1984, reports that it also represents about 15,000 medical students and residents of Indian origin about 10 to 12 percent of the student body in the country's medical schools. The AAPI is the umbrella organization for about 130 professional physician associations and chapters formed by Indians in the United States. Many of these are broken down by region and reflect linguistic differences. For instance, the Baroda Medical College Alumni Association of North America represents about 1,500 alumni from Gujarat. Medical graduates from the Indian states of Kerala and Tamil Nadu also have their own associations. These associations are the most recent conduits of information for becoming a medical doctor in the United States. Their transnational activities, such as the AAPI's thirty continuing medical educational programs in India, update doctors there on the latest medical and technological developments, thus linking Indian immigrant doctors in the United States with potential immigrant doctors in India (see www.aapiusa.org).

3. Jainism does not accept the authority of the Vedas, as in much of contemporary Hinduism, but rather promotes devotion to the prophet Mahavir. Jainism's worldview is grounded in five different kinds of knowledge that are attained through strict ascetic practices (Radhakrishnan and Moore 1957). These practices require the shedding of all material wealth and adherence to the philosophy of nonviolence (*ahimsa*), which historically has influenced the practice of vegetarianism among Hindus. Conversely, Hindu caste practices have influenced Jains even though Jainism does not officially profess to follow a caste system.

4. Notwithstanding the importance of hubs or central actors, Bashi's (2007) hub and spoke model cannot be generalized to all of the networks sampled in this study. In some networks there were hubs or central nodes in networks that controlled the selection of others for migration and employment. However, many of the Gujarati networks in both New York and London followed more of a chain model as they conformed to family reunification restrictions for immigration or used a more dispersed set of network ties to gain valuable resources and information over the course of years.

5. See Koskoff (1981) for a fuller description of the global diamond trade. Also see Westwood (2000) for a depiction of the role of Jains and other Indians in the trade.

6. Many Patidars were originally from the lower Kanbi caste and achieved upward caste mobility through emigration and return migration. Their cumulative success in commerce in East Africa eventually elevated their entire caste community in India. See Chandra (1997) for a detailed discussion of this process, Tambs-Lyche (1980) on the Patidars of London, and Pocock (1972) for a more general discussion of Kanbi and Patidar in India.

Chapter 4

Portions of this chapter are related to a previously published book chapter: Poros, Maritsa V. 2004. "Networks of Inclusion and Exclusion in the Economic Concentrations of Asian Indian Immigrants in New York and London," in Nancy DiTomaso and Corinne Post, eds., *Diversity in the Workforce. Volume 14: Research in the Sociology of Work*, 35–61. Amsterdam: Elsevier.

1. Niche employment is often embedded in ethnic economies. Ethnic economies consist of three types (Light and Gold 2000). An ethnic ownership economy includes business owners and their coethnic workers who may serve the wider population in addition to coethnics. Ethnic enclave economies are ethnic ownership economies that are geographically concentrated and typically serve a coethnic population that is concentrated in that enclave. And ethnic-controlled economies exist when coethnic employees exert significant power and economic control over a particular economic industry or sector.

2. From *Understanding Hinduism*, published by the Sri Swaminarayan Mandir in Neasden, London NW10 8JP, UK.

3. The Neasden Swaminarayan temple is dominated not only by Gujaratis but most prominently by the Patidar community. It is located in a sorely unattractive northwest London neighborhood. Surrounded by dilapidated terraced housing, enormous shopping centers, and the M25 beltway, which heavily pollutes the area, the temple seems to rise from the ashes as one approaches it. Built of marble and limestone, it was carved by artisans in India and shipped to London in approximately 26,000 pieces. The temple has become such a strong status symbol that it has been dubbed the "face of Hinduism in Britain." See Williams (2001) on Swaminarayan Hinduism, generally.

4. See www.leuvapatidarsamaj.com/.

5. This information comes from the 1998 Annual Report of the Brent Indian Association, funded by Brent Council, 116 Ealing Road, Wembley, Middlesex HA0 4TH, UK.

6. See the AAHOA website: www.aahoa.com/.

7. See www.aahoa.org/html/aahoa-history.htm.

Chapter 5

1. These dynamics of migrant selectivity in the case of Gujarati immigrants have been explained more fully in Chapter 2.

2. This is a point about which Zolberg (1997) has criticized Massey; see also Massey (1999).

3. Miguel Ceballos, in an unpublished paper (2001), comes closest to a relational approach in his revision of Massey and colleagues' theory (Massey et al. 1998). Ceballos argues that social networks are indeed the causal mechanisms that initiate and perpetuate migration. He focuses on the density (number of social ties), intensity (degree of obligation or solidarity within ties), and encapsulation (degree of embeddedness in the networks) of social networks. In contrast, I argue for a revised way of defining networks in which the types of social ties and the transactions within them are the most important causal properties of migration processes. The next subsection on "What Is a Network?" provides a more detailed discussion.

4. Social network theorists and migration theorists generally do not talk to each other very much. Two exceptions are theoretical discussions by Portes (1995) and Waldinger and Lichter (2003) on the economic sociology of immigration. However, most network studies of migration simply choose to ignore the contributions of social network studies and vice versa. This lack of communication has led to underdeveloped ideas about network structure and dynamics in migration studies. For instance, although Bashi (2007) goes further than most migration researchers in her analysis of migrant networks, she also eschews use of the networks literature. Thus, she terms central actors *hubs* in her study, even though centrality is an established measure in social network research. I have attempted to integrate a discussion of the two literatures in this chapter to further what we can learn about migrant networks and their dynamics.

5. This is a broader conception than that presented by Goss and Lindquist (1995), who show that migrant institutions (those organizations created and directed by co-ethnic migrants) are instrumental in encouraging the migration process.

6. I experienced this inequality firsthand when I once became the object of Jagdish's and Pravin's exchange negotiations: On the day that I first met and interviewed Pravin in London, he escorted me around his neighborhood to meet various significant persons in his social network of friends. He also enthusiastically suggested that I interview his cousin, Jagdish, an important employee of a well-known transnational firm, owned by a prominent Indian family from Uganda. Pravin phoned Jagdish in my presence to ask if he would talk to me. After listening to their ten-minute conversation in Gujarati, I spoke to Jagdish on the phone as he desperately tried to beg off my request for an interview. Instead, he suggested that I speak to various organizations and so on, but I gently persisted, and he agreed to meet me. It was quite clear to me that Jagdish was annoyed at this intrusion by his lower-status cousin. However, when I visited Jagdish and his wife at their home (wearing my American, middle-class, academic status) they were immediately warm and welcoming and very generous with their time and hospitality.

7. The concept of the ideal type was introduced by Max Weber in 1904 in "Objectivity in Social Science." Weber proposed the use of the ideal type as a conceptual and methodological tool that would allow the sociologist to observe and study, in an objective way, the inherent subjectivity of historical phenomena or empirical reality.

8. Bashi (2007) argues that West Indian migration looks more like a hub-and-spoke network rather than a chain. However, I have included her study along with others that reflect chain migration because they share an emphasis on the importance of interpersonal ties that facilitate migration processes, even when the initial flows began with organizational ties as in the case of recruits. This process of recruits becoming chains is also evident in the West Indian population studied by Bashi. Although she does not describe it in this way, most of the hubs in her study were recruited into the health professions, as nurses, for instance, and then sponsored interpersonal others, thus transforming a flow of recruits (which included similar others) into one of chains. See the following section on recruits for an example from her book, *Survival of the Knitted*.

9. Most migration studies focus on the migration of one ethnic group or sending region to one destination. This tendency results in a migration discourse that is often based on national/regional or ethnic origins or, in other words, methodological nationalism. I have argued against this tendency; however, I use the migration scholarship to point to existing studies that document chain migration streams in a way that exemplifies the relational approach—at least implicitly.

10. These data come from personal communication in December 2000 with the Central Placement Office of the Federal Employment Service, Press Office, Bonn, Germany (Zentralstelle für Arbeitsvermittlung der Bundesanstalt für Arbeit [ZAV], Pressestelle).

Bibliography

Abbas, Tahir. 2005. *Muslim Britain: Communities under Pressure*. London: Zed Books.

Abbott, Andrew. 2001. *Time Matters: On Theory and Method*. Chicago: University of Chicago Press.

Abraham, Margaret. 2000. *Speaking the Unspeakable: Marital Violence among South Asian Immigrants in the United States*. New Brunswick, NJ: Rutgers University Press.

Alba, Richard, and Victor Nee. 2003. *Remaking the American Mainstream: Assimilation and Contemporary Immigration*. Cambridge, MA: Harvard University Press.

Allen, Sheila. 1971. *New Minorities, Old Conflicts: Asian and West Indian migrants in Britain*. New York: Random House.

American Medical Association. 2007. International Medical Graduates in the U.S. Workforce: A Discussion Paper. October.

van Amersfoort, H. 1995. From workers to immigrants: Turks and Moroccans in the Netherlands 1965–1992. In Robin Cohen, ed., *The Cambridge Survey of World Migration,* 308–312. Cambridge, UK: Cambridge University Press.

Aneesh, A. 2000. *Rethinking Migration: High-Skilled Labor Flows from India to the United States*. Working Paper 18, The Center for Comparative Immigration Studies, University of California, San Diego.

Anwar, Muhammad. 1998. *Between Cultures: Continuity and Change in the Lives of Young Asians*. London: Routledge.

Australian Education International 2006. Year 2006 International Student Enrollments in Australia from Top 10 Source Countries, 2002 to 2006. Retrieved on June 9, 2010, from http://aei.gov.au/AEI/MIP/Statistics/StudentEnrolmentAndVisaStatistics/2006/2006Annual_Stats.htm#2006.

Bacon, Jean. 1996. *Life Lines: Community, Family, and Assimilation among Asian Indian Immigrants*. New York and Oxford, UK: Oxford University Press.

Bakalian, Anny, and Mehdi Bozorgmehr. 2009. *Backlash 9/11: Middle Eastern Americans Respond*. Berkeley: University of California Press.

Bakrania, Falu. 2008. Roomful of Asha: Gendered Productions of Ethnicity in Britain's "Asian Underground." In Susan Koshy and Rajagopalan Radhakrishnan, eds., *Transnational South Asians: The Making of a Neo-Diaspora*. New Delhi: Oxford University Press.

Ballard, Roger. 2001. The Impact of Kinship on the Economic Dynamics of Transnational Networks: Reflections on Some South Asian Developments. Workshop on Transnational Migration, Center for Migration and Development. Princeton, NJ: Princeton University.

Banks, Marcus. 1994. Why Move? Regional and Long Distance Migrations of Gujarati Jains. In Judith Brown and Rosemary Foot, eds., *Migration: The Asian Experience*. Oxford, UK: St. Martin's Press.

Barot, Rohit, ed. 1993. *Religion and Ethnicity: Minorities and Social Change in the Metropolis*. Kampen, the Netherlands: Kok Pharos Publishing House.

Barrett, Giles A., Trevor Jones, David McEvoy, and Chris McGoldrick. 2002. The Economic Embededdness of Immigrant Enterprise in Britain. *International Journal of Entrepreneurial Behavior & Research* 8(1/2): 11–31.

Barrett, Giles A., and David McEvoy. 2005. Not All Can Win Prizes: Asians in the British Labour Market. In *Asian Migrants and European Labour Markets: Patterns and Processes of Immigrant Labour Market Insertion in Europe*, 21–41. London: Routledge.

Barth, Frederik. 1969. *Ethnic Groups and Boundaries*. Boston: Little Brown.

Bashi, Vilna. 2007. *Survival of the Knitted: Immigrant Social Networks in a Stratified World*. Stanford, CA: Stanford University Press.

Basok, Tanya. 2003. Mexican Seasonal Migration to Canada and Development: A Community-Based Comparison, *International Migration* 41, 2: 3–26.

Batalova, Jeanne. 2007. The "Brain Gain" Race Begins with Foreign Students. *Migration Policy Institute*, January 1.

Baumann, Gerd. 1996. *Contesting Culture: Ethnicity and Community in West London*. New York: Cambridge University Press.

Beteille, André. 1996. Caste in Contemporary India. In C. J. Fuller, ed., *Caste Today*. Delhi: Oxford University Press.

Bhagwati, Jagdish. 1993. *India in Transition: Freeing the Economy*. Oxford, UK: Clarendon Press.

Bhardwaj, Surinder, and M. Rao. 1990. Asian Indians in the United States: A Geographical Appraisal. In Colin Clarke, Ceri Peach, and Steven Vertovec, eds., *South Asians Overseas: Migration and Ethnicity*, 197–218. Cambridge, UK: Cambridge University Press.

Bharot, Rohit. 1999. Local, Global and Transnational: The Case of the Swaminarayan Movement. Paper presented at the Transnational Communities Seminar, May 27, at Oxford University.

Bhat, Ashok, Roy Carr-Hill, and Sushel Ohri, eds. 1988. *Britain's Black Population: A New Perspective*. Brookfield, UK: Gower.

Bhatia, Sunil. 2007. *American Karma: Race, Culture, and Identity in the Indian Diaspora*. New York: New York University Press.

Bhatt, Chetan. 2003. *Hindu Nationalism: Origins, Ideologies and Modern Myths*. Oxford, UK, and New York: Berg.

Bhatt, Chetan, and Mukta, Parita. 2000. Hindutva in the West: Mapping the Antinomies of Diaspora Nationalism. *Ethnic and Racial Studies* 23, 3: 407–441.

Bhatti, Ghazala. 1999. *Asian Children at Home and at School: An Ethnographic Study*. London: Routledge.

Biao, Xiang. 2006. *Global "Body Shopping": An Indian Labor System in the Indian Information Technology Industry*. Princeton, NJ: Princeton University Press.

Birla, Ritu. 2009. *Stages of Capital: Law, Culture and Market Governance in Late Colonial India*. Durham, NC, and London: Duke University Press.

Borjas, George. 1990. *Friends or Strangers: The Impact of Immigration on the American Economy*. New York: Basic Books.

———. 1999. *Heaven's Door: Immigration Policy and the American Economy*. Princeton, NJ: Princeton University Press.

Bowers, John Z., and L. Rosenheim. 1971. *Migration of Medical Manpower*. New York: Josiah Macy Jr. Foundation.

Boyd, Monica. 1989. Family and Personal Networks in International Migration: Recent Developments and New Agendas. *International Migration Review* 233: 638–680.

Bozorgmehr, Mehdi. 1997. Internal Ethnicity: Iranians in Los Angeles. *Sociological Perspectives* 49: 387–408.

Brass, Paul. 1994. *The New Cambridge History of India, The Politics of India since Independence*, 2nd edition. Cambridge, UK: Cambridge University Press.

Braudel, Fernand. 1981a. *Civilization and Capitalism*, Volume II: *The Wheels of Commerce*. Translated by Sian Reynolds. New York: Harper and Row Publishers.

———. 1981b. *Civilization and Capitalism*, Volume III: *The Perspective of the World*. Translated by Sian Reynolds. New York: Harper and Row Publishers.

Breman, Jan. 1985. *Of Peasants, Migrants and Paupers: Rural Labour Circulation and Capitalist Production in West India*. Delhi: Oxford University Press

———. 1993. *Beyond Patronage and Exploitation: Changing Agrarian Relations in South Gujarat*. Delhi: Oxford University Press.

Brettell, Caroline, and J. Hollifield, eds. 2000. *Migration Theory: Talking Across Disciplines*. New York and London: Routledge.

Brubaker, Rogers. 2004. *Ethnicity without Groups*. Cambridge, MA: Harvard University Press.

Burt, Ronald. 1982. *Toward a Structural Theory of Action*. New York: Academic Press.

Burt, Ronald, and Michael Minor. 1983. *Applied Network Analysis*. Beverly Hills: Sage.

Casson, Lionel. 1989. *The Periplus Maris Erythraei*. Text with Introduction, Translation, and Commentary by Lionel Casson. Princeton, NJ: Princeton University Press.

Castles, Stephen. 2001. Migration and Community Formation under Conditions of Globalisation. Presented to the International Center for Migration, Ethnicity and Citizenship, March 12, in New York, The New School.

———. 2007. The Factors That Make and Unmake Migration Policies. In Alejandro Portes and Josh DeWind, eds., *Rethinking Migration: New Theoretical and Empirical Perspectives*, 29–61. Oxford, UK: Berghahn Books.

Castles, Stephen, and Mark Miller. 2003. *The Age of Migration*, 3rd edition. London: Macmillan.

Cavalli-Sforza, Luigi Luca, and Francesco Cavalli-Sforza. 1995. *The Great Human Diasporas: The History of Diversity and Evolution*. Cambridge, MA: Perseus Books.

Ceballos, Miguel. 2001. Social Networks and Social Capital as Mechanisms for Explaining the Initiation of International Migration. Unpublished manuscript.

Census of India 2001. C-Series, Population by Religious Communities. Available at: www.censusindia.gov.in/Census_Data_2001/Census_data_finder/C_Series/Population_by_religious_communities.htm

Chandra, Vibha P. 1997. Remigration: Return of the Prodigals—An Analysis of the Impact of the Cycles of Migration and Remigration on Caste Mobility. *International Migration Review* 31, 1117: 162–170.

Chandrasekhar, Sripati, ed. 1982. *From India to America: A Brief History of Immigration, Problems of Discrimination, Admission and Assimilation*. La Jolla, CA: Population Review Publications.

Chaudhuri, K. N. 1990. *Asia before Europe: Economy and Civilisation of the Indian Ocean from the Rise of Islam to 1750*. Cambridge, UK: Cambridge University Press.

Chisti, Muzzafer, and Claire Bergeron. 2008. USCIS Receives 163,000 H-1B Applications for Fiscal Year 2009, April 15. Washington, DC: Migration Policy Institute.

Chiswick, Barry. 2000. Are Immigrants Favorably Self-Selected? An Economic Analysis. In Caroline Brettell and J. Hollifield, eds., *Migration Theory: Talking Across Disciplines*. New York and London: Routledge.

Chung, Angie Y. 2005. "Politics without Politics": The Evolving Political Culture of Ethnic Non-profits in Koreatown, Los Angeles. *Journal of Ethnic and Migration Studies* 31, 5: 911–929.

Clark, Ken, and Stephen Drinkwater. 2007. *Ethnic Minorities in the Labour Market: Dynamics and Diversity*. Bristol, UK: The Policy Press.

Cohen, Robin. 1997. *Global Diasporas: An Introduction.* Seattle: University of Washington Press.

Coleman, David. 1994. The United Kingdom and International Migration: A Changing Balance. In Heinz Fassmann and Rainer Munz. Laxenburg, eds., *European Migration in the Late Twentieth Century: Historical Patterns, Actual Trends, and Social Implications.* Aldershot, UK: Edward Elgar.

Collett, Elizabeth. 2008. *The Proposed European Blue Card System: Arming for the Global War for Talent?* Washington, DC: Migration Policy Institute.

Commissariat, Manekshah Sorabshah. 1957. *A History of Gujarat*, Volumes 1–3. Bombay and New York: Longmans, Green & Co.

Cordero-Guzmán, Hector. 2005. Community Based Organizations and Migration in New York. *Journal of Ethnic and Migration Studies* 31, 5: 889–909.

Cowe, Roger. 1999. Superstore Curbs to Be Lifted. *The Guardian,* June 16: 1.

Crisp, Jeff. 1999. *Policy Challenges of the New Diasporas: Migrant Networks and their Impact on Asylum Flows and Regimes.* Geneva, Switzerland: UNHCR Policy Research Unit.

Curtin, Philip D. 1984. *Cross-Cultural Trade in World History.* Cambridge, UK: Cambridge University Press.

Dale, Stephen F. 1994. *Indian Merchants and Eurasian Trade, 1600–1750.* Cambridge, UK: Cambridge University Press.

Daniel, Caroline, and K. Merchant. 2001. Indian IT Centre Boosts Skilled Immigration Drive. *The Financial Times* UK, January 26.

Das Gupta, Monisha. 2006. *Unruly Immigrants: Rights, Activism, and Transnational South Asian Politics in the United States.* Durham, NC: Duke University Press.

Dasgupta, Shamita Das. 1998. *A Patchwork Shawl: Chronicles of South Asian Women in America.* New Brunswick, NJ: Rutgers University Press.

Desai, Rashmi. 1963. *Indian Immigrants in Britain.* London: Oxford University Press.

Detention Watch Network. 2008. Tracking ICE Enforcement. Retrieved on June 9, 2010, from www.detentionwatchnetwork.org/node/2382.

Dhingra, Pawan. 2009. The Possibility of Community: How Indian American Motel Owners Negotiate Competition and Solidarity. *Journal of Asian American Studies,* 12, 3: 321–346.

Domrese, Robert J. 1970. *The International Migration of High-Level Manpower.* New York: Praeger.

Donato, Katherine, Jorge Durand, and Douglas Massey. 1992. Changing Conditions in the U.S. Labor Market: Effects of the Immigration Reform and Control Act of 1986. *Population Research and Policy Review* 11, 2: 93–115.

duBois, Martin. 1997. Scandal Imperils Antwerp Diamond Hub: Money Laundering Probe Raises Fears of Dealer Exodus. *Wall Street Journal,* July 3: A8.

Dumont, Louis. 1972. *Homo Hierarchicus.* London: Paladin.

Dundas, Paul. 2002. *The Jains*, 2nd edition. New York: Routledge.

Durand, Jorge, Douglas Massey, and Emilio Parrado. 1999. The New Era of Mexican Migration to the United States. *The Journal of American History* 86, 2: 518–536.

Dwyer, Rachel. 1994. Caste, Religion and Sect in Gujarat: Followers of the Vallabhacharya and Swaminarayan. In Roger Ballard, ed., *Desh Pardesh: The South Asian Presence in Britain*. London: Hurst & Company.

Ellis, Jean, and David Appleton. 1989. *Breaking New Ground: Community Development with Asian Communities*. London: Bedford Square Press.

Emirbayer, Mustafa. 1997. Manifesto for a Relational Sociology. *American Journal of Sociology* 1032: 281–317.

Emirbayer, Mustafa, and J. Goodwin. 1994. Network Analysis, Culture, and the Problem of Agency. *American Journal of Sociology* 996: 1411–1454.

Engineer, Asghar Ali. 1980. *The Bohras*. New Delhi: Vikas Publishing House.

———. 1989. *The Muslim Communities of Gujarat: An Exploratory Study of Bohras, Khojas and Memons*. Delhi: Ajanta Publications.

Fainstein, Susan S., and M. Harloe. 1992. Introduction: London and New York in the Contemporary World. In Susan S. Fainstein, I. Gordon, and M. Harloe, eds., *Divided Cities: New York and London in the Contemporary World*. Oxford, UK, and Cambridge, MA: Blackwell.

Faist, Thomas. 2000. *The Volume and Dynamics of International Migration and Transnational Social Spaces*. Oxford, UK: Clarendon Press.

Federal Register. 2007. Department of Commerce, International Trade Administration. U.S. Electronic Education Fairs for China and India, 72, 103, 29971-2, May 30. Washington, DC: U.S. Government Printing Office.

Fisher, Maxine. 1980. *The Indians of New York City: A Study of Immigrants from India*. Columbia, MO: South Asia Books.

Foner, Nancy. 2000. *From Ellis Island to JFK: New York's Two Great Waves of Immigration*. New Haven, CT, and London: Yale University Press; and New York: Russell Sage Foundation.

Frank, Andre Gunder. 1998. *ReOrient: Global Economy in the Asian Age*. Berkeley and Los Angeles: University of California Press.

Gandhi, Maneka. 1992. *The Penguin Book of Hindu Names*. New Delhi: Viking.

Gibson, Campbell, and Kay Jung. 2006. *Historical Census Statistics on the Foreign-Born Population of the United States: 1850–2000*, Working Paper No. 81, Population Division. Washington, DC: U.S. Census Bureau.

Gibson, Campbell, and Emily Lennon. 1999. U.S. Census Bureau, Working Paper No. 29, Historical Census Statistics on the Foreign-Born Population of the United States: 1850 to 1990. Washington, DC: U.S. Government Printing Office.

Glick-Schiller, Nina, L. Basch, and C. Blanc-Szanton, eds. 1992. *Towards a Transnational Perspective on Migration: Race, Ethnicity and Nationalism Reconsidered*. New York: The New York Academy of Sciences. 645.

Goffman, Erving. 1967. *Interaction Ritual: Essays in Face-to-Face Behavior*. New York: Pantheon.

Goldstone, Jack. 2001. The Rise of the West—or Not? A Revision to Socio-Economic History. *Sociological Theory* 18, 2: 175–194.

Goody, Jack. 1996. *The East in the West*. Cambridge, UK: Cambridge University Press.

Goss, Jon D., and B. Lindquist. 1995. Conceptualizing International Labour Migration: A Structuration Perspective. *International Migration Review* 29: 317–351.

Gowan, Peter. 2009. Crisis in the Heartland: Consequences of the New Wall Street System. *New Left Review* 55, January–February: 5–29.

Granovetter, Mark. 1973. The Strength of Weak Ties. *American Journal of Sociology* 787: 1360–1380.

———. 1974. *Getting a Job: A Study of Contacts and Careers*. Cambridge, MA: Harvard University Press.

———. 1985. Economic Action and Social Structure: The Problem of Embeddedness. *American Journal of Sociology* 913: 481–510.

———. 1995. The Economic Sociology of Firms and Entrepreneurs. In Alejandro Portes, ed., *The Economic Sociology of Immigration*. New York: Russell Sage Foundation.

Greene, Molly. 2002. *A Shared World: Christians and Muslims in the Early Modern Mediterranean*. Princeton, NJ: Princeton University Press.

Gregory, Robert. 1993. *The South Asians of East Africa: A Social and Economic History*. Boulder, CO: Westview Press.

Grieco, Margaret. 1987. *Keeping It in the Family: Social Networks and Employment Chance*. London and New York: Tavistock.

Gujarat Samachar—Discover India. 1999. The British Council in India. April: 48–50.

Gurak, Douglas T., and Fe Caces. 1992. Migration Networks and the Shaping of Migration Systems. In Mary M. Kritz, Lin Lean Lim, and Hania Zlotnick, eds., *International Migration Systems: A Global Approach,* 150–176. Oxford, UK: Clarendon Press.

Hall, Kathleen. 2002. *Lives in Translation: Sikh Youth as British Citizens*. Philadelphia: University of Pennsylvania Press.

Haniffa, Aziz. 1998. Third Annual Wharton India Economic Forum. *India Abroad* 28, 23, March 6.

Hardiman, David. 1996. *Feeding the Baniya: Peasants and Usurers in Western India*. Delhi: Oxford University Press.

Harding, L. 2000. German Visa Offer Fails to Tempt India's IT experts: Xenophobia and Low Pay Means That "Green cards" Find Few Takers. *The Guardian*, May 22: 1.

Heimer, Carol. 1992. Doing Your Job and Helping Your Friends: Universalistic Norms about Obligations to Particular Others in Networks. In Nitin Nohria and R. Eccles, eds., *Networks and Organizations: Structure, Form, and Action*. Boston: Harvard Business School Press.

Held, David, Anthony McGrew, David Goldblatt, and Jonathan Perraton. 1999. *Global Transformations: Politics, Economics, Culture*. Stanford, CA: Stanford University Press.

Helweg, Arthur. 2004. *Strangers in a Not-So-Strange Land: Indian American Immigrants in the Global Age*. Belmont, CA: Thomson Wadsworth Publishing.

Helweg, Arthur, and Usha Helweg. 1990. *An Immigrant Success Story: East Indians in America*. Philadelphia: University of Pennsylvania Press.

Herbert, Joanna. 2008. *Negotiating Boundaries in the City: Migration, Ethnicity, and Gender in Britain*. Aldershot, UK: Ashgate.

Hernández-León, Rubén. 2008. *Metropolitan Migrants: The Migration of Urban Mexicans to the United States*. Berkeley: University of California Press.

Hiro, Dilip. 1973. *Black British, White British*. New York: Monthly Review Press.

Hoefer, Michael, Nancy Rytina, and Bryan C. Baker. 2009. Estimates of the Unauthorized Immigrant Population Residing in the United States: January 2008. *Population Estimates, Office of Immigration Statistics Policy Directorate*. Washington, DC: Department of Homeland Security.

Hoerder, Dirk. 2002. *Cultures in Contact: World Migrations in the Second Millennium*. Durham, NC, and London: Duke University Press.

Holmes, Colin. 1988. *John Bull's Island: Immigration and British Society, 1871–1971*. Hampshire, UK, and London: Macmillan Education.

Hondagneu-Sotelo, Pierrette. 2001. *Doméstica: Immigrant Workers Cleaning and Caring in the Shadows of Affluence*. Berkeley: University of California Press.

House of Commons Committee of Public Accounts. 2006. *Home Office Resource Accounts 2004-05 and Follow-up on Returning Failed Asylum Applicants, Sixtieth Report of Session 2005–06*. London: House of Commons.

HT Horizons. 2008. "And Now, a Smarter B-School." *Delhi*, September 24: 5.

Hussain, Yasmin. 2005. *Writing Diaspora: South Asian Women, Culture, and Ethnicity*. Burlington, VT: Ashgate.

Hussain, Yasmin, and Paul Bagguley. 2007. *Moving on Up: South Asian Women and Higher Education*. Stoke on Trent, UK: Trentham Books.

Hyder, Rehan. 2004. *Brimful of Asia: Negotiating Ethnicity on the UK Music Scene*. Burlington, VT: Ashgate.

India Brand Equity Foundation. 2008. Indian Investments Abroad. Retrieved on February 24, 2009, from: www.ibef.org/artdispview.aspx?art_id=21420&cat_id=599&in=37

Institute of International Education. 2007. *Open Doors: Report on International Educational Exchange*. Washington, DC: U.S. Department of State, Bureau of Educational and Cultural Affairs.

Jackson, Peter, and Susan Smith, eds. 1981. *Social Interaction and Ethnic Segregation*. London: Academic Press.

Jacobson, Matthew Frye. 1999. *Whiteness of a Different Color.* Cambridge, MA: Harvard University Press.

Jain, Neelu, and Benjamin Forest. 2004. From Religion to Ethnicity: The Identity of Immigrant and Second Generation Indian Jains in the United States. *National Identities*, 63: 277–297.

Jain, Usha. 1989. *The Gujaratis of San Francisco.* New York: AMS Press.

Jensen, Joan M. 1988. *Passage from India: Asian Indian Immigrants in North America.* New Haven, CT: Yale University Press.

Joshi, Khyati Y. 2006. *New Roots in America's Sacred Ground: Religion, Race and Ethnicity in Indian America.* New Brunswick, NJ: Rutgers University Press.

Julca, Alex. 1997. Domestic, International, and Intergenerational Andean Networks of Labor Migration, 1940–1996. PhD dissertation. Department of Economics, New School for Social Research.

Kalra, Virinder S. 2000. *From Textile Mills to Taxi Ranks: Experiences of Migration, Labour and Social Change.* Aldershot, UK: Ashgate.

Kanjanapan, Wilawan. 1992. The Immigration of Asian Professionals to the United States: 1988–1990. *International Migration Review* 291: 7–32.

Kanjilal, Tanmay. 2000. *Indian-Americans: Participation in the American Domestic Political Process.* Calcutta: Anuradha Kanjilal.

Karp, Jonathan. 1999. Call Them Icemen: India's Anagadias Tote Diamonds in the Rough—To Deliver the Gems, They Defy Robbers and Train Wrecks; It's "Too Risky" for FedEx. *Wall Street Journal,* March 9: A1.

Khagram, Sanjeev, Manish Desai, and Jason Varughese. 2001. Seen, Rich, but Unheard? The Politics of Asian Indians in the United States. In Gordon Chang, ed., *Asian Americans and Politics: Perspectives, Experiences, Prospects.* Washington, DC: Woodrow Wilson Center Press.

Khandelwal, Madhulika. 2002. *Becoming American, Being Indian: An Immigrant Community in New York City.* Ithaca, NY, and London: Cornell University Press.

Khare, Brij B. 1997. *Asian Indian Immigrants: Motifs on Ethnicity and Gender.* Dubuque, IA: Kendall/Hunt Publishing Company.

Khilnani, Sunil. 1999. *The Idea of India.* New York: Farrar, Strauss, and Giroux.

King, Russell. 2005. Albania as a Laboratory for the Study of Migration and Development. *Journal of Southern Europe and the Balkans* 72: 133–155.

Kloosterman, Robert, and Jan Rath 2001. Immigrant Entrepreneurs in Advanced Economies: Mixed Embeddedness Further Explored. *Journal of Ethnic and Migration Studies* 272: 189–201.

Kolb, Holger. 2005. Die Deutsche "Green Card," *Kurzdossier.* November 3.

Koskoff, David E. 1981. *The Diamond World.* New York: Harper and Row Publishers.

Kotecha, Bhanubahen. 1994. *On the Threshold of East Africa.* Translated by Lenore Reynell. The Jyotiben Madhvani Foundation.

Krackhardt, David. 1992. The Strength of Strong Ties. In Nitin Nohria and Robert Eccles, eds., *Networks and Organizations: Structure, Form and Action*. Boston: Harvard Business School Press.

Krissman, Fred. 2005. Sin Coyote Ni Patrón: Why the "Migrant Network" Fails to Explain International Migration. *International Migration Review* 391: 4–44.

Kurien, Prema. 2007. *A Place at the Multicultural Table: The Development of an American Hinduism*. New Brunswick, NJ, and London: Rutgers University Press.

Kyle, David. 2000. *Transnational Peasants: Migrations, Networks, and Ethnicity in Andean Ecuador*. Baltimore and London: Johns Hopkins University Press.

Kyle, David, and Rey Koslowski. 2001. *Global Human Smuggling: Comparative Perspectives*. Baltimore and London: Johns Hopkins University Press.

LaBrack, Bruce. 1988. *The Sikhs of Northern California, 1904–1975*. New York: AMS Press.

Lach, Donald F., and E. J. Van Kley. 1993. *Asia in the Making of Europe. Volume III: A Century of Advance*. Book Two: South Asia. Chicago and London: University of Chicago Press.

Lal, Vinay. 2008. *The Other Indians: A Political and Cultural History of South Asians in America*. Los Angeles: UCLA Asian American Studies Center.

Lau, Annie Christine. 2000. *South Asian Children and Adolescents in Britain*. London: Whurr Publishers.

Leadbeater, S. R. B. 1993. *The Politics of Textiles: The Indian Cotton-Mill Industry and the Legacy of Swadeshi 1900–1985*. New Delhi: Sage Publications.

Lee, Everett S. 1966. A Theory of Migration. *Demography* 3: 47–57.

Leonard, Karen. 1992. *Making Ethnic Choices: California's Punjabi Mexican Americans*. Philadelphia: Temple University Press.

Lessinger, Johanna. 1995. *From the Ganges to the Hudson: Indian Immigrants in New York City*. Boston: Allyn & Bacon.

Levitt, Peggy. 2001. *The Transnational Villagers*. Berkeley: University of California Press.

Lewis, Philip. 2007. *Young, British and Muslim*. London: Continuum.

Light, Ivan, and S. Gold. 2000. *Ethnic Economies*. San Diego: Academic Press.

Lobo, Arun, and J. Salvo. 1998. Changing US Immigration Law and the Occupational Selectivity of Asian Immigrants. *International Migration Review* 323: 737–760.

Logan, John, Richard Alba, Michael Dill, and Min Zhou. 2000. Ethnic Segmentation in the American Metropolis: Increasing Divergence in Economic Incorporation, 1980–1990. *International Migration Review*: 98–132.

Lubman, Sarah. 2000. High Tech's Imported Brainpower: Indians Recruited by Temp Firms Create Flourishing Subculture. *San Jose Mercury News*, January 16.

Ludden, David. 1999. History along the Coastal Zone of Southern Eurasia. Presented to the Southern Asia Institute in New York: Columbia University.

Lyon, M. H., and B. J. M. West. 1995. London Patels: Caste and Commerce. *New Community* 21:3: 399–419.

MacDonald, Dwight. 1989. *The Ford Foundation: The Men and the Millions.* New Brunswick, NJ, and Oxford: Transaction Publishers.

Magat, Richard. 1979. *The Ford Foundation at Work: Philanthropic Choices, Methods and Styles.* New York and London: Plenum Press.

Mahler, Sarah. 1995. *American Dreaming: Immigrant Life on the Margins.* Princeton, NJ: Princeton University Press.

Maira, Sunaina. 1999. "Identity Dub: The Paradoxes of an Indian American Youth Subculture," *Cultural Anthropology,* 14, 1: 29–60.

———. 2000. "Henna and Hip Hop: The Politics of Cultural Production and the Work of Cultural Studies," *Journal of Asian American Studies,* 3, 3: 329–369.

———. 2009. *Missing: Youth, Citizenship, and Empire after 9/11.* Durham, NC: Duke University Press.

Malik, K. N. 1997. *India and the United Kingdom: Change and Continuity in the 1980s.* New Delhi: Sage.

Marsden, Peter. 1982. Brokerage Behavior in Restricted Exchange Networks. In Peter Marsden and N. Lin, eds., *Social Structure and Network Analysis.* Beverly Hills: Sage.

Martin, Philip, and Jonas Widgren. 2002. International Migration: Facing the Challenge. *Population Bulletin* 571: 1–43.

Marx, Karl, and Friedrich Engels. 1975. *Economic and Philosophic Manuscripts of 1844, Collected Works,* Volume 3. New York: International Publishers. (Originally published in 1844.)

Mason, David, ed. 2003. *Explaining Ethnic Differences: Changing Patterns of Disadvantage in Britain.* Bristol, UK: The Policy Press.

Massey, Douglas. 1999. International Migration at the Dawn of the Twenty-First Century: The Role of the State. *Population and Development Review* 25, 2: 303–322.

Massey, Douglas, J. Arango, J. Durand, and H. Gonzalez. 1987. *Return to Aztlan: The Social Process of International Migration from Western Mexico.* Berkeley: University of California Press.

Massey, Douglas, J. Arango, G. Hugo, A. Kouaouci, A. Pellegrino, and J. E. Taylor. 1998. *Worlds in Motion: Understanding International Migration at the End of the Millennium.* Oxford, UK: Clarendon Press.

Massey, Douglas, Jorge Durand, and Nolan Malone. 2002. *Beyond Smoke and Mirrors: Mexican Immigration in an Era of Economic Integration.* New York: Russell Sage Foundation.

Massey, Douglas, and Kristin E. Espinosa. 1997. What's Driving Mexico–US Migration? A Theoretical, Empirical, and Policy Analysis. *American Journal of Sociology* 102, 4.

Masuzawa, Tomoko. 2005. *The Invention of World Religions or, How European Universalism Was Preserved in the Language of Pluralism.* Chicago: University of Chicago Press.

Mattausch, John. 1998. From Subjects to Citizens: British "East African Asians." *Journal of Ethnic and Migration Studies* 241: 121–141.

McDonald, Hamish. 1996. Rebel Mine Sparks Off Diamond Price War. *South China Morning Post,* September 1, 4.

McDowell, Edwin. 1996. Hospitality Is Their Business: One Ethnic Group's Rooms-to-Riches Story. *The New York Times* March 21: D1.

McGee, Marianne Kolbasuk. 2008. Who Got H-1B Petitions Approved Last Year: Look at the List. *Information Week,* April 2.

McPherson, Kenneth. 1993. *The Indian Ocean: A History of People and the Sea.* Delhi and New York: Oxford University Press.

Mehta, Nanji Kalidas. 1987. *Dream Half-Expressed, An Autobiography,* 2nd edition, I. K. Agarwal, Suresh M. Kothari Publishers.

Mejia, Alfonso, H. Pizurki, and E. Royston. 1980. *Foreign Medical Graduates: The Case of the United States.* Lexington, MA: D. C. Heath and Co.

Mendelson, Margot, Shayna Strom, and Michael Wishnie. 2009. *Collateral Damage: An Examination of ICE's Fugitive Operations Program.* Washington, DC: Migration Policy Institute.

Menjívar, Cecilia. 2000. *Fragmented Ties: Salvadoran Immigrant Networks in America.* Berkeley: University of California Press.

Metcalf, Hilary, Tariq Modood, and Satnam Virdee. 1996. *Asian Self-Employment: The Interaction of Culture and Economics in England.* London: Policy Studies Institute.

Meyer, Jean-Baptiste, and Mercy Brown. 1999. *Scientific Diasporas: A New Approach to the Brain Drain.* Paris: UNESCO-MOST Discussion Paper No. 41.

Min, Pyong Gap. 2008. *Ethnic Solidarity for Economic Survival: Korean Greengrocers in New York City.* New York: Russell Sage Foundation.

Minocha, Urmil. 1987. South Asian Immigrants: Trends and Impacts on the Sending and Receiving Societies. In James Fawcett and Benjamin Cariño, eds., *Pacific Bridges: The New Immigration from Asia and the Pacific Islands.* New York: Center for Migration Studies.

Mistry, P. J. 1994. Personal Names: Their Structure, Variation and Grammar in Gujarati. In Raja Ram Mehrotra, ed., *Book of Indian Names.* New Delhi: Rupa & Co.

Moch, Leslie Page. 1992. *Moving Europeans: Migration in Western Europe since 1650.* Bloomington: Indiana University Press.

Mollenkopf, John, and Manuel Castells, eds. 1991. *Dual City: Restructuring New York.* New York: Russell Sage Foundation.

Mukhi, Su Sunder. 2000. *Doing the Desi Thing: Performing Indianness in New York City.* New York: Routledge.

Mukta, Parita. 2000. The Public Face of Hindu Nationalism. *Ethnic and Racial Studies* 233: 442–466.

Musterd, Sako, and W. Ostendorf. 1996. Ethnicity and the Dutch Welfare State: The Case of Amsterdam. In Curtis, Roseman, H. D. Laux, and G. Thieme, eds., *Ethni-City: Geographic Perspectives on Ethnic Change in Modern Cities*. Lanham, MD, and London: Rowman & Littlefield.

Narayan, Anjana, and Bandana Purkayastha. 2008. *Living Our Religions: Hindu and Muslim South Asian-American Women Narrate Their Experiences*. Sterling, VA: Kumarian Press.

Ngai, Mae. 2004. *Impossible Subjects: Illegal Aliens and the Making of Modern America*. Princeton, NJ: Princeton University Press.

Nielsen, Waldemar A. 1972. *The Big Foundations*. New York and London: Columbia University Press.

Ong, Aiwha. 1997. Chinese Modernities: Narratives of Nation and of Capitalism. In Aiwha Ong and D. M. Nonin, eds., *Underground Empires, The Cultural Politics of Modern Chinese Transnationalism*. New York and London: Routledge.

———. 1999. *Flexible Citizenship: The Cultural Logics of Transnationality*. Durham, NC, and London: Duke University Press.

Oommen, T. K. 1987. India. In Yogesh Atal and Luca Dall'Oglio, eds., *Migration of Talent: Causes and Consequences of Brain Drain, Three Studies from Asia*. Bangkok: UNESCO.

Overdorf, Jason. 2008. When More Is Worse: India's Vast Plan to Build a Bevy of New Schools Will Fix Only Half the Problem: Quantity, Not Quality. *Newsweek*, August 18–25.

Pais, Arthur J. 1998. Growing Presence. *India Today International*, December 28.

Papademetriou, Demetrios, and Aaron Terrazas. 2009. *Immigrants and the Current Economic Crisis: Research Evidence, Policy Challenges, and Implications*. Washington, DC: Migration Policy Institute.

Parekh, Bikhu. 1985. India and America: The Story of an Uneven Educational Encounter. In Robert M. Crunden, ed., *Traffic of Ideas between India and America*. Delhi: Chanakya Publications.

Passel, Jeffrey S. 2006. The Size and Characteristics of the Unauthorized Migrant Population in the U.S.: Estimates Based on the March 2005 Current Population Survey. Washington, DC: Pew Hispanic Center.

Patel, Parvin, and M. Rutten. 1999. Patels of Central Gujarat in Greater London. *Economic and Political Weekly* April 17–24: 952–953.

Peach, Ceri. 1984. Asians in Britain: A Study in Encapsulation and Marginality. In Colin Clarke, David Ley, Ceri Peach, and Paul Paget, eds., *Geography and Ethnic Pluralism*. London: G. Allen & Unwin.

Peak, Steve, and P. Fisher, eds. 1998. *The Media Guide*. London: The Guardian.

Piore, Michael J. 1979. *Birds of Passage: Migrant Labor and Industrial Society*. Cambridge, UK: Cambridge University Press.

Pocock, David F. 1972. *Kanbi and Patidar: A Study of the Patidar Community of Gujarat*. Oxford, UK: Clarendon Press.

Poros, Maritsa V. 2001. The Role of Networks in Linking Local Labour Markets: The Case of Asian Indian Migration to New York and London. *Global Networks* 1, 3: 243–259.

———. 2004. Review of *Remaking the American Mainstream: Assimilation and Contemporary Immigration*, by Richard Alba and Victor Nee. *City and Community*, 3, 4: 425–427.

———. forthcoming. Asian Indians in America, 1870–1940. *Encyclopedia of Immigration*. Santa Barbara, CA: ABC-Clio Publishers.

Portes, Alejandro. 1995. Economic Sociology and the Sociology of Immigration: A Conceptual Overview. In Alejandro Portes, ed., *The Economic Sociology of Immigration: Essays on Networks, Ethnicity and Entrepreneurship*. New York: Russell Sage Foundation.

———. 1998. Social Capital: Its Origins and Applications in Modern Sociology. *Annual Review of Sociology* 24: 1–24.

———. 2000. The Two Meanings of Social Capital. *Sociological Forum* 15, 1: 1–12.

Portes, Alejandro, and R. Bach. 1985. *Latin Journey: Cuban and Mexican Immigrants in the United States*. Berkeley: University of California Press.

Portes, Alejandro, Luis Guarnizo, and William Haller. 2002. Transnational Entrepreneurs: An Alternative Form of Immigrant Economic Adaptation. *American Sociological Review* 7, 2: 278–298.

Portes, Alejandro, and Rubén Rumbaut. 1996. *Immigrant America: A Portrait*, 2nd ed. Berkeley: University of California Press.

Portes, Alejandro, and J. Sensenbrenner. 1993. Embeddedness and Immigration: Notes on the Social Determinants of Economic Action. *American Journal of Sociology* 98, 6: 1320–1350.

Prashad, Vijay. 2000. *The Karma of Brown Folk*. Minneapolis: University of Minnesota Press.

Purkayastha, Bandana. 2005a. *Negotiating Ethnicity: Second-Generation South Asian Americans Traverse A Transnational World*. New Brunswick, NJ: Rutgers University Press.

———. 2005b. "Skilled Migration and Cumulative Disadvantage: The Case of Highly Qualified Asian Indian Immigrant Women in the US," *Geoforum* 36: 181–196.

Radhakrishnan, S., and Charles Moore. 1957. *A Source Book in Indian Philosophy*. Princeton, NJ: Princeton University Press.

Rajagopal, Arvind. 2000. Hindu Nationalism in the US: Changing Configurations of Political Practice. *Ethnic and Racial Studies* 233: 467–496.

Ram, Monder, and Trevor Jones. 2005. Asian Business Strategies in the United Kingdom: A Qualitative Assessment. In *Asian Migrants and European Labour Markets: Patterns and Processes of Immigrant Labour Market Insertion in Europe*, 222–237. London: Routledge.

Rangaswamy, Padma. 2000. *Namaste America: Indian Immigrants in an American Metropolis*. University Park: Pennsylvania State University Press.

Ratcliffe, Peter 1996. "Social Geography and Ethnicity: A Theoretical, Conceptual and Substantive Overview," in Peter Ratcliffe, ed., *Ethnicity in the 1991 Census. Volume Three. Social Geography and Ethnicity in Britain: Geographical Spread, Spatial Concentration and Internal Migration*. London: HMSO Office for National Statistics.

Rees, Philip, and D. Phillips. 1996. Geographical Spread: The National Picture. In Peter Ratcliffe, ed., *Ethnicity in the 1991 Census. Volume Three. Social Geography and Ethnicity in Britain: Geographical Spread, Spatial Concentration and Internal Migration*. London: HMSO Office for National Statistics.

Rendall, Michael, and John Salt. 2005. The Foreign-Born Population. *Focus on People and Migration*. London: Office for National Statistics.

Richards, John F. 1993. *The New Cambridge History of India, The Mughal Empire*. Cambridge, UK: Cambridge University Press.

Robinson, Sara. 2000. Workers Are Trapped in Limbo by INS. *New York Times*, February 29: A12.

Robinson, Vaughan. 1979. *The Segregation of Asians within a British City: Theory and Practice*. Oxford, UK: University of Oxford.

———. 1986. *Transients, Settlers,and Refugees:Asians in Britain*. Oxford, UK: Clarendon Press.

———. 1996. The Indians: Onward and Upward. In Ceri Peach, ed., *Ethnicity in the 1991 Census, Volume Two, The Ethnic Minority Populations of Great Britain*. London: HMSO Office for National Statistics.

Robinson, Vaughan, and M. Carey. 2000. Peopling Skilled International Migration: Indian Doctors in the UK. *International Migration* 381: 89–107.

Ronad, Gladson. 1998. Getting into US Engineering Schools. *The International Indian* 61: 52.

Rudiger, Katerina. 2008. The UK and India: The Other "Special Relationship." Provocation Series, 4, 3. London: The Work Foundation.

Rudrappa, Sharmila. 2004. *Ethnic Routes to Becoming American: Indian Immigrants and the Cultures of Citizenship*. New Brunswick, NJ: Rutgers University Press.

Rutten, Mario. 1995. *Farms and Factories: Social Profile of Large Farmers and Rural Industrialists in West India*. Delhi: Oxford University Press.

Said, Edward W. 1979. *Orientalism*. New York: Vintage Books.

Salt, John. 1992. Migration Processes among the Highly Skilled in Europe. *International Migration Review* 26, 2: 484–505.

Saran, Parmatma. 1985. *The Asian Indian Experience in the United States.* Cambridge, MA: Schenkman Company.

Saran, Parmatma, and Edwin Eames, eds. 1980. *The New Ethnics: Asian Indians in the United States.* New York: Praeger.

Sarkar, Cara Gupta. 2008. Test Time: Take TOEIC if Applying for Jobs in BPOs and Multinationals Worldwide. *HT Horizons,* Delhi, September 24: 5.

Sassen, Saskia. 1995. Immigration and Local Labor Markets. In Alejandro Portes, ed., *The Economic Sociology of Immigration: Essays on Networks, Ethnicity and Entrepreneurship.* New York: Russell Sage Foundation.

———. 1999. *Guests and Aliens.* New York: New York Press.

———. 2001. *The Global City: New York, London, Tokyo,* 2nd edition. Princeton, NJ: Princeton University Press.

Saxenian, AnnaLee. 1999. *Silicon Valley's New Immigrant Entrepreneurs.* San Francisco: Public Policy Institute of California.

Schrover, Marlou, and Floris Vermeulen. 2005. Immigrant Organizations. *Journal of Ethnic and Migration Studies* 31, 5: 823–832.

Schütz, Alfred. 1944. The Stranger: An Essay in Social Psychology. *American Journal of Sociology* 496: 499–507.

Sen, Amartya. 1983. *Poverty and Famines: An Essay on Entitlement and Deprivation.* Oxford, UK: Oxford University Press.

Sengupta, Somini. 2007. India Attracts Universities from the U.S. *The New York Times,* March 26.

Shah, A. M., 1998. *The Family in India: Critical Essays.* London: Sangam Books.

Shah, A. M., and I. P. Desai. 1988. *Division and Hierarchy: An Overview of Caste in Gujarat.* Delhi: Hindustan Publishing Corporation.

Shankar, Lavina D., and Rajini Srikanth, eds. 1998. *A Part, Yet Apart: South Asians in Asian America.* Philadelphia: Temple University Press.

Sharma, Sanjay, John Hutnyk, and Ashwani Sharma, eds. 1996. *Dis-Orienting Rhythms: The Politics of the New Asian Dance Music.* London: Zed Books.

Sicar, Arpana. 2000. *Work Roles, Gender Roles, and Asian Indian Immigrant Women in the United States.* New York: The Edwin Mellen Press.

SiliconIndia. 2001. The UK and India. January: 91.

SiliconIndia. 2008. Banks' Collapse to Affect Campus Hiring at IITs, IIMs. September 16.

Simmel, Georg. 1955. *Conflict. The Web of Group Affiliations.* New York: Free Press.

———. 1971. *On Individuality and Social Forms,* Heritage of Sociology Series, edited by Donald N. Levine. Chicago: University of Chicago Press.

Smelser, Neil, and Richard Swedberg. 1994. *The Handbook of Economic Sociology.* Princeton, NJ, and New York: Princeton University Press and the Russell Sage Foundation.

Smith, Robert C. 2006. *Mexican New York: Transnational Lives of New Immigrants.* Berkeley: University of California Press.

Sodeman, William. 1971. United States Programs to Strengthen Medical Education in Developing Countries. In John Z. Bowers and L. Rosenheim, ed., *Migration of Medical Manpower*. New York: Josiah Macy Jr. Foundation.

Somerville, Will. 2007. *The Immigration Legacy of Tony Blair*. Washington, DC: Migration Policy Institute.

Soysal, Yasemin. 1994. *The Limits of Citizenship: Migrants and Postnational Membership in Europe*. Chicago and London: University of Chicago Press.

Spencer, Ian R. G. 1997. *British Immigration Policy since 1939: The Making of Multi-Racial Britain*. London and New York: Routledge.

Spener, David. 2001. Smuggling Migrants through South Texas: Challenges Posed by Operation Rio Grande. In David Kyle and Rey Koslowski, eds. *Global Human Smuggling: Comparative Perspectives*. Baltimore and London: Johns Hopkins University Press.

Srinivasan, Shaila. 1995. *The South Asian Petty Bourgeoisie in Britain: An Oxford Case Study*. Aldershot, UK: Avebury.

Srivastava, Raj Krishnan, ed. 1998. *Vital Connections: Self, Society, God, Perspectives on Swadhyaya*. New York: Weatherhill.

Stark, Oded. 1991. *The Migration of Labour*. Cambridge, UK: Basil Blackwell.

Stinchcombe, Arthur. 1989. An Outsider's View of Network Analyses of Power. In R. Perrucci and H. Potter, eds., *Networks of Power: Organizational Actors at the National, Corporate, and Community Levels*. New York: Aldine de Gruyter.

Sun, Lena. 1998. Merchants Share Heritage, Hard Work, Tragedy. *The Washington Post*, November 3: B1.

Takaki, Ronald. 1998. *Strangers from a Different Shore: A History of Asian Americans*. New York: Little, Brown and Company.

Tambs-Lyche, Harald. 1980. *London Patidars: A Case Study in Urban Ethnicity*. London: Routledge & Kegan Paul.

Terhune, Lea. 2007. Businesses Urged to Back U.S.–India Education Partnerships. *The Indian Star*, March 28.

Thomas, W. I., and Florian Znaniecki. 1918–1920. *The Polish Peasant in Europe and America*. New York: Alfred A. Knopf.

Tilly, Charles. 1978. Migration in Modern European History. In W. S. McNeil and R. Adams, eds., *Human Migration: Patterns and Policies*, 48–72. Bloomington: Indiana University Press.

———. 1990. Transplanted Networks. In Virginia Yans-McLaughlin, ed., *Immigration Reconsidered*. New York: Oxford University Press.

———. 1998. *Durable Inequality*. Berkeley: University of California Press.

———. 1999. Relational Origins of Inequality. *Anthropological Theory* 13: 355–372.

———. 2005. *Identities, Boundaries, and Social Ties*. Boulder, CO, and London: Paradigm Publishers.

Tilly, Charles, and C. H. Brown. 1967. On Uprooting, Kinship and the Auspices of Migration. *International Journal of Comparative Sociology* 8: 139–164.

Tilly, Chris, and Charles Tilly. 1998. *Work under Capitalism*. Boulder, CO: Westview Press.

Tinker, Hugh. 1977. *The Banyan Tree: Overseas Emigrants from India, Pakistan, and Bangladesh*. Oxford, UK: Oxford University Press.

Todaro, Michael P. 1976. *Internal Migration in Developing Countries*. Geneva: International Labour Office.

Tripathi, D., ed. 1984. *Business Communities of India: A Historical Perspective*. New Delhi: Manohar Publications.

UK Higher Education Statistics Agency. 2008. Top Ten Non-EU Countries of Domicile in 2006/2007 for HE Students in UK HEIs. Retrieved on June 9, 2010, from www.hesa.ac.uk/index.php/content/view/1158/161/.

UK Trade and Investment. 2006. Wipro: Harnessing the Entrepreneurial Spirit of the UK. January 30. Available at: www.ukinvest.gov.uk/story/10159/en-IN.html

U.S. Department of Education. 1997. *Degrees Earned by Foreign Graduate Students: Fields of Study and Plans after Graduation*. Washington, DC: National Center for Education Statistics.

U.S. Embassy, New Delhi. 2007. The U.S. Department of Commerce Announces Broadcast of U.S Electronic Education Fair for India. December 4. Available at: http://newdelhi.usembassy.gov/pr120507.html

Varadarajan, Tunku. 1999. A Patel Motel Cartel? *The New York Times Magazine*, July 4: 36.

Varma, Pavan. 1998. *The Great Indian Middle Class*. Delhi: Viking.

Vertovec, Steven. 2009. *Transnationalism*. London: Routledge.

Visram, Rozina. 1986. *Ayahs, Lascars, and Princes: The Story of Indians in Britain 1700–1947*. London: Pluto.

Waldinger, Roger. 1990. The Making of an Immigrant Niche. *International Migration Review* 281: 3–30.

———. 1995. The Other Side of Embeddedness: A Case Study in the Interplay of Economy and Ethnicity. *Ethnic and Racial Studies* 183: 555–580.

———. 1996. *Still the Promised City? African-Americans and New Immigrants in Postindustrial New York*. Cambridge, MA: Harvard University Press.

———. 1999. Network, Bureaucracy, and Exclusion: Recruitment and Selection in an Immigrant Metropolis. In Frank D. Bean and Stephanie Bell-Rose, eds., *Immigration and Opportunity: Race, Ethnicity, and Employment in the United States*, 228–259. New York: Russell Sage Foundation.

Waldinger, Roger, and Michael Lichter. 2003. *How the Other Half Works: Immigration and the Social Organization of Labor*. Berkeley: University of California Press.

Washbrook, David. 2007. India in the Early Modern World Economy: Modes of Production, Reproduction and Exchange. *Journal of Global History* 2: 87–111.

Weaver, Warren. 1967. *U.S. Philanthropic Foundations: Their History, Structure, Management, and Record*. New York, Evanston, and London: Harper & Row Publishers.

Weber, Max. 1949. Objectivity in Social Science. *The Methodology of the Social Sciences*, edited and translated by Edward A. Shils and Henry A. Finch. New York: Simon & Schuster, The Free Press. (Originally published in 1904.)

Werbner, Pnina. 1989. *The Migration Process: Capital, Gifts and Offerings among British Pakistanis*. New York: St. Martin's Press.

Westwood, Sallie. 2000. A Real Romance: Gender, Ethnicity, Trust and Risk in the Indian Diamond Trade. *Ethnic and Racial Studies* 235: 857–870.

Williams, Raymond B. 2001. *An Introduction to Swaminarayan Hinduism*. Cambridge, UK: Cambridge University Press.

Wilson, Amrit. 2006. *Dreams, Questions, Struggles: South Asian Women in Britain*. London: Pluto Press.

Zimmer, Catherine, and H. Aldrich. 1987. Resource Mobilization through Ethnic Networks: Kinship and Friendship Ties of Shopkeepers in England. *Sociological Perspectives* 304: 422–445.

Zolberg, Aristide. 1999. Matters of State: Theorizing Immigration Policy. In Charles Hirschman, Josh DeWind, and Philip Kasinitz, eds., *The Handbook of International Migration: The American Experience*. New York: Russell Sage Foundation.

Index

Note: Figures and tables are indicated by *f* or *t*, respectively, following the page number.